Books are to be returned on or before
the last date below.

08 OCT 97

2 4 F

T539.10.£37.50

KCN L
(Tor)

THE FORMATION OF PROFESSIONS

V

0803982518

scАsss

THE SWEDISH COLLEGIUM FOR ADVANCED STUDY IN THE SOCIAL SCIENCES

The Swedish Collegium for Advanced Study in the Social Sciences is a national scientific institution established in 1985. Its main objective is to promote theoretically innovative research with a comparative and long-range orientation.

Also in this series

Professions in Theory and History
Rethinking the Study of the Professions
edited by Michael Burrage and Rolf Torstendahl

The Firm as a Nexus of Treaties
edited by Masahiko Aoki, Bo Gustafsson and Oliver E. Williamson

The Shaping of Social Organization
Social Rule System Theory with Applications
Tom R. Burns and Helena Flam

THE FORMATION OF PROFESSIONS

Knowledge, State and Strategy

edited by Rolf Torstendahl
and Michael Burrage

SAGE Publications
London • Newbury Park • New Delhi

© Swedish Collegium for Advanced Study
in the Social Sciences 1990

First published 1990

SAGE Publications Ltd
28 Banner Street
London EC1Y 8QE

SAGE Publications Inc
2111 West Hillcrest Drive
Newbury Park, California 91320

SAGE Publications India Pvt Ltd
32, M-Block Market
Greater Kailash – I
New Delhi 110 048

British Library Cataloguing in Publication Data

The formation of professions: knowledge, state and
strategy. – (SCASSS Series).
1. Professions – Sociological perpectives
I. Torstendahl, Rolf   II. Burrage, Michael   III. Series
305.553

ISBN 0–8039–8251–8

Library of Congress catalog card number 90–60583

Phototypeset by Input Typesetting Ltd, London
Printed in Great Britain by Billing and Sons Ltd, Worcester

Contents

Foreword

This book emerges in a new series of scholarly anthologies which are the outcomes of work within SCASSS, the Swedish Collegium for Advanced Study in the Social Sciences, and published by Sage.

The book is a product of a three-year-long discussion among the authors and some other scholars. The initiative was taken in 1985 by Rolf Torstendahl as one of the directors of SCASSS. Three major conferences on the theme of theory of professionalism and several minor workshops and meetings have taken place since then. Some of the authors have also had the opportunity to work together as fellows at SCASSS.

The present volume is accompanied by another one, simultaneously published in the same series under the title *Professions in Theory and History: Rethinking the Study of the Professions.*

The editors would like to express their gratitude to all the contributors for their willingness to adapt their various drafts to the outlines for the two volumes presented by the editors. Thanks are also due to the publishers for their unfailing cooperation.

Rolf Torstendahl and Michael Burrage

Notes on the contributors

Tony Becher is Professor of Education at the University of Sussex. He has worked extensively with problems of the university system, especially in its English form. His books include *Process and Structure in Higher Education* (with Maurice Kogan, 1980), *British Higher Education* (1987) and *Academic Tribes and Territories* (1989).

Margareta Bertilsson is Associate Professor of Sociology at the University of Lund. Her research has been directed mainly towards sociological theory and theorists. At the time of writing she is studying the law profession in Sweden and its relation to the legal system. She has published several books and articles (in Swedish) on her main themes.

Randall Collins is Professor of Sociology at the University of California, Riverside. His books include *The Credential Society: An Historical Sociology of Education and Stratification* (1979) and *Theoretical Sociology* (1988).

Aant Elzinga is Professor of Theory of Science and Research at the University of Gothenburg. He has published several books and articles on the history and development of science and on the relation between scientific and social systems. His works include *Nursing Care Research: The Emergence of a New Scientific Specialty* (with J. Bärmark and G. Wallén, 1981).

Inga Hellberg is Associate Professor of Sociology at the University of Gothenburg. She has concentrated her research on problems regarding labour relations and groups on the labour market, especially professionals, and her publications (in Swedish) include a book on the rise of the veterinary profession in Sweden.

Lucien Karpik is Professor of Sociology at the Ecole des Mines, Paris, and a member of the Centre de Sociologie de l'Innovation. He has written extensively about large industrial firms in France and edited *Organization and Environment: Theory, Issues and Reality*. He is currently making a study of French advocates as part of a larger work on French justice.

Magali Sarfatti Larson is Professor of Sociology at Temple University in Philadelphia, PA. Her work *The Rise of Professionalism: A Sociological Analysis* (1977) gave rise to a debate where she participated with a series of articles on the theme. Her current research is directed towards the profession of architects.

Charles E. McClelland is Professor of History at the University of New Mexico, Albuquerque. He has written books and articles on German education and professionalism, among them *State, Society and University in Germany, 1700–1914* (1980) and *The German Experience of Professionalization: The Development of Modern Learned Professions and their Organization* (in press).

Raymond Murphy is Professor of Sociology at the University of Ottawa. In a series of articles he has discussed and analysed the concept of closure in Weber's theory and its application to modern society, including modern professionalism. The main results are published in *Social Closure: The Theory of Monopolization and Exclusion* (1988).

Lennart G. Svensson is Associate Professor of Sociology at the University of Gothenburg. His main research has been devoted to the Swedish university system and he has published three main volumes in Swedish on this theme as well as *Higher Education and the State in Swedish History* (1987). His present research relates to professional practice in different groups.

Rolf Torstendahl is Professor of History at Uppsala University and Director of SCASSS. He has published several works on Swedish historical problems, including technical education. He has written *The Dispersion of Engineers in a Transitional Society: Swedish Technicians 1860–1940* (1975) and *Bureaucratisation in Northwestern Europe 1880–1985* (in press).

1

Introduction: promotion and strategies of knowledge-based groups

Rolf Torstendahl

Starting-points for a theory

When a field in social science has become established and theories settled, it is often fruitful to question the very first assumptions for its theories and theses. The basic assumption regarding profession-alism and professionalization has for long been that we know what a professional is. Theories have been developed on the general phenomena of professionalism and professionalization, but most research has been concentrated on individual professions. In fact, two professions, lawyers and doctors, have dominated the dis-cussion on professions, and the perspective on these two cases has been focused on their appearance in nineteenth- and twentieth-century Britain and America.

There are other investigations. Especially quite recently several researchers have widened the sphere of interest to other times and other countries. With the hegemony of American social science after World War II, its problems were transferred to continental Europe and parallel investigations were made. The normal pro-cedure has been to compare the types which have been established in Britain and the United States and to regard them not only as specific types but rather as ideal-types in Weber's sense. The same holds true for investigations of other occupational groups, when they are not – as was the case especially in the 1960s and 1970s – dismissed as semi-professional, which means, of course, that they fall short of the standard set by the ideal-type.

If we do not take for granted that we know what a professional is, the whole field of studies of professionalism becomes open and complicated. A rationale must be found for the separation of cer-tain occupations from others and for their specific behaviour. The chapters in *Professions in Theory and History: Rethinking the Study of the Professions*, published simultaneously, are all concerned with the problem of finding a starting-point for a theory of professionalism when traditional demonstrative definitions are not accepted.

The chapters in this book are concerned with the connecting link between the groups which aspire to the status of professionalism; that is, their knowledge base, how they use it in order to strengthen their position in the labour market (their strategy) and how they relate themselves to the state and how the state relates itself to them.

Knowledge systems and problem-solving

In any definition of 'professions' knowledge systems will play an important role. The theory of professionalism has to do, in one way or another, with how knowledge (and/or skill) is used by its owners as a social capital and not only for purposes connected with the immediate problem-solving to which the system itself may refer. Most often the professions are centred on typical 'problem-solving' systems of knowledge and/or skill: the traditional core professional groups are lawyers and doctors, the one specialized in social, the other in bodily, problems. Other people, clients or employers or both, present these problems – their own problems – for the 'typical' professionals. Researchers, who 'invent' their problems, do not form a 'typical' professional group. The difference has to do with the use of knowledge systems, which does not refer immediately to the problem-solving use of them. Clients and employers define social relations between the members of knowledge-based groups towards society at large and to one another in forms which may be competitive or cooperative. Researchers have not got the same incentive for a clearly defined group sentiment founded on the use of their knowledge, even if they have their employers. They defend their autonomy in problem-setting and problem-finding vigorously against their employers when they are in a university environment, and these researchers tend to look down on those who have sold their freedom of selecting research to industry or government.

Problems are posed and solved in a conceptual framework. These concepts and their relation to one another tend to be used by convention in one way and not in another, and those who have the appropriate education or training know how to use it. The knowledge of the problem-solving groups contains an important moment of jargon. Within the knowledge base the ability to handle the conceptual instruments forms part of a 'discourse'. This discourse provides a basis of mutual understanding among the professionals, which is not shared by others (see the chapters by Sarfatti Larson and Svensson).

The problem-solving capacity inherent in the knowledge systems of professional groups is an important characteristic. The technical problems, bodily problems and social problems on which these knowledge systems are centred were, in the early nineteenth century, still mainly stated by individuals as persons. When this changed during the nineteenth century and problems became defined more and more often by organizations, either private enterprises or public agencies, professionals became more and more often related to organizations where such problems were defined. They became employees, selling their labour (as a competence in handling a specific knowledge system) rather than selling services to individuals (or companies).

The crucial characteristic of the knowledge systems of professionals, as they have been perceived in the discussions on professionalism of recent years, is to what extent they really serve a problem-solving purpose which in turn gives prestige and power to the owners of this capacity, or to what extent the knowledge is a symbolic value that serves the purpose of being something that can be brought forward in other people's eyes as important but which has no clear relation to the problem-solving capacity of professionals.

There are good arguments for both these standpoints. Randall Collins, who has most clearly advanced the idea that knowledge systems serve in the first instance a symbolic purpose, seems to mean that knowledge systems function primarily as prestigious ideological bases in order to give to the professionals high occupational status honour. The ritualistic and ceremonial moments in practising their professions impress the laymen. Those who have the knowledge have also the privilege of being in contact with a higher world – it may be a divine world in the true sense as for the clergy, or a secular higher world of ideas that gives to these people a serene capacity that is the real background for the honours given to them.[1] Murphy, who has called attention to the difference between Collins and Parkin in this respect, has emphasized that Collins does not give a precise statement on the eventual realistic background to problem-solving capacities of the professionals.[2] In fact, Collins does not exclude the possibility that professionals can solve problems within their field. What he wants to stress is that the occupational honour given to professionals is not dependent on this problem-solving capacity. It stems from other sources, sources that he wants to trace far back in history when the servants of gods and the servants of the sword guarded their fields of authority against intruders. Professionalism is a modern variety of (or just a continuation of) primitive and feudal usurpations of functions that asked for veneration.

There is an important difference between the symbolic interpretation of professionalism that Collins has given and the theory of symbolic capital that Bourdieu has created. Bourdieu's theory is a theory primarily on the heredity of symbolic capital in society and the veneration for these systems. This means that he deals with the transmission of knowledge systems, but also with the content of symbolic capital, but his theory is not in the first instance related to the questions of where veneration starts out or its sources.[3]

In contrast to the position that Collins has taken, others want to invest much more importance in the acquisition of knowledge systems for professionals. They imply – mostly without an explicit argument – that knowledge systems and a skill acquired in a professional learning process give to professionals the capacities that they use not only for actual problem-solving but also for their standing in society. A society that needs problem-solvers of a special kind (such as technical specialists or social workers) will create the proper teaching for these categories and reward them for their abilities in their field. The reasoning is in many ways market-oriented, and we may call this the economic interpretation of professionalism. Once a demand has become defined, a supply system is created and the suppliers are rewarded accordingly. The professional organization is, then, regarded as a restriction in the market functions – monopolies of competence and cartels are concepts used in this connection (see Sarfatti Larson and Åmark)[4] – and primarily as a disturbing factor in a market which need not be idealized by these authors. What has still not been thoroughly investigated is the question if it makes a difference in the marketing of professional abilities whether it is state-organized business or private individuals that create the demand.

It is important to point out that both the symbolic and the economic interpretation of professionalism have close links to the Weberian inspiration for the analysis of professional groups. None of them is, however, dependent on Weber and they might both be combined with other sources of inspiration as well.

Knowledge-based groups

The fundamental conclusions from the essays in this volume on state and knowledge are, first, that there are groups based on a shared problem-solving knowledge, which have acted as groups in very different social settings in European and American history, and, second, that knowledge-based groups have never been characterized by a total autonomy and that those with the most extended autonomy (for example university researchers) are not the most 'typical' professionals. Instead, two other characteristics have been deemed most important in the different shapes of knowledge-based groups. First, they are found in quite different social environments in different societies and their strategies are accordingly formed in different ways. Second, they are granted a 'jurisdiction' of their problem area[5] by their employers, collaborators, clients or indirect financers (the taxpayers in many cases) which can be withdrawn or changed in scope when the surroundings demand a change.

The emphasis in this volume is therefore on social change, state demands and professional variation. Societies have been different in different times and knowledge-based groups have also been different and have acted differently. There are hardly any two countries where professions have been quite like each other, and everywhere they have changed. This does not mean that there are no knowledge-based groups any more where 'de-professionalization' may be detected. This term is coined because of the limitation in the conceptual frame. Only when a demonstrative reference group is known to be 'the professionals' can we also discern 'de-professionalization'. Otherwise we have to concentrate, instead, on the exciting study of the change of professional habits and work through the different adaptation of knowledge-based groups in different societies.

The state has been the most important friend of the professions (in order to domesticize them, of course) in some societies and it has been abhorred by them in others at certain times. Knowledge has always been used by both state and industry in general terms, and the groups which have had the problem-solving capacities or, at least, have managed to give the impression that they have these capacities, have been asked, implored or ordered to help.

Sometimes a group has diligently managed to manoeuvre strategically in this situation in order to establish itself in a very privileged position, while another group has not been able to do so. Some knowledge-based groups have become part of the elite in their societies while others have not, and there is a wide status gap between elite professions and the non-elite, knowledge-based groups. There are many variables which have been of importance in deciding their treatment by others and their own strategic actions. The transfer of knowledge is one: by imitation (Britain), by attendance at certain prestigious schools (France), by attendance at certain specialist types of schools (Germany) or by attendance in high-quality education (the United States). The indicated types are never quite unambiguous and no sharp differences are noticeable in many instances, but the loyalty pattern of the nineteenth-century French engineers to their old school (Polytechnique, Central and so on) ought to be compared to the German engineer from the type of school that was called Technische Hochschule and the British engineer who was trained by a certain master. Similar differences may be found in other professional groups.

A second variable is the type of the knowledge base. Different knowledge bases have in fact served the bearers of the knowledge in different ways. A medical knowledge base, though of partly different content, is used by both doctors and nurses. Even if it is completed by different other elements in the two cases, the structure of education in higher and lower seems to be fundamental and only reinforced through the gender organization of these knowledge-based groups. This may be compared with engineers, who have, mostly, competed for the same posts in private industry independently of their level of education. Even if those with the higher education have, on average, got the better positions, they have not succeeded in their repeated efforts to close the upper ranks for those with the higher education. Third, we may also take doctors and lawyers and engineers into consideration from another point of view. They may all specialize in their education but there is also a vast variation in their careers independently of specialization. These careers are sometimes organized into specific professions: attorneys, solicitors, barristers and so on are not in the same profession even if they have (in many countries) basically the same education.

Another variable of importance is the shape of the state. The currently rising interest in the state as something with an explanatory power in itself, which cannot be reduced to class interests or individual motives,[6] makes it urgent to take a standpoint on the content of the relation between professions and state. States have been different in the types of networks of which they consist – that is, the relation system between the decision-making political and administrative bodies, which forms the individual state. Knowledge-based groups have found different places in these settings. Official recognition by the state is no general prerequisite, but it is very common that knowledge-based groups have acquired a charter or other official acknowledgement to certify their position in society.

Further, states have incorporated the expertise of the professionals – their problem-solving capacity – in different ways. Sometimes they have been made central for state functions (for example, in France); sometimes they have been recognized as (semi)-independent bodies of experts, whose advice may be taken when found relevant, and whose status is only partly dependent on recognition by the state (such as in Britain). All types of variation between the extremes are found, such as the creation of special bodies, organized by the state, for experts in certain fields with the privilege of exerting the functions of the profession in question. As noticed by Burrage, this form of state organization of the knowledge-based groups deserves special note and may be called 'cameralism' from '*Kammer*', the German term for these organizations.[7]

One of the main sources of state influence has been the educational system. In those countries where the state has had control over the professions – mainly continental Europe and Scandinavia – professional schooling has been organized mainly through the state. Privately organized schools (with less paradigmatic replicas organized by states) have been common in the United States, and individual training, often organized by the professions themselves, has been the usual form for acquiring the professional knowledge base in Britain. These ways into professionalism have been regarded, in the classical literature on the professions, as the 'typically professional' bases for getting into the professional groups. This Anglo-American bias has brought about a presupposition that professions should be characterized by an anti-state attitude. Thus either continental and Scandinavian knowledge-based groups are not 'professional', or there is something wrong with the concept 'professional' used in this way.

Clients and employers are other variables. Clients become clients because they have met problematic situations and they transfer their problems to 'their' doctor, solicitor, construction engineer, sanitary inspector or whoever may come into consideration. Clients of seventeenth-century Europe were most often aristocrats who asked for submissiveness rather than for advice from their preachers, orators, master builders and scribes. In the late twentieth century the individual client has become less common and is often at best an equal in status to the professional whose services he will engage. On the other hand, collective clients have become much more numerous in all types of professional activity and, depending on the importance of the collectivity, they may be demanding in their relationship to the practitioner in the professional field.

This means that the difference between the private practitioner and the employed professional is less apparent now than it was a century ago. On the other hand, the distinction becomes blurred again if one goes further back in European history. The aristocrat would not make a great difference between a man whom he had on his payroll and a man to whom he gave an occasional sum for good services.

Historicity

As Magali Sarfatti Larson has shown, the historicity of professions is nothing specific to the countries (that is, the national systems) where professions are tied to rule systems formed by the state. She has discussed professionalism in an Anglo-American context, and her examples from the last century are mainly of American origin. These examples show that a major change took place when professions were generally built into a bureaucratic surrounding from the 1890s and onwards. In this phase, which she calls the corporate economy, professions have established new normative systems in order to cope with the new situation with which they have been faced. They have not 'lost' their autonomy in their new roles but they have, to a varying degree, adapted their code-books to the new relations that professionals have come into.[8]

There are several other studies of American professionalism that show the same thing: American professionals have been related to a changing society and have adapted to the changes of the society. American professionalism is not determined by the state, as is continental and Scandinavian European professionalism, but has all the same been the object of a historical development. There has not been a 'once-for-all professionalism' either in the United States or in Europe. Professional activities – labelled professional or not – have changed in content and legitimation according to the environment. This environment has been determined in continental and Scandinavian Europe primarily by the state and in the Anglo-American world primarily by private sector enterprise, which means that the relations between professions and society ought to be interesting to compare systematically. The chapters in this volume make evidently clear that knowledge-based groups behave in some specific ways in the most different social settings, but that they are, at the same time, very dependent on the crucial variables of these social settings. Knowledge transmission, type of knowledge base, state organization, clients, employment and possibly a couple of more crucial variables have to be treated intensely in each case in order to clarify both the historical process in the development of certain knowledge-based groups and also the common grounds for such knowledge-based groups.

The contributions to this volume

The contributors take up different aspects of the problematic. In the first essay Randall Collins shows what in his opinion are the main changes in the conceptual framework which has been used by sociologists when they have dealt with the professions. He also presents a systematic view on professions and discerns a continental model of professionalism as an alternative to the Anglo-American.

The next two contributions deal with knowledge and discourse. Magali Sarfatti Larson discusses the characteristics of the knowledge bases of the experts, their discursive fields and their relation to other groups in society. The discourse is used, according to her, both as a tool for understanding and as a defence against attack. Lennart G. Svensson approaches the problem of discourse from another angle. He wishes to show in which ways professionals, exemplified by architects and psychologists, use textbook knowledge and other forms of knowledge in their actual work situations. He concludes that the knowledge transmitted through formal education is not the only or even most important knowledge for professionals in their conversationally defined situations of practice.

The following three chapters all deal with the relation between professionals and politics; that is, the state and its actors. For Raymond Murphy the perspective on how the standing of professionals has changed must be broader than a very limited theory of professionalism. His own perspective is a Weberian theory of closure, and the relation to state and market are the explanatory factors for changes among professionals. Charles McClelland shows that even if German knowledge-based groups were not exactly like the British or American, they were certainly professional in a sense, even if the role of the state was a very active one and even if their autonomy was limited. He also emphasizes the historicity of professionalism and its relative weakness. Margareta Bertilsson, in her contribution, emphasizes another transformation of professionalism. She shows that the welfare professions have become involved with the state so that they have assumed, or been invested with, a mediating function between the state and the citizens. For citizens are clients of the welfare professions in the welfare state, in her conception.

The next two contributions deal with the knowledge content of specific professional groups. Tony Becher shows that those who teach and those who are taught do not necessarily share the same ideas and ideals. His examples are from pharmacists, nurses and teachers, and he compares the teacher–practitioner relation in these three fields. They share a knowledge base in each case but, as he found in an interview investigation, their attitudes and loyalties differ. Aant Elzinga, on the other hand, has investigated the professionalism in a certain field in Sweden where the struggle between groups has been intense. The efforts to establish 'nursing care' as a scientific field of study have been closely connected with the ambition to confirm a progressional status for nurses and to give them a different knowledge base from that of doctors.

The two last contributions deal with two specific professions, veterinarians (in Sweden) and lawyers (in France). Inga Hellberg, in her study of veterinarians, shows both the historicity of the form of professionalization and the importance of the active role of the state. The periodization of the development of the profession is closely connected with the ambitions that the state had for it. Lucien Karpik, in his study of French *avocats*, shows that this profession relies not only on a technical but also on a political knowledge base. In historical situations the professionals have been able to emphasize the one or the other part of their knowledge base which has given to the profession different fields of action and connected it differently with the state.

In sum, material is presented in this volume to show how professional groups in a wide sense are dependent on the use of knowledge bases, relations to state, clients and employers and strategic actions and attitudes of the groups in specific historical situations. Flexibility seems to be a more fundamental criterion of professionalism than any set of properties that might be invented. Professionals exist in the form in which society – market or state – finds use for their knowledge base.

Notes

1 Collins, 1979.
2 Murphy, 1983; also in Murphy, 1988, ch. 2, pp. 15–42.
3 Bourdieu and Passeron, 1970; Bourdieu, 1984.
4 Larson, 1977/1979; Åmark, 1990.
5 Abbott, 1988, defines professionalism according to the concept of 'jurisdiction'.
6 See, especially, Evans, Rueschemeyer and Skocpol, 1985. This book has stimulated a debate which cannot be cited here.
7 M. Burrage in an unpublished manuscript on cameralism.
8 Larson, 1977/1979.

2

Changing conceptions in the sociology of the professions

Randall Collins

Areas of research in the social sciences seem to have a life-cycle. After some unfocused preliminaries (frequently in adjacent topics or applied/ideological areas), there comes a 'classic period' of research and theory which explicitly generates an explanatory paradigm (or competing paradigms). Then comes a time of revisionism, a new upsurge of research and theory. But after this the area dies down, little work is done in it because the main contours seem to be known. The field drifts back into applied issues, and the narrower focus here, together with the fact that little research or new theory is being done, give the impression that the field is dead. This seems a peculiar problem of the social sciences, part of our lack of cumulation: our very successes in achieving consensus on an area leads researchers to move away from it, and we have little institutional memory of what we learned that isn't immediately in our research front.

The preliminary period of concern for the professions, from the 1930s to the early 1950s, was not strictly focused upon the nature of the professions *per se*, but found professions, so to speak, standing in the way of a discussion of some larger topic. Kotschnig's *Unemployment in the Learned Professions* for instance, centred on the political theme that the expansion of education in Europe had produced large numbers of persons whom the economy could not absorb, resulting in dissatisfactions which contributed to Nazism.[1] Mannheim also saw professions in a political context, but regarded them more as saviour than threat, in effect as the institutionalization of the 'free-floating intellectuals', free of ideological ties, who could produce a technocratic solution for the ills of modern society.[2]

As professionalization theory emerged as a topic in its own right, it was set in the context of issues of bureaucratization or politics. Parsons developed his sociological theory of professions to counter the notion that modern society was becoming more rigidly bureaucratic, and to introduce an altruistic element into capitalist occupations.[3] The first point was the perceptive one that modern organizations are not merely bureaucracies characterized by hierarchy and centralization. Professional experts within bureaucracies introduce horizontal connections to other experts and to their professional communities; their activities are carried out by delegation of authority and with a degree of autonomy. Parsons' second point was more ideological. Where a Marxian or instrumentalist viewpoint would see modern capitalism as motivated by nothing but self-interested pursuit of profit or wages, Parsons argued that professions are motivated by altruistic motives of service and maintenance of standards. Since the professions, in Parsons' argument, are the technically most important of modern occupations, their altruism can be viewed as comprising the centre of the modern economy, and the Marxist position is reversed.

As empirical field research on professions began to be done, it focused largely on the first of these points – the relationship between the professions and organizational authority structure – although some discussions (rather than empirical research itself) reiterated the argument about altruism. Research began on specific professions. The sociology of science developed by Merton and Barber was in many ways parallel to Parsons' more general argument about the professions.[4] Scientists were depicted as oriented towards their community and to upholding altruistic ideals of universalism, disinterestedness and competence. This argument was directed against political opponents of liberal democracy, both against the Marxists (Hessen, Stern) who began the sociology of science in the 1930s, and against the Nazis, who exemplified the values antithetical to the practice of science.

The first round of research on specific professions was done primarily around the issue of role conflicts and lines of authority in organizations. The theme of professions versus bureaucracies, of expert versus line authority, was something of a paradigm found not only in the studies of professions but also in the more general field of organizational studies as well. A particular prominent case concerned the role conflicts of engineers.[5] Kornhauser's book bears the characteristic title *Scientists in Industry: Conflict and Accommodation*.[6] In general, this research work studied some profession in its organizational context. The empirical sociology of science focused on what happened in laboratories, but not from the point of view of the social production of knowledge (a theme that was later to be pushed by the radical social constructionists of the 1970s), but rather to discover the conditions for efficient organizational functioning.

Thus the tendency was to study the professions in regard to

external issues in sociology, especially their effect upon some other sphere of social activity. Medical sociology emerged in relation to social problems interests. Again, Parsons developed his theory of medicine as a set of normative roles, making a functional contribution to the society as a whole.[7] Lawyers were studied especially from a political point of view; as an influential elite based on restricted mobility channels,[8] as well as an occupation split by internal stratification.[9] Professions were set against the theme of occupations in a mass society.

As this research built up, however, it gradually acquired some autonomy as a subject of theoretical concern. Theoretical controversies emerged. Symbolic interactionists disputed the external and normative interpretation of professions, countering with their own emphasis on situational flexibility and self-creation of identities.[10] Although the tendency had been to treat professions in the general context of other occupations, the question became more pointed as to what constituted the difference between professions and ordinary occupations. Some occupations, moreover, were in a middle position as 'semi-professions'. Was there a sequence that occupations went through, such that we observed them at different phases at any given point in time?

The classic period of professionalization theory culminated in Wilensky's 1964 article, 'The Professionalization of Everyone?' Wilensky continued some of the 'external' themes regarding occupational and political trends, but his judgement was largely negative. Not all occupations could become professions; that is, fields of work whose practitioners had gained control of their own training, admission to practice and evaluation of standards of performance. Professionalization thus became viewed as a matter of power, a high degree of success in the struggle for autonomy; the formation of a self-regulating community was seen as the key to such success, and the altruistic codes of conduct put forward by such communities as part of their collective identity in the face of distrustful outsiders. Although many occupations may aspire to this kind of power and status, they succeed only in degree, because success here depends upon conditions not available to everyone: control of areas of uncertainty, and the capacity to organize for collective validation of work in such areas.

The 1960s and 1970s experienced a second upsurge of research on professions, in this case a revisionist wave. Professions were seen as part of the stratification of society; but instead of being extolled as altruistic and liberalizing, they were critically scrutinized as part of the structure of privilege. Research on stratification and social mobility focused upon educational attainment as the main channel to higher positions; together with Wilensky's model which stressed professional control of its own training and admission to practice, this led to historical analyses of the process by which professional education and credentialling were established. Especially high-status professions such as medicine were now analysed as successful monopolies reaping the benefits of their market controls in the form of high incomes.[11] Critical analyses of the credentialling process assessed the component of educational requirements attributable to skills, versus the component due to the inflationary movement of credentials in response to expanding educational systems.[12] An explicitly conflict-oriented theory of the professions was put forward on the basis of comparative and historical evidence.[13] This in turn was incorporated into an even more general theory of the production of inequality through social closure, building upon Parkin by Murphy.[14]

Since the revisionist sociology of the professions was riding a political wave of its time, one might say that it became institutionalized all too easily. The older functionalist and idealizing view of professions fell rather rapidly into disfavour; the conflict view of professions was accepted readily because it fitted the mood of the times. Thus in a sense the sociology of the 1980s, now far removed from the old political/ideological disputes regarding functionalism versus conflict theory, has let the sociology of the professions slip into an unexciting routine. Although there is some truth in this assessment, it should be noted that the breaks between different phases in the theory of the professions are not so sharp as an external/political viewpoint would suggest. It was empirical research building up during the 1940s and 1950s that made it possible to separate out professions as a phenomenon in its own right. The culmination of this, Wilensky's 1964 model, was itself a theory about differences among occupations, based on specific conditions which allow them to construct varying degrees of autonomous control. Wilensky's model really stands at the watershed between the 'classic' and 'revisionist' theories. Although it looks backwards in laying out a sequence through which all professions presumably pass, it looks forward in so far as it is a model of occupational closure based upon power. In a sense, the revisionist theories took Wilensky further, by emphasizing the privileges that follow from having attained this closure; and by paying more attention to the historical dynamics by which professional closure develops, especially in the expansion of educational credential systems.

In the same way, there is a continuity between the revisionist theory and the 'post-revisionist' sociology of professions which is now emerging. A major theme of the current work revitalizing the field is to capture historical variation. All professions do not go through the same pathways, nor do they arrive at the same outcomes. We have instead a kind of family resemblance among different professions, and current work is concerned with charting those multiple paths. An exemplar of such 'post-revisionist' work would be Burrage's demonstration of how the major professions of law and medicine were shaped along different channels in their respective countries by the English, American, and French revolutions.[15]

'Anglo' and 'Continental' models of professions

In the interest of maximizing the cumulation of knowledge, let me attempt to pull together some themes from past work, and relate them to the condition of current research. Classic sociology of the professions was organized around the belief that there is a single, ideal-typical entity, towards which everything is evolving (or against which everything is judged). This model has been much criticized, for teleology, for evolutionary Utopianism (or ideology) or for insensitivity to historical variations. But this does not necessarily mean that any theoretical conception must dissolve into an endless variety of particular kinds of occupational constellations.

A reasonable strategy which emerges from current research would be to suggest there are two principal models of this wondrous occupation we are tracking down: (1) the Anglo-American, which stresses the freedom of self-employed practitioners to control working conditions; and (2) the Continental, which stresses elite administrators possessing their offices by virtue of academic credentials. The two models have something in common: they both are idealized and ideologically defined (which is why they are dangerous concepts for us to take at face value); and they both refer to occupations which organize themselves 'horizontally', as communities with a certain style of life, code of ethics and self-conscious identity and boundaries to outsiders. This gets us part of the way to an overall definition: we are dealing with occupations which are also a Weberian 'status group' (*Stand*) – more precisely, an elite status group (since low-ranking occupations can also become status communities, in this case negative).

It appears that there are several ways in which occupations acquire this kind of social organization and prestige. A typical continental route was via the transformation of employment in a bureaucratic hierarchy, under the impetus of academic credentializing and against the backdrop of the legalistic *Standestaat*, and the taming of the aristocracy in the absolutist state. Here we have the nobility as the model status group, which gives its aura to bureaucrats; then the credential revolution carries this aura further and further afield to other occupations. In seventeenth- and eighteenth-century France, the nobility of the robe gradually displaced the nobility of the sword; in Prussia, Russia and elsewhere, the bureaucracy of the absolutist state became the counterweight to the military aristocracy. Thus one old, closed elite occupational community not only gave up part of its privilege to a newer occupational group, but the newer group modelled itself on the status privileges of the old.

The driving force for the development of continental professions was primarily the growth of the state. Political struggles, whether revolutionary or reformist, typically pitted different factions against one another based on these changing structures of state-supported privilege. In Prussia, the reform movement at the time of the Napoleonic wars was a victory for university-educated bureaucrats, who were able to extend credential requirements into a monopoly on government careers. As the bureaucratic model of organization spread into the private sector in the nineteenth century, the elite occupational sector was built up around the ingredients which carried on the status traditions of the past. Thus Weber, writing around 1914, built into his definition of bureaucracy the monopolization of offices by academically trained experts with a distinctive status honour.[16] Bureaucracy, academic credentialling, and a quasi-aristocratic life-style became fused to a degree which characterizes the Continental much more than the Anglo image of a profession.

A typical Anglo route, by contrast, was the formation of a monopolistic practitioner group operating on a market for services. An occupation became a high-status profession by forming itself apart from the state. English lawyers spun off official roles from the royal law courts into a private, guild-like structure; medical practitioners acquired licensing monopolies from the Crown. Here the image of an elite profession was not that in the service of the state, nor indeed within any bureaucratic framework modelled after the state. Occupational prestige, rather, resided in having one's own self-regulating organization. Such organizations, of course, are not oblivious of the state; but they attempt to use the state merely to give it privileges, and to back up its power of monopolization and of self-regulation over its members. With this as a leading structure, numerous occupations may attempt to raise their status by organizing themselves into professional associations in emulation of older professions. Their success depends on a kind of decentralized, democratic occupational politics, perhaps best represented by the proliferation of quasi-professions and would-be professions in the United States.

The 'Continental' and 'Anglo' models which I have sketched are ideal-types. More analytically, we can say that the resources and historical conditions by which occupations struggle to raise their status and privileges include two broadly differing types: political struggle for control of positions within an elite bureaucratic hierarchy; and the struggle to form private governments within occupations, backed up by the delegation of state powers to regulate a market. In any historical case, variations on these two types of conditions may lie anywhere along the continuum, and may involve mixtures of both types. Thus there are numerous routes across the generations leading up to whatever occupational structures may exist at any point in time. Concretely these will be structured by the particular histories of the English, German, French, American and other states, and their surrounding organizations and status groups.

This typology is not analytically exhaustive. there are also occupations which we certainly should take as 'professions' of some sort, which do not depend on government position or licensing for their closure and control of work conditions: a strong example is the scientist (and in archaic societies, the magician), occupations which are intrinsically esoteric and tied together by in-group networks of apprenticeship and validation. That is to say, some professional communities may lack even a minimal relationship to the state, but are organized by their inner relationships. Here again, we are dealing with ideal-types, which are capable of being mixed with other structures. Thus scientists may come into some relationship with the state (such as has developed since 1940); and at some point in time, various of the politically based professions may attempt to make a structural alliance with scientists. We must be clear in such cases what we are seeing. One ideology about the professions, especially prominent in the professional self-identification of the later twentieth century, derives all their claims and privileges from their knowledge; this is as if to say that professionals are simply possessors of specialized scientific knowledge. This definition drops out all the political and organizational structures, reduces all the ideal types down to one. What we need, rather, is a relationship among ideal-types. And as we shall see, even in the case of the knowledge-centred professions (science itself) there is a crucial social structure.

Analytically, there is some unity behind all the occupational variants that we might call 'professions' of one kind or another. The broad outlines of our territory comprise *socially idealized occu-*

pations organized as closed associational communities. We can add on to this the various traits by which particular occupations may acquire these status structures: these might include 'bureaucratic office-holders', 'licensed market-monopolizers', and 'esoteric knowledge-holders' and combinations thereof. And we can investigate the degree to which occupations actually obtain high status, self-governing powers and community organization.

Knowledge as power versus social monopolization of knowledge

In the 'post-revisionist' discussion of the professions, the nature of 'knowledge' has come in for renewed discussion. What is the nature of the expertise that professions monopolize? And what social consequences follow from what kind of knowledge and what modes of appropriation? The issue is not merely whether particular occupations hold particular kinds of knowledge, but whether their knowledge is the basis of their prestige and closed organizational structure.

Let us make some comparisons. There is no doubt at all that engineers have valid scientific knowledge (and indeed have had it, in such forms as military engineering and construction skills, for at least 2,000 years). But engineers have had the greatest difficulty in getting themselves organized as a self-governing occupational group, and they have rarely had high prestige; in the traditional army, these technical skills generally carried the lowest status, compared to more ostentatiously ceremonial combat officers. Even today, when our 'high-tech' civilization depends far more on engineers than on anyone else, they have neither the rewards nor the tight communal structure found among doctors, lawyers and others. Here we see that technical knowledge is not enough to determine the occupational structure, even knowledge for which there is a very strong demand. A similar case is mechanics: the people who repair one's car and household appliances, and who keep factory and office machinery running. These are clearly the indispensable experts, without whose knowledge our civilization would quickly collapse – something that could not be said about the withdrawal of services by any of the high-prestige professions of today.

What is the lesson? It is not the existence of knowledge that is crucial, but how it is socially organized. The theory that the 'professions' owe their high material and non-material rewards to their knowledge is essentially a market model: services which are very valuable must be paid a high price in social respect, autonomy and power as well as income. But this is a very crude market theory. Price depends on how much of a demand there is for this knowledge, and how large a supply. The demand for the services of mechanics is very high in our civilization, but they are not treated particularly well; that would appear to be because the supply of mechanics' skills is also quite large. Tracing this further back, the reason for this large (and rather flexible) supply is that these skills are learned through practical experience; and it is very difficult to make them mysterious and impressive however much we rely on them practically. The problems of engineers getting themselves organized to acquire high respect are similar.

Is the difference academic knowledge versus practical knowledge? Perhaps there is a correlation here; but it is not of the sort which the skills-market model predicts. The market model should give the highest rewards for the highest payoff in services; why then should genuine practical services get lower rewards than services which are embellished by additional years of attendance in a non-practical setting? The conclusion must be that the knowledge which brings professional privileges is knowledge embellished by its status image.

I will add three more considerations about the academic basis of 'professions'. First, there is a great deal of empirical evidence that extended academic training does not usually enhance practical effectiveness very much.[17] The content of schooling typically does not provide direct practical skills; those students who have the highest grades do not turn out to be the best performers; most practical skills are learned on the job; comparisons of performance of credentialized and uncredentialized members of the same occupations do not show any superiority of the former. This does not necessarily mean there is no such thing as 'professional' knowledge. But it does tell us that the academic organizational structure has a social rather than a technical impact: it affects the way in which an occupation is organized, but not the amount of skilled performance. The point is not to claim that a doctor or an academically trained engineer is a fraud; they may have real skills, but these skills could also be acquired another way. But without the academic organizational structure, they find it much more difficult to acquire the same 'professional' status.

Second, the market model depends not merely on whether there is a skill which is provided, but on that skill being in relatively short supply. Hence the high-status occupations ('professions') are those which are able to organize themselves to limit the supply of skills. Doctors, for example, monopolize not only the practice of medicine by their licences, but also monopolize the sale of medical drugs by legal prescriptions. In the modern professional structure, doctors make a living mainly by monopolizing the right to sell temporary licences to patients to buy small supplies of drugs. An alternative structure would exist if knowledge about how to make medical diagnoses, and which drugs to take for which symptoms, were widely disseminated in the population. This could exist if medical testing laboratories sold their results directly to the public; medical drugs were sold commercially without restriction; and the media and educational system spread medical knowledge widely so that everyone could take maximal advantage of these services and products, without having to go through the doctor as monopolistic 'middle-man'. In other words, if medical knowledge were not so strongly monopolized, the prestige and rewards of doctors would be much more like ordinary occupations, and their occupational structure would be much less like a closed status group.

Third, when an occupation does acquire academic credentialling requirements, an additional market consideration comes into play. It is no longer a matter of the supply of skilled performers (persons able to provide certain services); there is also a supply of credentials, and a social demand for them. This credential market has its own dynamics, quite apart from whatever level of skill the education provides.[18] The occupational payoff of a given level of education responds to the supply of educational credentials; and the content of education which goes into credentials responds to the process of academic competition, rather than to the skill requirements of jobs. Credential inflation is not the same issue as monopolization, although educational credentialling can be a mechanism through which monopolization may proceed. But the credential market adds another layer of social organization to the occupational structure, one that is particularly important in shaping the social identity of twentieth-century occupations.

Extrinsic versus self-created demands for solving problems

The above examples are cases where there is a 'real', extrinsic skill: that is, there is a demand for the knowledge, which exists whether or not a 'professional' status organization is the form in which it is provided. Some of the skills of 'professionals', however, are answers to self-created problems; the skill is intrinsic to the professional structure itself, and does not exist without it. Law, for example: a lay person needs a lawyer to make a way through the mazes of legal procedures, codes and precedents; but that is because the legal problems have been created by the previous activities of the profession of lawyers. Without lawyers, there would be no legal problems; that is, there would be problems, but they would not be legal ones: they would be matters of politics, tradition, personal negotiation, conflict and so on. Similarly, with the oldest profession, of theology/divinity; whether one is saved or damned, feels a need for absolution of sins or defences from witchcraft, depends on the prior existence of the religious profession. Without the professionals, the problems would not exist.

A third example of a profession serving self-created demands is science. Scientists become eminent by solving intellectual problems posed by other scientists. Their knowledge, and the issues to which it is an answer, are intrinsically connected; neither would exist without the community which defines the issues and socially validates what is accepted as an answer to them. This is why scientists are so strongly organized, even without the enforcement power of the state licensing; and also without university credentials – a structure which has been added on to an already flourishing scientific community only within the last century and a half.

Law and theology are two of the oldest and most important 'professions'; other occupations have attempted to raise their status by piggy-backing off the structures which these have created for themselves. It was the church which created the universities; and the state connection is the core of the lawyers' position. Hence I would suggest that the model of 'self-created' problems – and the 'professional' knowledge which is a solution to them – may be the most important component for a theory of idealized occupational status groups. As I have indicated above, of course, a general theory of the professions must be multi-dimensional, and this is only one component of it. The scientific community has been another piece of these puzzles, at least within the last century, as various status-striving occupations have attempted to make alliance with it. And for some occupations, there are extrinsic sources of demand for their expertise (along the line of medicine), which adds another mechanism: the social processes of monopolizing real skills. Any particular profession thus derives its power from some combination of these different sources.

The future of research on professions

Clearly, there are plenty of problems to be solved in the sociology of the professions, and hence opportunities for yet further phases of development. One broad set of problems is historical and comparative. I believe we have advanced to the point of being able to see, not just massive historical variation, but also some of the analytical themes which underlie them. There are broad 'Continental' and 'Anglo' routes to professional status and closure; analytically this means struggles over bureaucratic position on one hand, and struggles for decentralized market-regulating associations on the other. Politics thus becomes an increasingly central part of our researches: both the massive revolutionary events which Burrage has described, and the more intimate levels of organizational politics within every institutional sphere.

On another front, there are questions of theory *per se*, such as the nature of professional monopolization, and group closure generally. This is an area in which broader sociological theory has been making considerable strides, towards a general model of the relationship between markets, networks and organizations. Theory of the professions thus has a link to more general questions of economic, political and social organization. What the analysis of the professions can add uniquely to this discussion, I suggest, are two things: our special concerns for how knowledge enters into social conflicts and forms of organization; and our current emphasis on historical sequences and comparisons. The study of the professions has raised the question clearly of when and how knowledge affects social structure, and conversely of what social conditions determine who will control what kinds of knowledge. Since expertise as the basis of power is a prevailing ideology in late twentieth-century societies, the sociology of professions gives us a vantage point for seeing through some of the major struggles of our times.

The sociology of professions also has the analytical advantage of now being grounded in historical comparisons. The more general field of markets and organizations, by contrast, has yet to achieve this broadening; it is still mostly focused upon models of organizations derived from narrow slices of time in one or a few societies. (There is a similar narrowness in the empirical base for the study of markets.) The danger of becoming historical is that a field simply fragments into particular case studies, and loses its analytical edge in sheer description. But the strength of historical sociology is its potential for reconstructing our theories on a broader basis, one which is capable of accounting for variations and for the dynamics of change itself.

A current intellectual frontier is the challenge to make all our theories historical in the analytical sense: that is, as referring to social processes unfolding through time. History is like a process of endlessly mixing a salad, in which new ingredients are constantly being thrown into the bowl, while the old ingredients disappear only slowly. This means, first of all, we have to be analytical: we need specific theories of how each set of ingredients (for example, bureaucratic, scientific or market-regulating structures) operates; and second, we need to be aware of the combinations among these ideal-type models which make up an actual society at any point in time. And there is a third point: the sequence in which different ingredients are thrown in affects how the latter will operate. I have suggested this is the way in which the 'Continental' professions have chain-linked themselves on to the bureaucratic official *Stand*, and that in turn derived from struggles to supersede the old military aristocracy. Every modern occupation carries some historical influence within it in this sense.

As a final instance of dynamic processes, I would suggest attention to historical declines in the power of professions. We have freed ourselves by and large from linear evolutionary models of social change. Many of the most interesting issues concern occupations which lose ground in the struggle for privilege. Divinity is one such case: in medieval Europe, it was virtually *the* profession, its monopoly enforced by heresy trials. It has declined over the centuries to a modest position in the occupational array. Where it survives most prominently, as in the United States, it is as a market-centred competition among religious entrepreneurs, whose commercial tactics create scandals and further threaten the occupation's status. Our overall theme, the formation of professions of various structural types, is analytically part of the same question as the decline of professions. Whether something goes up or goes down is the same question; our problem is to explain position and movement.

Notes

1 Kotschnig, 1937.
2 Mannheim, 1935.
3 Parsons, 1939:457–467.
4 Merton, 1949; Barber, 1952.
5 See the summary in Perrucci and Gerstl, 1969.
6 Kornhauser, 1962.
7 Parsons, 1951:428–479.
8 Smigel, 1964.
9 Ladinsky, 1963:47–54.
10 Bucher and Strauss, 1961:325–334; Becker, 1961; Freidson, 1970a.
11 Berlant, 1975; Starr, 1982.
12 Collins, 1979; Barbagli, 1982.
13 Larson, 1977/1979; Collins, 1979:131–181.
14 Parkin, 1979; Murphy, 1988.
15 Burrage, 1990.
16 Weber, 1968:958–963, 998–1002.
17 Collins, 1979, and many other studies.
18 Collins, 1981.

3

In the matter of experts and professionals, or how impossible it is to leave nothing unsaid

Magali Sarfatti Larson

Speaking of the relations between sociology's generalizing concepts and the more empirical concerns of history and ethnography, Clifford Geertz quotes a marvellous analogy from the great art historian Erwin Panofsky: generalizing and specifical approaches in the social sciences are like two neighbours who are allowed to hunt in the same district, but one has the gun and the other all the ammunition.[1] To state what I think that a theory of professions should be, many years after I first told one particular story and many particular stories after that one, makes me feel without either gun or ammunition.

Ten years ago, in *The Rise of Professionalism*, I had proposed not a theory, but an interpretation of the modern professional phenomenon in Anglo-American societies. My reading questioned the evolutionary implications of functionalism and its neglect of historical diversity; it was based on specific historical cases – medicine, the law, engineering and, in our century, 'techno-bureaucratic' specializations such as social work or planning – and compared professionalization movements in England and in the United States from the early nineteenth century to our time. Nevertheless, despite its limited theoretical intentions, this interpretation rooted in specificity appeared as an alternative to the functionalist 'story' and seemed thus to be pursuing a measure of generalization.

On one hand, my reading linked the partial phenomenon of professionalization and its specific cases to the general restructuring of society in two exemplary instances of liberal capitalism. On the other hand, the analysis of different professional projects clearly indicated that they all shared the goal of creating a protected institutional market for services or for the work of individuals whose competence also had to be institutionally demonstrated. This goal suggested that the leaders of professional reform movements would all have to carry out the structural task of linking certified knowledge to markets of services or labour, although it was clear that they could only do so in particular circumstances and in historically variable forms.

The study of professionalization in the core countries of Anglo-American capitalism led me inevitably to exaggerate the import-ance of a protected market for these social movements, which had had the experience of highly competitive markets. Anglo-American professionalization movements rose from the civil society but necessarily addressed to the state their demands for a guarantee of the monopolistic mechanisms required by their project. On the other hand, as my critics pointed out, I had also exaggerated to the point of distortion the discontinuity of professional practices 'before' and 'after' the Industrial Revolution, where a more attent-ive observation of history would have revealed multiple continuit-ies. It is clear that a historical process as long, as complex and as unevenly developed as the 'Great Transformation' could never provide us with clear cuts in historical practice. The discontinuity of structure between 'pre-modern' and 'modern' professional phenomena is analytical and theoretical: it could never be uniformly translated in empirical reality and it can only be observed in periods and in social spaces that must be carefully specified.

I believe now that it is less productive to work towards a general theory of professions than it is to think of questions which go beyond the professions and address the larger and more important theme of the construction and social consequences of expert knowl-edge. The first part of this chapter is placed under the sign of historical specificity: in tracing the outline of the intellectual path I have followed, I shall be seeking to highlight its gaps and its limitations. However, the general structural area to which pro-fessional phenomena are attached includes the production of knowledge, as an essential component of the activity of experts. The second part of the chapter will therefore be abstract, as I examine the production of 'learned' discourse and its implications for the professional phenomenon. Here, I will attempt to put some aspects of Michel Foucault's fundamental work into a properly sociological key.

I therefore take the risk of affirming that all professional or professionalizing phenomena must be theoretically linked to the social production and certification of knowledge. At different levels and in different social locations, we should nevertheless always find within professional phenomena practices and codes of behaviour which are justified by reference to 'learned' or 'knowledgeable' discourse. Now, individual professionals and professional groups have different capacities to appropriate authoritative and authorizing discourse. This differential capacity constitutes a singular and characteristic dimension of social inequality.

In conclusion, I examine some instances (always particular and limited) where groups of experts have attempted to translate their competence and their authorized power over specific discourses into more directly and overtly political power. It is in instances such as these that we can study with the utmost clarity both the relations between 'knowledge' and 'power' (relations that explain the genesis of power and the varying functions of knowledge) and the negative political consequences of knowledge that cannot be directly challenged.

Professionalization: a limited story

Professionalization in the United Kingdom and the United States consisted in a variety of efforts, led from the late eighteenth century on by elites or counter-elites within the 'classic' occupational fields of medicine and the law and others that followed.[2] I deliberately ignored the military and the clergy, thereby limiting my argument to occupations that transacted their services or their labour on markets. These markets, for a large part, had to be created as much as protected. On the strength of tautology, I assumed that 'profession' in the Anglo-American world would be that which modern professionalization movements were trying to establish.

Despite profound differences, both countries were in the process of organizing nation-wide (indeed, world-wide) market economies and committed at least ideologically to *laissez-faire*. Except for purposes of defence, expansion and internal repression, the growth of the state apparatus and the centralization of power were seen with suspicion by the entrepreneurial bourgeoisie and the architects of its ideology. Government should intervene in society only to ensure the free operation of the market. In the bourgeois mind, as we know well, this principle admitted the provision of trade's physical and legal infrastructure, but not the regulation of its most invidious practices at the point of production, nor the self-defensive union of the workers.

It is in this general context that the leaders of professionalization movements, responding to both the expansion of market opportunities and the decline of traditional warrants of moral probity, strove to obtain the backing of the state for their 'exclusionary shelters in the market'.[3] They justified their claims by 'non-market' principles: disinterestedness, which derived from the gentry's sense of 'noblesse oblige', and superior learning, which, at least in England, could not be quite the same as that of their rivals in the traditional learned professions.[4] Gentlemanly status was something that the 'new' professionals both used as legitimation in their quest for protected market shelters, and hoped to affirm through their behaviour and style of life. The complex social project of modern professional reform thus intertwined market and non-market orientations, disparate ideological and intellectual resources that fed back upon each other. Certified knowledge was obviously a most significant resource in the professions' self-presentation to the public, but it cannot be assumed that it was sufficient to establish the superiority of trained professionals *vis-à-vis* their rivals. The place and importance of professional knowledge in the panoply of resources of each profession changed, thus, with the character of the available technologies and with each profession's fortune.

As I said before, the selection of Anglo-American cases led me to place undue emphasis on *market* professions and professionalization projects that emerged from the civil society. Yet, at first sight, many examples from similar professions in continental Europe do not seem that different. Matthew Ramsey says of the medical profession that 'the Old Regime so clearly lacked a uniform professional monopoly that it would be an anachronism to apply the current concept of "illegal practice" to the eighteenth century'; in the nineteenth century German states, for instance, the guilds – first abolished during the French occupation, then restored in some areas after 1815 – coexisted side by side with stiff regulations before being swept away, as in northern Germany, by a freedom of practice that medical elites themselves had supported.[5]

What needs to be underlined, however, is that the organization of medicine was by far not the most compelling model. The earliest alternative model was the officer corps of absolutist monarchies, a most significative *ancien régime* legacy for the organization of expertise. Napoleon applied it in the construction (or the reconstruction) of his two elite schools for state engineers, the Ecole Polytechnique and Ponts et Chaussées, the military and the civilian *génie*. The French state engineers did not only enjoy the social benefits of elitist schooling, but also, more precisely, the security and the instant authority that the French state bestowed upon its agents.[6] Most other professions were far from attaining comparable prestige; the architects of the Ecole des Beaux-Arts, like some sectors of medicine, tried hard during the nineteenth century and beyond to obtain a similar status, without quite reaching it.[7] It bears repeating, therefore, that there is no pattern of social closure around an occupation that is not inflected by the latter's past, its specific activity and typical context of performance or, as we shall see, by the political context within which closure is obtained.

Matthew Ramsey's comparative study of medical monopoly shows that the effective protection of a strong state can grant a profession social power *before* it has demonstrated technological superiority (or independently of it). He distinguishes four basic models of control of the medical profession that are useful to keep in mind. First, is the *ancien régime* corporate monopoly, in which the state conferred 'exclusive right to practice in certain regions . . . to members of chartered bodies and those persons they choose to co-opt'. The history of British physicians until the Medical Act of 1858 shows that this monopoly was as effective and wide-ranging as its enforcement powers and that success can be maintained for as long as the challengers neither gain clienteles nor the ear of the state. Second, in the model of bureaucratic regulation, typical of Prussian enlightened absolutism and adopted by nineteenth-century France, a state agency identifies qualified individuals, gives them alone the right to practise and punishes their unauthorized rivals. Third, the radical free field, where anybody can attempt to heal or prescribe, is only typical of unsettled outlying areas, though it was adopted in core areas during the French Revolution and in the United States at mid-century, and fourth, the modified free field, where practitioners are certified by a designated official agency, given certain exclusive privileges (such as that of testifying in court or being forensic doctors) and where the *use of the title*, but not the practice itself, is a monopoly enforceable at law. The United Kingdom, Germany, three Swiss cantons in the nineteenth century, Norway in 1871 and Sweden in 1915 adopted this model, which is still the common form of protection enjoyed by professions other than medicine.[8]

Ramsey argues first, and undisputably, that monopoly – granted that such protection is desirable for the practitioners whom it englobes – is a *political* phenomenon. As such, it depends on strictly political conceptions of what the state's role should be. Therefore, in his period, it depended more on the fortunes of economic liberalism than practically any other factor, *including* the profession's cognitive and technical achievements or even its organized power. In support of this, he follows the fate of medical libertarianism in both France, so deeply marked by the Napoleonic restoration of regulation, and the four 'free fields'. In France, he says, criticism of monopoly by Catholic and liberal physicians in the second half of the nineteenth century was not well received by the rank and file:

> Whatever their qualms about government interference in the medical domain . . . the doctors remained protectionists, fearful of competition from empirics, foreign physicians and even their French colleagues . . .

Although the state administration oversaw education and admission to practice . . . [the profession did not have to] sacrifice its independence in return for monopoly. Only the empirics had reason to fear *gendarmes* looking over their shoulders.[9]

In the United States, bacteriology explains the gradual elimination of unorthodox healers from the licensing boards better than it explains the reinstitution of medical monopoly itself, which *preceded* 'the first major applications of microbiology in the 1890s'. The regulation of medicine was part of the 'search for order' moved by the fear of excessive competition after the major economic crises of the last decades of the century.[10] Ramsey's research deals with official monopoly, not with its actual enforcement; it is nevertheless quite clear from his account that the *efficacy* of monopoly did not depend exclusively on the state's effectiveness, but also, and arguably as much, on the profession's organization and demonstrable technical superiority.[11]

The French state controlled the secondary school system and higher education. This gave governments the power to manipulate access by changing the examinations and degree requirements.[12] This power would only seem exceptional from the perspective of the non-interventionist state of Anglo-American nations, although even there the state was ultimately always called upon to assist social closure, guaranteeing the credentials obtained in the private sector and the licensing process. What seems characteristic of the French state is the direct and deliberate interventions, from Napoleon on, in re-casting the occupational and class structures through the educational system and the reconstitution of *corps* and orders.[13] The direct impulses provided by the state of a bourgeois liberal nation to the persistence of social inequality could be interpreted as a response to revolutionary discontinuity, rather than simply as another effect of the long tradition of French *dirigisme*.[14]

In sum, it is sound to argue that the inaction of the state may have been a major factor prompting Anglo-American professional leaders to take the initiative in organizing mechanisms of closure and protection around their fields. Nevertheless, in any case they had to address their claims to the state. Ramsey shows that in the emotionally charged context of medicine, both the ideology of *laissez-faire* and the reactions against it, may have had a more determining influence on the response of law-makers than the rational evaluation of the wares that the 'professionalizers' had to offer. However, after the initial reaction, professional issues were decided like others by the normal interplay of political forces.[15] Undoubtedly, there was and there is more than one model of professionalization. Political climate and general political expectations about the role of the state in society shaped the ambitions of both successful and aspiring professionals.[16] Where, as in France, the model of a civil service elite was associated to authority and prestige, it appeared to influence even the classic *professions libérales*.

The existence of distinct models of status closure alerts us to the fact that profession is always a historically specific concept. However, the meaning of 'profession' – whether it emerges from the Anglo-American experience or the French-European – must perforce include the central function that professions (or their counterparts) have in the social practice of most advanced societies: that of *organizing the acquisition and certification of expertise in broad functional areas, on the basis of formal educational credentials held by individuals*. If this can be accepted, then I think that a general structure of profession can be identified beyond the contingencies of politics, social status or nominal labels.[17]

Whatever the origin of professionalization, it results in translating one order of scarce resources (expertise created through standardized training and testing at the higher levels of the formal education system) into another (market opportunities, work privileges, social status or bureaucratic rank). 'Profession' is thus a name we give to historically specific forms that establish *structural links between relatively high levels of formal education and relatively desirable positions and/or rewards in the social division of labour*.

The content and the meaning of each of the terms changes historically, but the inclusion of formal higher education in the definition clearly locates this kind of structural link in societies that have some concept of the university. Again, by 'university' I only intend an institution that collects, transmits and eventually produces knowledge (supposedly at high levels of sophistication and complexity), determines its conditions of validity, and transforms the acquisition of knowledge into an asset, materialized into credentials. What those assets mean in economic terms is obviously variable; but the economic value of the diploma cannot be 'purely' economic nor severed from the status that the credential confers, if nothing else by contrast with the uncredentialled.[18] A degree of control over access to the credential, linked to the protection of *scarcity* (if not necessarily monopoly), is an integral part of this conception of professionalization. In societies that value specialized expert knowledge and are also structurally unequal, scarcity or monopoly have two kinds of interdependent rewards: opportunities in markets of services or labour, on the one hand, and, on the other, status and work privileges in an occupational hierarchy, including bureaucratic position. From both forms of shelter special rent or benefits can be extracted.

One of these benefits is the professional's autonomy in the exercise of his or her specialized functions. Autonomy, which has occupied a special analytical place in the sociology of professions, is justified in principle by the professionals' claim of possessing a special and superior knowledge, which should therefore be free of lay evaluation and protected from inexpert interference. However, in societies that are structurally unequal but ideologically egalitarian, cognitive superiority is not by itself a persuasive legitimation.

The organization of compulsory and hierarchical systems of *public* education strengthens the meritocratic justification of inequality with all the force of institutional objectivity. Knowledge, indeed, must appear to be accessible to all who are willing to learn and capable of learning. Certification, which is a central mechanism of professionalization projects, requires a basis of homogenized and standardized knowledge. Moreover, the very meaning of 'profession' implies that this knowledge will be applied in the world of work: in modern societies both the market and the bureaucratic form of work organization also demand standardization and uniformity of training.

In theory, thus, codification and standardization make knowledge accessible to all, while defining a universe of discourse to which all certified knowers have equal access. However, just as knowledge is not really accessible to all in the same manner or measure, not all certified knowers have the same authority to speak within their field. The boundary that protects cognitive fields toward the outside (roughly coincident, for the professions, with credentialling and certification) means that only the knowers themselves will define what are valid subjects of knowledge and valid criteria of pertinence and truth. The standardization of training appears to guarantee this privilege to all the certified knowers; but it is, in fact, only the homogeneous background upon which the lines that stratify and hierarchicize these special 'communities' of discourse can be drawn. The unequal ability to produce or appropriate authoritative statements distinguishes the leaders from the led, the official from the unofficial spokesmen, the orthodox from the marginals or the dissenters, the prestigious from the more obscure institutional roles and even, after all that, the talented from the less talented.

This is a form of inequality characteristic of all specialized cognitive fields. It may be more or less synchronous with the particular institutional development, collective social position, internal organization and public authority of given professions at given times.

In what follows, I shall examine some hypothetical patterns of relationship between the sociological organization of professional fields and the production of discourse.

Professions and discourse

A theory of professions should be centrally concerned with the conditions under which knowledge is produced and applied in ways that make a difference for the life of others. I shall return in my conclusion to the manner in which 'making a difference' is usually understood in American sociology. It seems to me now that any implicit allusion to the adjacency between knowledge and power must come to terms, sociologically, with the towering shadow of Michel Foucault. I can only sketch here what I think this would involve. As a preamble, I should state my conviction that the control of knowledge always ultimately depends on controlling the subjects who know.

In his inaugural lecture in 1970 at the Collège de France, Michel Foucault distinguished a variety of procedures for controlling the production of discourse, which corresponded to different stages of his work.[19] Among the basic procedures of exclusion in the production of discourse, interdictions come first; they reveal the close affiliation with power and desire of the discourses that have been stricken. The second basic exclusionary procedure is the distinction between reason and madness, which preoccupied Foucault at the beginning of his work. The third is the opposition between truth and falsity. Since Plato, says Foucault, it is typical of Western civilization that its will to know should concern itself essentially with what discourse *says* more than with its nature or efficacy.[20] The epistemic revolution of the seventeenth and eighteenth centuries instituted a new kind of will to knowledge which

> sketched out a schema of possible, observable, measurable and classifiable objects; a will to knowledge which imposed upon the knowing subject – in some ways taking precedence over all experience – a certain position, a certain viewpoint and a certain function (look rather than read, verify rather than comment), a will to knowledge which prescribed . . . the technological level at which knowledge could be employed in order to be verifiable and useful (navigation, mining, pharmacopoeia).[21]

The institutionalization of the scientific vision of truth transformed the practice of *all* forms of discourse: literature, economic practices, penal codes and penal institutions, all sought justification in specific regimes of truth. From a sociological perspective, we should expect to find that a growing number of practitioners within these fields felt compelled to show at the same time that what they said had *a* truth, and the truth of what they said.

At a different level from that of the basic exclusionary principles, Foucault distinguished several *internal* procedures that control the production of discourse, procedures that classify, distribute and order it. More interesting for the sociologist than the exegetic commentary is *authorship*. As a principle for the organization of discourses, a focus of their coherence, it has increasingly tended to disappear from science since the seventeenth century, while being reinforced in literature. But the constitution of science as a discourse ideally without authors fades in practice into the notion of *disciplines*, anonymous systems for the construction of new valid utterances, theoretical frameworks within which pertinent propositions must be placed in order to make sense.

Finally, the *sociological* principles that control access to the production of discourse are rituals, 'discourse societies', doctrinal groups and the large cleavages of social inequality. The latter, of course, form a matrix within which access and claims to all discourses occur. It is, I think, impossible to conduct a sociological and historical analysis (as something distinct from a purely textual one) and separate these principles from either the basic exclusions or the procedures of internal control. Foucault says:

> There is . . . a third group of [procedures] serving to control discourse. Here, we are no longer dealing with the mastery of the powers contained within discourse, nor with averting the hazards of their appearance; it is more a question of determining the conditions under which [discourse] may be employed, of imposing a certain number of rules upon those individuals who employ it, thus denying access to everyone else. This amounts to a rarefaction among speaking subjects: none may enter into discourse on a specific subject unless he has satisfied certain conditions or if he is not, from the outset, qualified to do so. More exactly, not all areas of discourse are equally open and penetrable; some are forbidden territory (differentiated and differentiating) while others are virtually open to the winds and stand, without any prior restrictions, open to all.[22]

The first exigencies and qualifications are presumably met by partly unconscious allegiance to the fundamental cultural exclusions: knowing what transgression means and how to avoid it; knowing how to walk on the precarious edge between madness and reason; accepting the 'regime of truth' that applies in specific discursive fields. As soon as we talk about *speakers* and their claims to partake in discourse, as soon as we talk about practices, we run into problems with the distinction and articulations between discourse and the practical field within which it is produced.[23]

Given the dominance of scientific discourse in our societies, it is tempting simply to assimilate the notion of discursive field to the sociological concept of scientific field proposed by Pierre Bourdieu.[24] The latter also is a system that does not quite coincide with any given institution, with any visible or invisible college, but it is clearly constituted by all the positions, relationships and strategies in which interrelated 'speakers' acquire, from one another and in different quotients, the authority to speak. The great merit of Bourdieu's elaboration is that it excludes any reductive determination of the content of discourse by the benefits the speakers expect from it. All benefits and rewards become contingent with respect to the primordial and specific reward expected in scientific fields: the authority to speak, which Bourdieu calls 'symbolic capital' because it accrues to initial investments and it can be accumulated. In fields where the governing discourse and the institutions where it originates can be as clearly identified as in the scientific disciplines, institutional positions (or the relative position of institutional units in competitive systems) coincide with gross or first-level attributions of discursive authority. Concretely, in a deeply stratified system of higher education such as that of the United States, at first glance, a full professor has accumulated more symbolic capital than an assistant professor and a scientist from Harvard is placed a priori in a superior category of 'authority' to a scientist from any state college or even almost any public university.

Things become more complicated when discursive fields do not coincide (in tendency) with any one institutional setting. Even in scientific fields, the studies of science policy clearly show that coincidence of the field with its official, 'autonomous', and university-based practitioners cannot be taken for granted, for increasingly important discourses and codes of practice originate in government and in industry.[25] The difficulties of delimitation and articulation are compounded in the case of professions which, by definition, are more open than the academy to regulatory agencies and to segments, at least, of their lay public. This openness makes them, I think, closer to a notion of discursive field derived from Foucault than to the stricter concept proposed by Bourdieu.

Discourse, as Foucault says in the previous quotation, includes both highly defended regions and others which seem accessible to any speaking subject. A discursive field is therefore something broader than a scientific field, since discourses are produced in areas of social practice that include both unauthorized and non-authoritative speakers. The difference is that between a 'discourse society', in which Foucault would include only the initiates, and a field where, for instance, science is taught to non-scientists or disseminated to a broad lay public, obviously without empowering members of this public to 'speak science'. Foucault has said in an interview:

> If I have studied 'practices' like those of the sequestration of the insane, or clinical medicine, or the organisation of the empirical sciences, or legal punishment, it was in order to study *this interplay between a 'code' which rules ways of doing things* (how people are to be graded and examined, things and signs classified, individuals trained, etc.), *and a production of true discourses which serves to found, justify and provide reasons for these ways of doing things. . . .* My problem is to see how men govern themselves and others by the production of truth (. . . not the production of true utterances, but the establishment of domains in which the practice of true and false can be made at once ordered and pertinent).[26]

It is clear that Foucault's domains of practice englobe actual institutional settings: those he has studied (the asylum, the hospital, the gaol, the confessional) and those he only implicitly alludes to (the school, the army, the courtroom, the factory, the social welfare agency, the publishing industry, the art gallery, the museum and so on). But a discursive field also goes beyond the institutions within which 'codes' are elaborated, learnt, applied, in conjunction with legitimating discourses. At some point, we must include fields that only have *a thematic ideological unity*, that are unified only because all their parts, all their actors, all their speakers, are concerned with the same thing and almost always with conflicting points of view. These are best seen as battlefields, wherein different kinds of experts fight for pre-eminence and where other, 'non-expert' forces also intervene. I want to argue forcefully that the degree to which these arenas of struggle are open to common citizens is both a measure of democracy and one of the stakes of democratic politics. While I do not think that the position social actors will take can ever be pre-judged on the basis of their class, race, gender (or even their profession!) or predicted independently of their engagement in the arena, these discursive fields are not dissimilar in my mind to the ideological level at which, for Marx and for many Marxists, political battles are first joined.

For example, the discourse on AIDS in the United States has become an enormously complex and multi-faceted discursive field where, at the core, true (or truest) discourses are produced by scientists about the disease, its etiology, its epidemiology and its therapy. However, the most efficacious discourses are the ones implicitly or explicitly mobilized in the battlefields where codes of practice are at stake. Thus, we have recently seen not at the scientific core of the field, but at centre stage, within the federal government, the battle between two forms of power: the power of science and medical professionalism, invoked by a Surgeon General who is personally a fundamentalist Protestant, and the power of another ideology, justified by a discourse echoing the views on sexuality, education and the family of the fundamentalist religious right, cynically represented by the former Secretary of Education, William Bennett. In turn, the movement for Gay Rights, in particular, has spawned associations that militantly oppose the stigmatization of homosexual victims, the discrimination against carriers of the virus, the proposals for mandatory testing and disclosure, while they demonstrate and lobby for medical funding and scientific research. It is a battle waged in different forms in countless war zones, enacted day after day on a background haunted, thanks to the press, by the patients and the 'innocent victims', who tend to become weapons in the fight.

These singularly contested discursive areas, where experts of different kinds converge with lay people upon important political issues, illuminate with a searing light the fundamental political importance that Foucault attributes to discourse *in itself*: it is 'not simply a translation of struggles and of systems of domination', he says, 'but that for which and by which the struggle is waged, the very power that is at stake'.[27] Therefore, the seemingly definitive appropriation of collective issues by state agents or independent experts of different kinds is a profound symptom of successful depoliticization.[28]

I shall try to propose on the basis of this reading of Foucault an elaboration of the notion of discursive field. I think that it can both clarify some questions that concern a sociology of professions and open up new ones. That link between higher education and the social division of labour that we call 'profession' has become, at least in capitalist societies, an almost ubiquitous way of *constituting expertise* – that is, creating, organizing, representing to both actors and spectators (or practitioners and clients) that here, vested in a person identified by particular badges, there is available specialized knowledge superior to that of other persons, who may well be even more knowledgeable and well-trained *but in other domains*. In fact, this way of constituting expertise presupposes the parallel constitution of *a lay public*, which cannot be composed of just anybody: lay men and women must have in common with the experts the knowledge that allows them to understand the marks of expertise, that is, the social/cognitive map on which the experts' 'superiority' has been placed, or the code within which expertise must be attributed. More fundamentally, lay men and women partake in their society's understanding of transgression, of reason and insanity.

The presence of a lay public is what distinguishes modern professional expertise from other forms of scarce and esoteric knowledge: it is, in principle, available, to the broadest public.[29] The making of a 'lay public' is due in large part to the systems of free and compulsory public education which, at the top levels, also produce the largest number of credentialled experts.[30] In advanced capitalist societies, press, radio and, above all, television, mass-communicate all along the life-cycle – longer, more frequently, more assiduously and often more effectively than the schools – messages by and *about* experts. What the 'mass media' do not impart is the direct experience of systems where knowledge comes fused with authority and where failure to master knowledge becomes a thoroughly personal failure, independent of the exclusions and maldistributions inherent in the school system. I believe that a lay public is constituted by the combined effect of a 'personalized' experience of education and a distracted and impersonal relation to the media. Sectors of the 'lay public' can mobilize themselves and challenge practices which are of concern to them. It is part of Foucault's general logic, as I read it, that they shall then enter the pertinent discursive field as speakers and confront the alleged truth of the discourse that justifies those practices.

A plurality of discourses coexist in a discursive field but they can seldom all be considered equally true. Truth is a matter of authorization and power, including the power to engage and provide the scientific demonstrations to which modern capitalist society accords (but not always) superior epistemological validity. The latter is bolstered by the structural links that modern societies establish between knowledge and practice, education and occupation, schools and work. Whether their expertise is, strictly speaking, scientific or not, credentialled experts always tend to occupy the core regions of discursive fields in our societies. But what do we understand by 'core region'?

Because discourse is spoken and appropriated by concrete social actors, the core region is that concrete and concretely protected social location from which the truer discourse (the most theoretically coherent or epistemologically valid) is issued in defence of dominant codes of practice – that is to say, the codes of practice favoured by social agents who have the power or the influence to make them be accepted. It is easy to see here a correspondence with the institutional domains which issue and apply authoritative practices, those which Foucault has brilliantly studied and the others. For scientific disciplines, the core region still is the research university, whose authority is disputed or shared in the case of practising professions. There is no doubt that discourse in professions such as the law are organized around 'practical' core regions – the courts and the legislature; but where the attempt to give such professions the legitimacy of a 'scientific' (or at least a dispassionate) claim to truth has been made, the institutional advancement of such claims has also been normally located in the university system.

In the core region (which can be institutionally differentiated or divided), speakers are distinguished by their relation to true discourse itself, by the authority that accrues to their position or to their name. If we think in terms of professions, the core region *tends* to coincide (but not always, as I observed above) with the research and training system. At the centre we find those who 'create' knowledge – researchers or systematizers of pertinent knowledge – surrounded by those who teach apprentices and, in a further removed concentric circle, by those who disseminate knowledge and make the profession visible in the press and the electronic media. But there are also managers directly involved with promulgating codes and sustaining institutional capabilities that support both the core and the outlying regions. In the latter, practitioners enact in their own way the applicable consequences of the true discourses emitted at the core. While managers must speak with funding and overseeing agencies, practitioners meet the 'lay public', which may consist of only their colleagues or their employers. It is there that different 'truths', different discourses are brought to bear upon codes of practice for which practitioners tend to invoke, as their foundation, the 'true' discourses produced at the core.

Professions can be distinguished by the nature and the structure of their discursive field. In our society, this is almost equivalent to saying that they can be compared, on one hand, by the degree to which their core discourse pretends to approach scientific validity; on the other hand, they must be compared by the extent to which the core region commands the outlying ones.[31] To consider them as discursive fields has interesting practical implications, because so many of our empirical data consist of what agents *say*, of their attempts to intervene in the production of discourse. I have implicitly proposed above that we consider the internal organization of professions by the relation of different categories of professionals to the production of discourse. At the core, we should be able to apply Bourdieu's elaboration of the scientific field: what matters most is discourse itself, the production of true knowledge about that part of natural or social reality that the profession addresses, the defence that it makes of its own manner of address, as necessary means for accumulating symbolic capital.

For administrators, however, the true discourse that matters is different: it must ultimately justify the codes of practice that they apply to be successful in their own form of 'capital accumulation', that is, power over resources and personnel. Administrators in professional fields are ultimately concerned with the materiality of the institution, and with its sustenance. The true discourses produced at the core of the professional field are only one argument in their justificatory elaborations; they are not interested in discourse production as much as in productivity. For average practitioners, the core is a distant area indeed. They are confronted with a multitude of 'truths', and their claim to being possessors of true discourse must be renegotiated in the different instances of their practice.

The various struggles and conflicts that emerge in professional fields can also be located with relation to the production of true discourses. First of all, the utterances of the participants reveal what codes of practice are placed in question and in what areas of the discursive field they belong. From what is said and the claims to truth that are being made, it is also possible to determine whether any challenge aims at the core region or is, instead, contained. And the audiences that are explicitly or potentially alluded to in the speakers' discourses tell us whether the overall boundaries of the field are respected or, on the contrary, expanded. In this last case, the conflict exceeds the limits implicit in its origins: as it becomes larger, as more speakers and more 'true' discourses are allowed in, the resolution of the conflict becomes a *general* political and public matter.

It is clear from the above that containing an issue within discursive fields controlled by professionals (regardless of where it has originally arisen) is an essentially depoliticizing strategy, which may or may not be followed by the professionals themselves and which may be employed by outsiders. Individual professionals can obviously act in any way they see fit regarding any issue. I believe, however, that there is a 'properly' or 'typically professional' mode of addressing conflictive issues that can be included within the profession's discursive field. The first and basic principle in the protection of something equivalent to what Bourdieu calls the *doxa* of scientific fields: the epistemological system by which claims to truth are recognized and validated. It obviously must not be touched, for, as he says, there is in scientific fields the deepest agreement about what are licit subjects of disagreement.[32] A second principle is attached to the basic interdiction: the norm of containing controversy within the field or, which is equivalent, the normative protection of its boundaries. A third principle is contained within the first two, and it is the defence of professional authority, the tendency to de-authorize non-expert speakers even when the issue at hand regards them. A consequence of this mode of addressing problems should logically be that 'properly' or 'typically professional' political programmes tend towards technocratic solutions. Conversely, conflicts which become political projects, exceeding and transforming the boundaries of the discursive field, tend to be fuelled and expanded from the outside or from the margins, by both unauthorized speakers and experts who abandon the professional mode. In concluding, I shall briefly consider a few examples where this has happened.

The variety of technocratic temptations

There is a strong hypothesis that takes the multiplying numbers of professionals and specialized credentialled workers, and ties them not only to the class structure but also to a political vision of their own. As a hypothesis, it does not address the question of authority within discursive fields but tends, rather, to assume a commonality that underlies them. Thus, Alvin Gouldner postulates a 'culture of critical discourse', common to both the technical intelligentsia and the humanistic intellectuals, which may provide a basis for their 'new class project'. The culture of critical discourse is both a 'context-free grammar' and a system for establishing the validity of claims, without making reference to the authority of the speaker. It is meant by this that the only authority that can be legitimately admitted is that conferred within the discursive field itself.[33] There is nothing here that extends the boundaries of discursive fields, but a common interest of experts and intellectuals (which, for Gouldner, may provide a basis for the making of the new class) in having their special languages recognized and establishing 'favorable exchange rates for their "cultural capital" '.[34] The culture of critical discourse is therefore wholly compatible with the exclusion of non-academic discourse and non-credentialled speakers.

It is in Eastern Europe, however, that the general thesis of experts and intellectuals as possible leaders of a political transformation that would obviously be in their collective benefit seems to have acquired the most strength. It is mainly through the work of Gyorgy Konrad and Ivan Szelenyi, first, and then through Szelenyi's remarkable auto-critiques, that the debate has reached us. In the post-Stalinist 1960s and early 1970s, they were mainly concerned with the warming up of *elite* sectors of the intelligentsia to the possibilities of reform that bureaucratic socialism still seemed to harbour. Their 'New Class project' was the classic technocratic one, Eastern European style: reform of the state apparatus from within and of society from above. 'The road to class power' passed through state power and its prerequisite was the displacement of old-line bureaucrats by new generations of well-qualified and committed socialists.

Until the early 1980s, the expert elites seemed to keep hoping for some form of coalescence with a renewed or self-reformed bureaucracy, for an alliance that would unify the 'red' and the 'expert', the technical and doctrinal prongs of the state's intellectual and moral hegemony, into one single scientistic *raison d'état*. This did not happen. After the fiasco of a second wave of reforms in 1982–1983 and the crushing of Solidarity in Poland, Szelenyi concludes that 'The New Class project got off track during the 1970s, in part because of the stubbornness of the bureaucracies and in part because of the success of the politics of concession by the dominant bureaucratic estate to small private business', primarily in agriculture.[35] Konrad and Szelenyi were extremely sceptical about the democratic vocation of the New Class, but, as Szelenyi insistently clarifies, their success depended on the vastness and effectiveness of popular mobilization for reform.[36] The 'intellectuals' road to class power' had, therefore, an uncharted and partly open destination.

The scenario of a 'new class' constituted of highly competent reformers within and around the state bureaucracies, interpreting broader reform aspirations, embarking simultaneously on the re-conquest of the state and the re-design of society, seems highly unlikely among the individualistic expert elites of capitalist societies. However, within the framework of a political party, or in periods of national danger or reconstruction, there have been cases that are strongly reminiscent of Konrad and Szelenyi's original hypothesis. The first efforts that come to mind are those of technocratic precursors, seated in the cradle of ideological anti-statism: the part played by a small group of career civil servants in the reform of the British state in the 1830s. Philip Corrigan and Derek Sayer have called this a process of 'making of the State', the material creation of both its forms of rule and its new rituals.

The government inspectors, partisans of efficiency and useful knowledge, yet distant from the pure utilitarianism of the entrepreneurs, were the vanguard of this movement.[37] Armed with (at least the idea of) statistics and a broadly understood educational mission, architects of the centralization of facts and knowledge in the hands of government, heroes of fact-gathering and consultative procedures, they appeared fully conscious and quite deliberate in their actions:

> First, as agents for that national system of Improvement which the more radical of them recognized was needed, they sought to secure not simply, in their different 'fields', a national minimum standard provision across the country, but to ensure that they would be a 'transmission belt' between the best examples and the rest of the relevant institutions. Second, they acted to establish and standardize a range of civic institutions . . . beyond the efforts (if any) of either individual paternalist capitalists or local groupings of the same.[38]

Despite the diversity of projects that preoccupied the Victorian professional and administrative elites, they had this in common: unlike the triumphant industrial capitalists, they did not shrink from requesting state intervention in the civil society beyond the repression of the 'dangerous classes', labouring or not labouring. The British inspectorate (as a symbol of other civil service elites) can best be seen as an equivalent of Napoleonic cadres, placed in their positions of battle, with a self-created *esprit de corps*; a particularly competent set of state servants, definitely interested in harnessing expertise of many kinds (committed, yes, with a sense of mission, but not necessarily 'certified') to the 'chariot of the state'. In its technocratic overtones, the inspiration of the project may appear *formally* similar to that of the reform-minded Eastern European cadres, fighting unreformed bureaucratic elites within the state apparatus.[39] The mid-nineteenth-century inspectors, however, were led by their own position and dedication to stand for the *build-up* of the machinery of government, for deepening, not releasing, its hold on the civil society. As James P. Kay wrote in 1853, the efforts of the inspectors,

> have also spread among the humbler classes a general sense of the vigilant care of the Government for their well-being, and thus . . . have promoted that political repose which has characterised the English poor, while the whole of Europe has been threatened with a socialist rebellion, has suffered the confusion of democratic revolutions, and the revulsion of military despotism.[40]

Projects that aim at improving the public welfare from above demand first of all the creation of appropriate mechanisms. Their general forms were established even in the 'passive' state of liberal ideology: consultative forms of variable effectiveness; autonomous task forces within the civil service; commissions of inquiry; advisory committees; national emergency boards, after World War I circumvent the bureaucratic apparatus of the state. But what is principally at stake is the direction of social planning and engineering. One kind of technocratic project, faced with an under-developed government, builds up the state apparatus for the protection of society. Another kind transforms the direction of state policies in order to release private energies. Both presuppose what Szelenyi calls 'counter-selection': the right people must be in the right places.[41]

Similarly, in the United States, the public service professionals who had forcefully begun to organize during Progressivism emerged from World War I with the conviction that their goals were the goals of the government. It is interesting to note that a seasoned activist in the field of housing like Clarence Stein was among the first to reject federal housing programmes: not because of any ideological resistance to government intervention, but out of contempt for a corrupt Congress and mistrust for an unreformed civil service.[42] For others in the fields of social work and public health, disappointment was slower to set in, as they pressed unsuccessfully for an expansion of the government's functions and adjusted their goals down from the federal to the state and municipal levels of government.[43] Already before the crash and the Depression they had envisaged many of the concrete measures within which massive federal aid could be channelled. As the Depression deepened, unemployment hit them too, adding self-interest to their principled call for public programmes. Most of the outspoken public service leaders were ready to welcome the New Deal, but the division in the ranks of social work professionals after 1932 stands for the two poles of professional involvement. On the one hand were those who had only been waiting for a government ready at least to hear them and who projected their own vision of a planned society on the partial and improvised measures that the Roosevelt government was taking under duress. On the other were those who, following the probing radical analysis of leaders like Mary van Kleeck, saw in the workers' movement a call for joining in a much larger project of reform.[44] Neither group, however, was ready to question the discourse on which their social activism was founded:

> Everyone agreed that reform had to be grounded firmly in planning, and everyone knew that planning was based upon some sort of relationship between present knowledge and future goals. It was that area of 'present knowledge' that brought the professionals into the picture, because their professionalism was built upon their . . . expertise. They seemed scarcely aware at the time that this 'knowledge' might be elusive or conjectural, that it might consist not only of facts, but of inferences drawn from those facts, and of projections made from those inferences, that it might be laced with value-judgments and that it might mislead them altogether.[45]

Thus, whether they are ensconced within the civil service like the British inspectorate, or functioning as advisers to a shadow government like the economists of the Stockholm school in the 1930s, or seeking alliances in the bureaucracy of governments that have lost their legitimacy as in Eastern Europe, or functioning as a special *corps* within the apparatus of the state like the French *ingénieurs*, or waiting for a government that would finally heed their programmes like the American public service professions during the Depression and the New Deal, all technocratic projects have in common with the clearly corporative project of professionalization the defence of a discursive field. The perimeter and the plurality of discourses and speakers within it vary in each case, but it is distinctive of expert speakers that they should not of their own initiative want to erase the enclosing barriers.

In conclusion, profession should be seen as a complex programme of research rather than a readily usable and unproblematic concept. *Structurally*, profession is a link between codified knowledge and practice, in a world of not-knowers or of less knowing laity. As a structural link between the hierarchic educational system and the hierarchic occupational order, profession seeks in both orders institutional guarantees which only the state can offer. Profession can thus become, structurally, a *material link between the state and the deployment of specialized knowledge in the civil society*. By their structural characteristics, professions are a necessary part in any theory of the *modern* state. But this would be a state that resembles Foucault's conception more than Weber's, which is necessarily founded on the ultimate control of physical force: a state that equips the society and is presented to all its citizens as a *positive* agency.

Historically, profession appears as a field where the relations between the apparent continuity of forms and the discontinuity of content and meaning can be fruitfully analysed. The specificity of profession as a historical phenomenon and its close dependence on particular socio-historical matrices are coupled with the transmission of rituals across space and time and the apparent permanence of conceptions of social 'pollution' and constructions of talent and honour.[46] The historical uses that corporate groups tending toward social closure make of symbolic systems and consumption patterns related to 'styles of life' are one example of the areas intimately related to our most contemporary notion of professional status. The constitution of protected markets by community of sellers, ready to act on the cues they visibly present to one another, is a path first opened by professions, at least in the Anglo-American countries. Furthermore, profession can embody a historical bridge between aristocratic knowledge, with the price it puts on theory, and practical bourgeois knowledge, which puts a price on instrumental results. In certain cases professions can appear as a symbolic hybrid between the past and the present of capitalist societies.[47]

From a *symbolic interactionist* point of view, profession contains the actual traces of all that professionals in theory claim to be. Because of the collective claims that professionals make, professional practice is the locus *par excellence* where lies can be revealed. The dissonance between profession and its practice, between theoretical knowledge and applications, between claims and reality, makes profession a particularly interesting field for the exercise of sceptical denunciation. The moral zeal involved in denunciation may account to some extent for the great preference that symbolic interactionism has shown for professions which have power in interpersonal relations, such as the law or, above all, medicine. Here power clearly presents itself as *agency*, far easier to comprehend than the anonymous functional power exercised by engineers, for instance, at the orders of an organization. Because responsibility can be easily assigned, the thorny question of the permanence and efficacy of structure can be suspended. But then, ultimately, at this level too we are confronted with the relations between knowledge, belief and power. Professionals and experts, whenever they are challenged, individually or collectively, retrench behind the boundaries of their discursive fields and retreat towards the protected core. To understand the real significance of the experts' collective appropriation of knowledge and the social complex that supports it, all the levels of questioning will have to be covered in the end.

Notes

1 Geertz, 1983:124–125.

2 Larson, 1977/1979.

3 The term 'exclusionary shelter' comes from Eliot Freidson (1986), and it is much better suited for the reality of what professionalization movements actually obtained than 'monopoly', the term I use. Nevertheless, the drive or the intentions of professionalization are, I would maintain, monopolistic.

4 Larson, 1977/1979, ch. 5.

5 Ramsey, 1984:234 and 254ff.

6 Throughout the nineteenth century, the engineers of Ponts et Chaussées, as John Weiss tells us, self-consciously cultivated their corporate unity, 'as a means of . . . ensuring that its members' status derived from a single source, service to the state, and found a single mode of expression, militarized scientific professionalism' (Weiss, 1984:31–32).

The recruitment of engineers into the Grandes Ecoles gradually narrowed as the state required a classic *baccalauréat* of all the learned professions. The engineers resisted it for a longer time but, after heated debates, it was imposed upon them too. By 1850, 'claims that the *baccalauréat* consecrated "all the high careers of social life" and the "civil staff officers of the country" were accepted even by those who regretted the degree and wished to abolish it' (Weiss, 1984: 22). Weiss argues that one of the powerful effects of the *baccalauréat*, besides the practical ones of opening the door to careers and restricting the number of entrants, is that it conferred upon its holders in the civil service and the professions that sense of being 'mandarins', not the equals but *the superiors* of the industrial and commercial strata (Weiss, 1984:22–23).

7 Lipstadt, 1979; Goldstein, 1984.

8 Ramsey, 1984:230–231.

9 Ramsey, 1984:240.

10 To complete briefly Ramsey's remarkable presentation: in Britain, to this day, abuses do not meet anything resembling the effectiveness of the French bureaucratic apparatus; even though the welfare state piles exclusive privileges upon qualified physicians, sharply distinguishing them from the unlicensed, private doctors have had to form a Medical Defence Association. The paradoxical German case, where the free field persisted, despite the illiberalism of the state and the world leadership of German medical science, is explained by the 'formidable political force of the unlicensed healers, who had emerged almost as a distinct profession'. When the Nazis finally instituted a single corporation and punishment for unauthorized practice, they recognized the empiricals in a grandfather clause, while none the less outlawing their schools (Ramsey, 1984:272 and 273–274).

11 Thus, in reference to what he says about the re-institution of monopoly in the United States: the sequence of events does not prove that the discovery of diphtheria antitoxin did not make a great effect on the legislatures which were always lobbied by regular practitioners against their rivals. In any case, the appropriation by medical leaders of successes that depended more on public health reformers than on their rank and file made monopoly both effective and beneficial. The 'scientificity' of medical schools was the cornerstone of the hierarchy that the Flexner report sought to establish with the full support of the medical elites. I fully agree, however, with the connections Ramsey makes, much more systematically than I did, between different foci of regulation and the passing of *laissez-faire* capitalism (Larson, 1977–1979:159–166 and ch. 9).

12 Weiss, 1984:17–28.

13 As Weiss reports, the official voice for the Ministry of Public Instruction, the *Gazette spéciale de l'instruction publique*, argued in 1841 that the students who prepared the entrance examination to the engineering *écoles* could not afford and should not be allowed to finish their classic education three years earlier than the non-technical students. Asserting that they were deficient in 'all that serves as a basis for political, religious and domestic society, all that gives charm in prosperity and consolation in unhappiness', the *Gazette* concluded more expediently: 'it will suffice to recall that it is from among the students of our government technical schools that Saint-Simon and Fourier found their most ardent disciples' (Weiss, 1984:24–25).

14 Geison, 1984; Burrage, 1990.

15 Ramsey, 1984; Calhoun, 1965.

16 It may even be shown, as Jan Goldstein does in a subtle study of the concept of 'moral contagion', that the pattern of professional aspirations shapes the content of knowledge. Dissatisfied with their social authority, French psychiatrists, from the eighteenth century onward, developed a theory of mental epidemics which, during the Second Empire, allowed them to take over, as agents of the state, where the 'witch-prosecuting judicial magistrates' of the seventeenth and eighteenth century had left off (Goldstein, 1984:216).

17 In my belief that there is something structural (and therefore general) in what modern professions have historically attempted to be or to become, I differ from Eliot Freidson, although I fully agree with both his words of caution and the provisional operational emphasis he chooses. Freidson writes: 'as a concept capable of dealing with more than prestige and the fact of formal knowledge, with the way professionals can gain a living, and with the institutions that shape the way they gain a living, *profession* must be used in a specific historical and national sense' (Freidson, 1986:35). After examining in the most careful and useful manner the occupational categories of the US Census under the light of the *Occupational Outlook Handbook*, he concludes:

> a critical criterion lies in some degree of *exposure to higher education and the formal knowledge* it transmits. But remembering the importance to potential understanding of the professions' capacity to exercise power and the problem of gaining a living, let us add the criterion that they are occupations for which *education is a prerequisite to employment* in particular positions. Formal education creates qualification for particular jobs, from which others who lack such qualification are routinely excluded. Such a circumstance is likely to mean that those occupations have developed *a coherent organization . . .* that succeeds in carving out *a labor-market shelter*, a social closure, or a sinecure for its members in the labor market. (ibid.:59, emphasis added)

The 'institutions that shape the way [professions] gain a living' vary and/or change, including the institutions of higher education. If the structural connection between higher education (a relative term, we should note!) and desirable occupational positions is severed, I would be ready to argue that the *concept* of profession is no longer operative, though the word may still be used.

18 Larson, 1977/1979, ch. 12; Larson, 1980.

19 And which, in fact, reproduced both the profundity of Foucault's work and its conceptual haziness.

20 As Jürgen Kocka points out, one could clarify Foucault by distinguishing, in Weberian terms, the kinds of knowledge that give power into *Heilswissen* (the revealed knowledge of priests), *Herrschaftswissen* (the knowledge, ultimately backed by force, of those who govern) and *Leistungswissen*, knowledge oriented to achievement, which can be tested and must produce some results in order to *be* a power (Kocka, 'Commentary at the First Symposium on Professions and Conflict Theory', Swedish Collegium for Advanced Studies in the Social Sciences, May 1986). The conditions of all these forms of knowledge define fields of practice, institutionalized or not, within which discourse attains its efficacy through other practices. The latter may be defined and regulated by discourse, but they are not part of it: the Catholic priest has a knowledge of rituals which allows him, by means of discourse, to instruct the faithful and strike them with proscriptions and interdictions. The rituals themselves are not discourse, however, even though rituals and the discourse that governs them are included within Catholicism and the latter can be viewed *also* as a discursive field.

21 Foucault, 1972:218.

22 Foucault, 1972:224–225.

23 Foucault names three kinds of 'systems of restriction': *rituals* define the qualifications that speakers must have in order to speak, their position in speech, the 'whole set of signs that must accompany discourse' and, he adds, 'the supposed or imposed efficacy of words'; when, for instance, a policeman reads to the arrested

his or her rights with the proper intonation (either solemn or rapid and dismissive to mark what the corps thinks of the Miranda decision!), in the proper circumstances and with the intended effect of preventing adverse judicial consequences. *Discourse societies* are illustrated by reference to the groups of rhapsodic poets, because the example from antiquity highlights the 'ambiguous interplay of secret and divulgation': restrictive initiation and training give access to a real group and to a knowledge that the listeners cannot appropriate. The modern counterparts that Foucault fleetingly cites are, precisely, professionalized discourses – scientific, technical, medical, political, economic. Ultimately, in these restricted groups, the speakers can only circulate and transmit parts of discourse to the initiated. *Doctrines* are different. In doctrinal groups, individuals whose number has no fixed limits belong together because of the set of discourses (the doctrine) they share. 'Doctrines tie individuals to certain types of utterances and therefore forbid all other types.' Doctrines are always the sign of affiliation and always include the inherent potential for heresy and orthodoxy (Foucault, 1971:39–45). Professions and academic disciplines are a kind of 'discourse society', within which doctrinal divisions define important lines of cleavage, conflict and strategy which may or may not overlap in part with divisions dependent on larger social inequalities.

24 Bourdieu, 1976.

25 Spiegel-Rosing, 1977; Crane, 1980; Gibbons and Wittrock, 1985; Nelkin, 1987.

26 Foucault, 1981:9; italics mine.

27 Foucault, 1971:12; my translation.

28 Larson, 1984.

29 Surely, as we know only too well, not everyone can pay for professional services, not everyone is eligible for what the welfare state provides, not everyone can go where services are bought or otherwise dispensed, but almost everyone in the fictional 'lay public' has an idea that such services exist.

30 The modern state and the capitalist corporation mobilize the expert information needed to govern society or to control production and markets. This is not open but 'classified' information, that is shrouded in secrecy and escapes any democratic controls. In a parallel, though not simultaneous movement, experts have appeared in the everyday life of ordinary people in advanced industrial societies – in some key sectors, as a result of deliberate government policy. I think it is through direct or symbolic (mainly through mass communication) contacts with professional experts that people get their notions of the usefulness of expert knowledge. But it also appears as something that can be appropriated for secret or private uses. The diffusion of expertise among people who are not experts would thus seem to carry with it an implicit vision of the conspiracies that can be formed in order to use it and a sceptical, albeit inexact, notion of the independence of experts *vis-à-vis* the powers of business and government.

31 If we take the academic profession as a particular self-enclosed illustration, disciplines tend to be ranked internally according to their scientific 'theoreticity'. Rankings are obviously contested matters, the object of incessant striving and not at all fixed attainments. What they imply in terms of outside resources is also variable: business administration, for instance, receives resources because of the importance in which it is held *outside* the academic profession and because students in recent years have flocked to it, but its academic practitioners try very hard to *also* acquire academic legitimacy through research and publications. In the academic profession more than in any other, new discourse produced at the core should in principle be registered immediately in the profession's practice, which is teaching,

and change both its contents and its practical methodologies. This happens, with some time lag, at the graduate level, but the outlying practitioners who teach undergraduates have the most leeway, and can be not in the least concerned by the implications of the latest theory about the diversification of portfolios or moral incentives, to keep with the business administration example.

32 Bourdieu, 1976.

33 Gouldner, 1979.

34 Disco, 1982:811.

35 Szelenyi, 1986–1987:130.

36 After the ebb of the reform movements, Szelenyi depicts a pervasive pragmatism: the 'New Class' reform alliance, joining with the new(er) yet petty bourgeoisie, might still continue 'the process of socialist embourgeoisement' in the economy and gradually undermine the political power of the bureaucratic elites in a Hungarian road to socialism. But it might also be possible for the cadres to retain their power in the state, leaving the economy to technocrats and entrepreneurs 'merged into a bourgeoisie', in a model similar to the Spanish regime in the last years of Franco (Szelenyi, 1986–1987:135).

The momentous events of October to December 1989, which have transformed Eastern Europe and the world, require at least a brief rejoinder. Without doing too much violence to the profound differences between Hungary and the other countries, it can be said that Konrad and Szelenyi's original thesis has been vindicated. Everywhere (even in Poland, the only country where a *workers'* movement led the attack against the post-Stalinist order, at least for a period) an *intelligentsia* is coming to power. Professor Szelenyi considers that Konrad and he had *underestimated* the extent to which the old communist elites were disintegrating. He could not have predicted either the rapidity of their collapse or the capacity of the intellectual leadership to mobilize vast sectors of the population behind the reform movements. He argues that the extraordinary fact of a communist party voting to dissolve itself (in Hungary) shows to what extent the party officialdom had become 'technocratic': of the 1400 party members participating in the vote, *1200 were party officials*! that they should have voted themselves out of their jobs shows their confidence in the convertibility of their skills. Obviously, the future now depends on what winning coalitions emerge and whether they are capable of directing the state towards the transformation of the economy, but, for all practical purposes, the old bureaucratic elites have been replaced (Personal communication, Professor Ivan Szelenyi, December 1989).

37 Roberts, 1960; Sutherland, 1972.

38 Corrigan and Sayer, 1985:125–126.

39 The British inspectors had had to fight for implementation of the Factory Act against the non-compliance of greedy mill-owners and against the children's own parents. Beyond the struggle for implementation, they had to lead a losing fight against the entrepreneurs' influence on their government and increasingly defend the Factory Act as their own (MacDonagh, 1977).

40 Quoted by Corrigan and Sayer, 1985:128.

41 Szelenyi, 1986–1987:113.

42 Kirschner, 1986:135.

43 The public health professionals, in particular, appear to have entertained oppressive measures without too many qualms. Thus, Hardy Clark, a public health physician from Long Beach, California, advocated the widespread use of the grading system in practice there: 'welfare nurses [were] empowered to administer a battery

of tests' which they used to grade families 'on such things as the quality of home atmosphere, . . . the remedial physical condition of children, . . . and the social or character qualities of children'. Children who failed the character test 'were sent to a municipal correctional center for character training – repeatedly if necessary' (Kirschner, 1986:137).

44 Kirschner, 1986:142–147.
45 Kirschner, 1986:150.
46 Abbott, 1981.
47 Tocqueville, 1945, vol. 2:45–47.

4
Knowledge as a professional resource: case studies of architects and psychologists at work

Lennart G. Svensson

Professionals have been essential actors in the formation of the bureaucratic state as well as the welfare state.[1] Studies of professionalization have attempted to show a close relationship and mutually strengthening processes between professionalization and state formation.

Bureaucracy and professionalism are two different, but in many respects compatible, methods of rational administration and state control. Both bureaucrats and professionals are expected to apply general rules, categories or other concepts that limit the need for information and facilitate decisions as to action. In the case of bureaucracy, it is a question of laws and regulations; in that of professionals, of more or less scientifically based generalizations or assertions.

We will thus distinguish between tasks which are connected with *interpreting rules and regulations*, applying administrative routines, or deciding where a given case belongs, and tasks connected with *giving explanations* on more or less scientific grounds and with using certain skills. The former tasks concern an organization, administration or apparatus of laws and rules which guide professionals' work. The latter tasks, however, have to do with professionals' education and affiliation, and their own system of rules, such as ethical ones – all that is considered to be the specific ability for work, separating the professionals from others in certain working tasks.

The former, too, constitute resources and frames which the organization or the bureaucratic administrations offer outside of the professionals' own work organization. These may be called 'organization assets'. The latter can be termed 'skill or credential assets or professional assets'.[2] The former have mainly to do with being able to lead and delegate, take policy decisions, employ and start new projects, and change the organization and arrangement of work. But they also have to do with the extent to which work is regulated, standardized and formalized through official descriptions and prescriptions as to how tasks must be prepared.

The institutionalization of formal knowledge has occurred chiefly through the higher educational system under some state control in the knowledge-producing centres.[3] There, the ideals for application of professional knowledge in the peripheral practices have been established for many professions. But which knowledge is actually applied in these professional practices, as compared to the assumed ideals? Which relationships exist between rational, formal knowledge and professionals' daily work? In criticism of the alleged links between education and work, there is often a lack of concrete studies of how professional work really proceeds in its limited daily contexts.[4]

The present chapter reports and analyses some empirical material of this kind from a study of individual professionals and professional groups at work. The focus is on professionals dealing with clients and their cases on a micro level. The study surveys the means and resources which professionals use and try to control in their work, against the background of their positions at work and their acquired knowledge. Individual professionals and smaller groups are thus studied in the context of their working organization, and as regards the more or less independently controlled professional education which they take to work.

Architects and psychologists are the chosen examples of professional groups for case studies within the project. These are two relatively small groups with quite different activities and character.

As representatives of a bureaucratic organization and of a knowledge-based profession, architects and psychologists exercise some state control over individuals as clients. Our main concern is to identify the means by which this occurs in daily work.

Architectural work is defined chiefly by the unique projects which sometimes stretch over several years and affect a range of office-holders, interests and professional groups. Meetings for planning are the form of work in which different consultants cooperate to develop and design a construction, and to produce the necessary drawings and proceedings. Three cases studied are to be reported below: a larger building project for private clients, a smaller one for public clients, and a freer working group which dealt with the design of a public street environment. These will be termed the large project, the small project and the free working group.

Psychological work is usually defined by cases. The basis for decisions is produced and presented mainly in conferences and discussion groups which consider how the cases should be prepared and treated. Four areas of work in psychology are to be covered below: an institute for readjustment to working life, child, youth and family psychiatry, a psychology group in social service at the welfare office, and a private group of therapists. They will be termed 'the institute', 'the clinic', 'the social service' and 'the therapy group'.

We have devoted a large part of the interviews and observations to specifying which actual resources are seemingly used by architects and psychologists in a number of different working tasks.

The problem of organization versus profession is much discussed in studies of professional work. The relative significance of both these origins of resources is an important issue in the present study. We combine it with a more general origin, which is connected with the rather personal ability to participate in conversation situations and to debate or persuade. In the following, we regard these resources as aids to architects and psychologists, as individuals and smaller groups, in applying their different qualifications.

Rules and regulations as resources

This is the type of non-material resources which is most closely connected with administrations and bureaucratic organizations. One aspect of it is the ability to make decisions about organization and arrangement of work, about employment and so on. Another aspect is the application of rules, regulations, ordinances and other codified norms. The latter aspect concerns the extent to which daily work is penetrated and controlled by administrative routines, sets of rules, descriptions of official duties and other elements, which can also be used as effective aids to fulfil working tasks and define relations with clients and the surroundings.

Applications of norms, rules and regulations are the encounters in which state control is exercised over people as clients. This is where the convergence or conflict between the public and private spheres takes place. The professional practitioner represents public interests, either directly as an official in an organization of the central or local state government, or indirectly as a free professional – yet following bureaucratic rules and professional ethics under any kind of public or collegiate supervision.

The building trade has become one of the most normatized fields, judging by the number of administrations, norms and control levels under which it operates. Here one finds starting permits, building permits, on-site inspection of construction works, inspection, quality control, standard approval certificates based on statutes, mandatory regulations, instructions, standards and advice. Some of these refer to the actual project process and the work, while others refer to the final product. Some, again, are connected with decisions of financing the construction.

The working tasks of architects, then, are penetrated by innumerable rules, norms and ordinances. Planning must take account of the ordinances from a variety of administrations.[5] In the free working group's discussions, constant reference is made to ordinances for different types of traffic, ordinances from administrations, rules and recommendations by trade unions, the legal status of building sites and so forth.

In the large project, many relationships concern the fact that the architects in official practice must satisfy the public interest with general recommendations and check the building standards against construction norms. The degree of exploitation becomes an issue for judgement and negotiation. In questions of getting permission to build, the architects may at times reject a proposal by referring to laws and norms. But then they have to know the law paragraph by paragraph. More commonly, they use arguments about solutions by building technique in order to turn down or modify a proposal. Still, they must make sure that the laws and rules are obeyed.

For architects in individual project work, rules make a constant impact through the building norms which must always be kept in mind. Much of this is memorized after some experience with similar working tasks. The rest has to be looked up.

Some psychologists can refer to their official duty descriptions as means of defining their relationship to the environment. Others have only a vague notion of what these contain. Most claim to feel very little control by laws, rules and regulations. In the recorded material from observation of the clinic's treatment conferences, there are no examples of anyone arguing by reference to administrative rules or paragraphs in the law of health and medical care or the law of social service. Either the latter are frameworks which scarcely affect daily treatment work, or else they are so obvious to everyone that they need not be mentioned.

In the psychologists' internal conference in the social service, examples are again lacking of appeal to laws, statutes or ordinances. On the other hand, a number of arguments occur which can be traced back to the existing work division and authority of different personnel groups in discussing who should do what. In the institute's client conference, there seems to be more common reference to rules and decrees on, for example, financial grants or the requirements for regarding a client as qualified for a particular measure. This area of psychological work is the one most affected, among the four examined here, by the need to test and apply rules. Yet the psychologists can leave most such tasks to other personnel.

Thus, the psychologists very seldom see administrative rules, laws and ordinances as obstacles or restrictions. Blank forms and rulebooks are conspicuously absent. By the same token, however, they lack ordinary, simple organizational resources for defining their relations to clients and consulting personnel. They can rarely refer to collected rules or single paragraphs which clearly show the client upon what grounds a decision is made and what preconditions must exist.

Like several other professional groups in both the social and technical spheres, the psychologists display a strong ambivalence to this issue – both wanting and not wanting to have unambiguous regulations for knowing which information can be considered relevant in an enquiry, and what can justify a decision or how it should be implemented. These would simplify relations to clients and greatly facilitate the legitimation of decisions before them, colleagues and the rest of the environment. The psychologists partly compensate for the lack of rules and administrative routines by ever more frequently formulating a contract with those who seek consultation, stating the purpose and limits of the psychologists' work and the obligations undertaken by the client or other contractee during the time covered by the work.

Psychologists' lesser dependence on legal, economic and technical rule systems, as well as their effort to attain a position as consultants with less subordination to the administrative leadership, makes them more dependent on ethical rules. Several statements show that the psychologists feel strongly bound by ethical rules, which seem in some cases to provide the basic relationship between the psychologist and other members in a working team. Expressed, too, is a very strong loyalty towards clients, patients and families, compared to collaborators from other professional groups.

The architects' working processes and products are, by contrast, penetrated continually by rules and instructions. The written documentation is quite exhaustive in virtually all working situations. Often several people are present at discussions and negotiations. In every project or application, several officials are involved. This makes control over the architects' work more direct, which in turn makes the architects less dependent on ethical norms. Their professional rules, too, are chiefly aimed at the private practice.

However, the architects' rules do not stress ethical responsibility for a good living environment and a good public environment for third parties, anything like as clearly as do the psychologists' rules in regard to their ethical responsibility for the lives of individual people. The aesthetic responsibility lies more on the politically composed building authorities, to which the architects can refer.

Knowledge and skills as resources

What one usually associates most closely with the ability of professionals are the knowledge and skills which they are assumed to have acquired during their special education. This ability is expected to let them know what is going on and what is to be done. Knowledge of theories and theoretical perspectives supplies concepts, classifications, models, figures of thought, connections, instances, and criteria of relevance. These are resources which often lie unexpressed as a background to what the professionals offer.

Knowing what to do is bound up with skills and the ability to handle tools and instruments, to use operative methods for making diagnoses, to obtain and process information, to carry through interpretations and carry out treatments. These are what the great majority of clients demand, and what they primarily associate with professional knowledge. A patient must be able to rely on a doctor's skill in diagnosis or treatment. He need not worry about which theories the doctor employs. A client for an aptitude test considers the psychologist's ability to use and interpret the test, not on which theories the test is based. But for the professionals themselves, and in studies of their practice, one of the most important points is to learn what theoretical knowledge they think they are using, and what they really seem to be using, apart from practical skills.

Historically, certain professions such as psychology have arisen within the traditional academic system and developed professional practices only later. Others – like engineering science and architecture – have seen their practices become theoreticized and embraced by the academic world. Some professions became paragons of the rational academic view of how knowledge should be objectivized and then applied, with a distinction between imparting or producing knowledge inside the profession's university-allied core and, on the other hand, applying knowledge outside at the profession's periphery.[6] We shall proceed from this view and examine the work of architects and psychologists with the rational model, before opposing it to another model which many psychologists and architects seem actually to follow in their work, despite their general advocacy of institutionalized formal knowledge in that core.

What connection exists between *theory and practice* in psychologists' and architects' work? We begin with psychologists.

First, in the institute and the clinic, the psychologists sometimes use formalized *tests and testing methods*. There it is stated what information is worth obtaining, and how this can be interpreted according to some particular theory. Whether or not the psychologist knows the theoretical background, a connection exists there between theory and practice when applying the test. It was also on such grounds that academic psychology acquired its practical areas of work, and professionalized its application of knowledge. The test became, for a psychologist, what the hammer and nail are for a carpenter – as expressed by one of the founders of pedagogical/psychological practice, Torsten Husen. But large areas of psychological practice do not have most such concrete tools.

Second, another type of connection occurs when the psychologist has a *hypothesis, model or explanation* which is, or can be, derived from some theory. This situation, however, turns out to be either extremely difficult to observe – both from the outside and by the practitioners themselves – or else of very rare occurrence. In the registered material from five occasions of supervision at the welfare office, there is only one example of a relatively clear hypothesis or attempt at explanation. This was asked about in the interviews and it was said to occur, but nobody could cite instances of such a hypothesis recently used in supervision. At the clinic it also seems very hard to report how theoretical orientations or explanatory models control ideas, interpretations and possible hypotheses. The personnel claim not to think consciously about such points of departure during their work, apart from what concerns the levels of individual, family and system, and how it is expressed. Everyone has an education and background which gives rise rather unconsciously to hypotheses or suggested interpretations. In subsequent analytical work, however, the connection between theory and practice may be clearer and more systematically experimental from various theoretical viewpoints.

As to private therapists, a psychologist also points to the close connection of theories and models with the therapists' personalities. One seldom thinks in terms of models in guidance situations.

A great deal of psychological work has to include the personality as an 'instrument'. This must be trained through work and supervision. Architectural work displays a certain analogy to it, in the originality and personal ability which are needed during parts of the project work. One may speculate as to what difficulties result when maintaining and developing common knowledge for groups such as a professional collective. One can also dwell upon what strategies are required in order to preserve and assert an independent area of knowledge, which might tend to disintegrate into an endless variety of personal styles. It is possible that the therapeutic orientation in several areas of psychology present just such a threat to the body of collective knowledge, and that a counter-strategy lies in developing the supervision. But as the interviews and other studies emphasize, the traits of a good supervisor are more concerned with being a competent practitioner and with accepting and supporting the people supervised, steering them towards independence and recognizing deficiencies in one's own competence, than with being stringent and verifying a certain application of theory.

Third, psychologists do, on the other hand, gladly place themselves within some *theoretical orientation* or tradition acquired from their basic education, self-therapy or further education. Yet being 'eclectic' is wholly acceptable. A frequent means for psychologists both individually and collectively is to pursue continuous education. Here lies an ever-changing background for seeking explanations and using models. It is, in part, a rather irrational process. The arsenal of theories and perspectives used must be tractable and surveyable. One must adopt what has somehow been actualized in recent literature or heard during education. One focuses on particular problems, observed reactions or patterns from a certain temporary perspective. This, too, is a kind of connection between theory and practice – while less rational than is stipulated by the rationalistic model of knowledge, as this quotation of a psychologist indicates: 'An example is Minuchin's structural family analysis. I then think a lot in those terms for a few weeks, and interpret much of what I hear in those terms. Next some other theme may enter, such as transference between parents and children.'

The theme may vary for many reasons: free-time experiences, mass-media information, what happens in the group and so on. It depends on which components of one's 'knowledge reservoir' are 'stimulated'. The psychologists think that, as supervisors among other things, they must have their 'reservoirs activated by impulses from outside'. But even newly won theoretical knowledge can be difficult to apply. Much psychological work consists of conversational situations, where material is gathered for enquiry, where it is processed until a decision and where treatment takes place. In the form of the free conversation, theories, models, themes and hypotheses often lie well-hidden. Yet choices of examples and models can illustrate or refer to a certain unexpressed theory. Those interviewed also say that such elements exist mainly in the back of their minds, as a less conscious background. One is only intuitively conscious of when, for example, one changes perspective from system theory to psychodynamics. Such a change of perspective can, for the most part, only be reconstructed afterwards.

Fourth, a further loose connection between theory and practice is found in a *jargon with labels and commonsense ideas*, which sometimes are a translation of theoretical concepts and explanations into simpler ways of representation. In supervisory conversations, the psychologists often refer to such ideas by means of images: 'letting off the pressure', 'airing our feelings', 'being a waste-bin', 'filling up a reservoir' and so on. The images may contain or point to certain models, and in some cases they may be allied to more systematic theories. But they are perhaps more frequently part of the psychologist's everyday outlook, which is often shared with other psychologists due to common education and experience. Images and further translations are a way of communicating to personnel who lack psychological education and the reference frame which psychologists have. In such situations, they can often indicate links, between reactions and causes, which may appeal to anybody and provide good explanations and plausible interpretations, while at the same time being concrete exhortations.

The links may also be referrable to more systematic theories which have other grounds than proven experience. But it is doubtful whether they consciously arise from such a theory or model at the moment of expression. A conversation proceeds rapidly and it must be difficult to leave time for such rational deliberations. However, interpretation may instead be drawn from earlier experience of similar cases, where an interpretation was used that has proved to be plausible; it can thus be linked to a theory by that route. Yet it may simply be taken from the psychologist's own experience of life, and then belongs to a different sort of competence from that of theoretical knowledge, even though it can be fairly substantial.

Hence, in many of the psychologists' working situations, it is unusual to find a connection between theory and practice which involves deriving an explanation from theories or general assertions in the traditional sense of applying theoretical knowledge. This, of course, need not mean that psychologists lack that kind of professional competence. On the contrary, perhaps more than any other comparable group, they devote themselves to further theoretical education as well. But it is possible that the theoretical knowledge has a quite different function from that of an immediate aid to their own productive work. Its function would then be to create unity and togetherness among psychologists, to strengthen the professional group by providing a common language and reference frames, through which they can discuss their working tasks and support each other, talk themselves out and diminish their own anxiety.

Let us now see something of how the architects use knowledge and skills in their work. With their emphasis on skills and experience, we can subsequently throw light on how the psychologists also make use of these while not emphasizing the fact or being able to report it in the same way as architects can. We thus pass to an alternative model of knowledge as compared with the rational one.

In the architects' role as projectors, the work involves being able to run a project and have all the social competence required for it. Here, theoretical knowledge of projecting as a process of information, decision, planning and working is highly significant. However, such knowledge is scarcely included in their education, but must be acquired as experience in work, and has been formalized to a very small extent.

During the planning work – and especially the phase which deals with elaborating the main proceedings, where architects choose alternative technical solutions – they apply theoretical knowledge from the arsenal of engineering science. This is relatively unproblematical, since they can choose solutions without needing to worry in detail about the underlying theories. They can calmly ignore the question of which orientation in, for example, the science of material strength is responsible for a given solution. They need not confess to any particular orientation or disavow any other 'paradigm'. Theories are rather irrelevant to their role as technicians.

The technical theories are laid down in construction norms, material and methods of manufacturing and building. The architects' dependence on theory lies, in this case, mostly beyond their possibilities, but at the same time it constitutes strong and stable frames of reference. The engineering work means that they use well-known principles, norms and standardized partial solutions. They frequently seek precedents in previous similar buildings and designs. They go through the office archives, look in journals and product catalogues.

In their role as artists, on the other hand, they have essential degrees of freedom to choose approaches. But since the rules and connections which typify special styles are so indirectly implied, even the architects must, in their artistic role, depend on example and on their own experiences. Thus, too, they go back to their own and others' solutions.[7] Rules and norms for artistic styles are bound up with examples and precedents, and with established preconceptions. Against this, the functionalist tradition sought to introduce a more rational working method, based on analysis and synthesis, and derived from the view of knowledge in rational scientific tradition. Study of how the actual projecting looked there was neglected. The project is characterized by having a sustaining idea, which is gradually subjected to modifying factors.[8]

But the analytical and synthetic method prepared another approach. One was to avoid sustaining ideas, preconceptions, rules of thumb and intuition. Instead, form was to be derived merely from the requirements set by the project situation itself, with quantifiable and objective information. Only at the later synthetic stage was this to be translated into linguistic and graphic information, three-dimensional in form, emphasizing creativity and originality.

> In the architectural education, the analysis/synthesis method becomes confusing. One phase calls for objectivity and avoidance of preconceived opinions while the other, synthesis, demands originality and innovativeness. The pupil is thus faced with two different and mostly unrelated strategies. The great majority save this situation by invoking types of solution taken from outside their education in trade journals or personal environments. It is actually these advance models which enable them to project.[9]

This also shows that the rational-scientific view of knowledge hardly suits the study and analysis of professional practice. Knowledge is applied there in ways differing from the hypothetico-deductive or inductive-deductive method. And this, in turn, brings us to non-theoretical knowledge.

Experience and example as resources

Hitherto, we have confined ourselves to what can be called *theoretical or asserted knowledge*. This may be partly knowledge about laws, regulations and ordinances connected with the work organization and with relations to clients. It may partly include the special theories, models and explanations which professional groups employ. In the following, we shall take a more detailed look at *skills* or *practical knowledge*, as well as what is called *tacit and experiential knowledge*. The latter involves good judgement, such as knowing styles and principles of form in order to judge architecture. This is often not formulated in words but made visible by carefully choosing and indicating examples and particular cases, where the underlying rules are concretized by being applied.[10] The rational model of knowledge is here opposed to the uncertainty, complexity, and instability which characterize the daily work of many professionals, with their tendency 'to converse in terms of the situation or the individual', or to proceed from a 'sustaining idea' as a 'preconceived opinion' and to let 'modifying factors' lead to a 'satisfying solution'. In both application of rules and explanation with the rational model, there are ready-made categories and classifications which provide 'selective attention' during the enquiry or the problem formulation. As a result, unstable and unique phenomena slip through. At the same time, there is a tendency to concentrate more on the solutions than on formulating the problems.[11]

In questions as to what architects and psychologists use as aids in their work, they have trouble in pointing out examples of rationally applying theoretical knowledge or assertations. Their answers are, rather, reminiscent of the following quotation: 'There are those who choose the swampy lowlands. They deliberately involve themselves in messy but crucially important problems and, when asked to describe their methods of inquiry, they speak of experience, trial and error, intuition, and muddling through.'[12] In this and similar ways, the active professionals throw into question the rational, formal and asserted knowledge which they themselves still mainly embrace in other contexts, and which their professions have historically upheld.

The architects' arguments in discussions and negotiations are supported chiefly by referring to concrete, personally experienced examples such as other buildings, other city environments and completed projects. The psychologists often point to earlier patients or clients whom everyone in the group knows, in order to make comparisons. They frequently draw parallels between cases. Some claim to collect and memorize cases, although unable to say which principles are used for gathering and subsequently exploiting such precedents.

When an architect is in the sketching phase of a project, various solutions are tested with the help of precedents, examples and previous experience. The work here is often creative and artistic. It builds to a high degree upon what the architects themselves describe as intuitive knowledge – their feeling for how different solutions should work, rather than conscious calculation and decision. The sketch method means that one works with different comprehensive solutions which are designed in rapid succession, tested and elaborated in a process of adjustment with regard to diverse subsidiary problems.[13]

Tacit and reflective knowledge

With the intimate or tacit knowledge of being able to use and judge examples, and the skill of using working tools in order to sketch, many of the steps in the process are unexpressed. For the most part, there is no need to formulate and articulate them. In other cases, this could be done only with great difficulty or not at all. Such knowledge and skill depend strongly on the individual and context. Whatever rules and principles the practitioners may use are hard to formulate generally apart from the person and situation.

Hence they become hard to discover and verbalize or to express discursively. They are best communicated through illustrative examples.

The ability to sketch, form and design is said to lie in one's fingers and eyes. When a person possesses a certain concept or has a certain piece of knowledge, it need not mean that he can express it in words or writing with terminology rather than solely through actions and experiences. Personal or subjective knowledge is acquired through training until it becomes an automatic habit.[14]

The ability to express knowledge or skills in words or other actions can be related to different degrees of consciousness. We may act with a practical consciousness without being able discursively to reproduce or report this.

> When we go about the spontaneous, intuitive performance of the actions of everyday life, we show ourselves to be knowledgeable in a special way. Often we cannot say what it is that we know. When we try to describe it we find ourselves at a loss, or we produce descriptions that are obviously inappropriate. Our knowing is ordinarily tacit, implicit in our patterns of action and in our feel for the stuff with which we are dealing. It seems right to say that our knowing is *in* our action.[15]

> Although reflection-in-action is an extraordinary process, it is not a rare event. Indeed, for some reflective practitioners it is the core of practice. Nevertheless, because professionalism is still mainly identified with technical expertise, reflection-in-action is not generally accepted – even by those who do it – as a legitimate form of professional knowing.[16]

Schön, cited above, then analyses a number of individual professionals' conversations, supplemented with interviews, in order to describe how they work, step by step, and which aids they use. A designer supervises and corrects a student's sketch proposal. Here the architect conducts a sort of conversation with the material in a given context. He sketches and talks in parallel, or carries out his inner dialogue aloud before the student, in a language of designing with many spatial references. They try to make these congruent between themselves. A fundamental principle for the drawing is to alternate between the part and the whole. Another, of which the architect is not conscious, is to work oneself forward in sequences. Aided by the sketching and the spatial language as media, he represents the buildings through experimental features. Every feature has consequences which are described and evaluated with a number of design domains. These have consequences which are conditions for the next feature, and create problems that must be described and solved in the next step.

The architect spins a web of features, consequences, implications, appreciations and new features. Sometimes the web becomes so comprehensive that he must ask 'What if?' and make a decision which becomes a sort of binding implication, with inescapable or irreversible conditions for the sequel.[17]

A psychoanalyst supervises a student in psychotherapy. He uses a repertory of meanings and patterns, to get the student to tell about his patient. This forms the material which the supervisor uses to test interpretations, which become interventions in the process that tests their viability. They will be viable if the patient finds them compelling.

Both the architect and the psychoanalyst regard the practical case as unique. They avoid using any standard solutions, and look for special circumstances which they try to liberate in order to formulate an intervention. This is a reflective conversation about a unique and uncertain situation. But they make no attempt to reflect on their own reflection-in-action. Hence they cannot show on a meta-level what they are doing.[18]

The architect begins with a form, a sustaining idea, and proceeds to test its consequences in the situation at hand. This method disagrees with the rational analysis/synthesis method, and can be better compared to deduction/conjecture/refutation. The practitioners have built up a repertoire of examples, viewpoints, understandings and actions. Through these, they see the situations as something they are already familiar with, without directly subordinating the unique situations to their precedents.

Such virtual worlds are created by all practitioners in their special way and with their special media. They form contexts for experiments, where they can disregard or win control over some of the hindrances of everyday life so as carefully to reflect in action. They constitute representative practical worlds in the sense of both exercise and practice.[19]

Such penetrating analyses as these in professional work indicate that large parts of the knowledge required for it lie embedded in its very execution. If so, it calls for a wholly different concept of knowledge from the usual one which lies behind formalized knowing in all public instruction – even that which is conducted for the majority of professions. It would mean affirming that social actors mostly know how one does things, that this knowledge is bound to contexts and constitutes resources only in these contexts, that it cannot be formalized in the same way as knowing what one does, and that it cannot be communicated by the same methods.

Among psychologists, there is a rapidly growing awareness of how knowing is bound to situations and contexts. The view is that solutions cannot be ready-made but must evolve in interaction with clients and collaborators. Their further education largely concerns learning to understand and use processes and processual thinking – which not seldom comes into opposition with experimental psychology, test psychology and other kinds of theoretical and asserted knowledge.

Perhaps the main cause of such an ongoing transformation in practical psychology is the ever-stronger orientation towards therapy on psychodynamic grounds. There a long tradition has existed of thinking and working with processes and allowing knowledge acquisition to be equated with the method of conducting therapy. But it is seen primarily in the ever more extensive systems for supervision, and the growing requirements of having one's own supervisor in a number of different working tasks as well as obtaining one's own training in supervision. The term 'supervision' stands, certainly, for a variety of things. Yet the choice to use it indicates the desire to emphasize apprenticeship and another method of communicating methodical knowing.

This method assumes that one must win knowledge through a personal creative effort. Theories and techniques must be made vital in a practical test of one's own work, where both the personality and the situation step in and shape knowing as a part of acting. Architectural and psychological work have this in common with several other professions. Such processes are analogous to artistic work, which could yield reasoning about how professional work rests not only on scientific foundations, but perhaps mainly on proven experience.

The architects repeatedly stress the enormous significance of experience. But this passes into the third category of resources, which concerns communication and conversation. It is naturally a resource or ability which belongs to organizational and professional resources, in that these cannot be used without communication and conversation. The latter, though, can be used independently of the former and, moreover, it constitutes a neglected aspect in studies of organizations and professions.

Conversation as a resource

Conversational acts are a hallmark of all intellectual work. For some professional groups, language enters all working situations; for others, it plays a lesser role in certain phases. But for most, it is relatively important during the investigatory phase. Here are posed questions to be answered and problems to be solved. Language then becomes the chief medium for collecting information and producing material through statements and accounts. Particularly in jurisprudence, these expressions are themselves subjected to closer scrutiny. In psychoanalysis, they may be a part of the treatment phase.

Many of the architects' and psychologists' working tasks occur as more or less formalized talks with clients, colleagues and other personnel. During enquiry, much of the information is gathered in this way. The psychologists must then often depend on second-hand information or hearsay which has run through several conversational situations. The processing towards a decision, and the actual decision situation, occur for the most part in groups where the forms of conversation, the participants and the rest of the context contribute to the result. Advice and treatment, too, often occur in various conversational situations.

An essential element of this resource is what the publicly employed architects possess in their organization. They must know how it functions and with which people one must, formally and informally, have good contact. This knowledge can scarcely be acquired from education, but is learned in time at work. The ability to create alliances before special issues and meetings can be decisive. In addition, they must learn to converse with clients. Generally, for all architects, this is a matter of creating confidence in different conversational situations. They claim to be strongly aware of who the clients and principals are, in order to know 'which arguments can strike home'.

Architects make use of the combination of verbal or written presentation with sketches or other illustrations. They may feel quite handicapped without their sketches.[20] In the often completely free conversational form of conferences, information is processed and decisions are taken, which are probably far more strongly tied to these situations' contexts than they may seem.

Self-therapy and supervision in therapy may be regarded as situations which exercise and train the ability to participate in and conduct conversations in order to gather information and give treatment. This occurs without the conversation as such becoming an object of analysis and instruction. The rules of conversation are communicated as implied skills. (Instruction in therapy can, of course, be called a systematic exercise in conducting a certain conversation, but based on other methods and theories than those of linguistics.)

The psychologists at the institute emphasize the guidance conversation at some cost to the formalized tests. They also emphasize other, more or less therapeutic conversations. They prescribe guidance in a group, whose conversational resources are made use of. The psychologists at the welfare office, and at the clinic, also devote most of their working time to conversations. They participate in strengthening the overall tendency of psychology to concentrate more closely on therapeutic conversations. They also take part in the general tendency within organizations to make decisions in group conversation without reflecting much on how the conversation's conditions control the production of decisions and other results.

Conversation, then, is an activity with strong ties to contexts, but it is also strongly linked to individuals. Personal traits play a very large role in the ability to engage in conversation, and in the results which can be attained. The psychologists are trained to make use of and develop their personal resources for conversation, while the architects hardly receive such training although they often employ such resources in their work.

Conclusions

The main types of resources differentiated above can more or less be related to a work organization, a professional group and conversational situations. Being a pure 'bureaucrat' would mean that one makes use only of organizational resources. Using only professional resources would mean being a kind of 'free professional' without subordination or access to rules, regulations or the like, and without belonging to a formal organization. Having only conversational resources would mean being a kind of entirely 'free intellectual'.[21]

We have tried to survey the combinations of resources which exist for architects and psychologists, those they seem to be able to exploit, and those by which they are at the same time limited and controlled. Competence is equivalent to being able to mobilize resources of different sorts for particular working tasks.

Architects' work is both organizationally and professionally permeated by rules, norms and regulations which are systematized in handbooks. Specialization in certain tasks leads to corresponding specialization in the norm system. At the office, an architect is set in a hierarchy and organization with great demands on efficiency, disciplined behaviour and organized participation in numerous gatherings and meetings. Such a situation also offers great opportunities for collaboration and the conducting of projects: resources which self-employed architects may lack, as the free working group illustrates.

Among psychologists, it is mainly those at the institute who are affected by rules and regulations, even if they too can leave most such questions to other personnel. On the whole, psychological work is very little regulated in these ways compared with architects' work. The lack of such rules for relations with clients and others who consult is compensated for by contracts.

Psychologists often refer to ethical issues and ethical rules, and thus strongly emphasize this aspect of professional unity. A certain lack of bureaucratic rules seems to be compensated for by the tremendous impact of professional ethics. Architects, for their part, do not refer nearly so frequently to aesthetic issues. Beautiful solutions are (unfortunately) discussed less often than solutions which are practical, economic, technical and politically possible.

Psychologists tend to exaggerate the significance of theoretical knowledge for their own working tasks. As we have seen, it is hard to see what the connection between theory and practice consists of, other than giving psychologists a common representational world and language. In the rapid conversational flow of many working tasks, such knowledge is scarcely used in any traditionally explanatory, derivative manner. Their dependence on theories and theoretical traditions is, nevertheless, very strong and may be caused by a certain lack of simple unambiguous rules, as well as by the uncertainty in which many decisions have to be made. In addition to this are the personal resources which psychologists must continually mobilize in close contact with clients and others. Most immediately point to themselves as their main aid in work. This is a professional as well as a communicative resource.

Architects' application of technical theories is unproblematical and occurs simply through their choice of particular technical solutions. Most of them have a complete disregard for theory in the social and behavioural sciences. What is controversial to them lies in choosing styles, which they do mainly by choosing or referring to examples of earlier solutions. They have a long tradition of familiarity with examples. They eagerly cite experience in selecting these, and skill in shaping and testing solutions.

Yet both architects' and psychologists' experiential knowledge should be regarded for the present as rather hypothetical, since such categories of knowledge have much of the character of remainder categories – giving a positive rubric to the unexplained. Tacit knowledge may then be only a legitimized self-image which is drawn in order to elicit confidence from the public and principals.

Finally, we have noticed resources which have to do with interaction and conversation. The architects use these in negotiation and in persuasion of the splendour of their proposals. Psychologists use them to create trust and, thereby, a will in the client or other principal to confess, open up and release information, and accept treatment.

Both professional groups depend strongly on methods which can create confidence. Psychologists are trained in these, while architects have to gather their own experience of such conversation situations. Here, too, are emphasized the practitioners' personal means of expression, which are often said to be the essential characteristic of both professions. For many architects, however, this remains largely wishful thinking, since they are strongly bound to technical and administrative rules and economic frameworks. For psychologists, by contrast, personal opportunities for development expand as long as the therapeutic orientation expands. Yet at the same time, psychologists are required to strengthen their ties with the ethical rule system. Architects' methods are more allied to social organization resources, whereas those of psychologists are a fairly independent, non-material resource allied to the profession and to conversation rather than to organization.

Among psychologists, therefore, means based upon professional resources are more important than those based upon organizational ones, while conversational resources are decisive although only practically conscious and not recognized in any linguistic sense. Among architects, means related to their social networks are very important in most phases of work, except for the sketch phase where the 'real' architectural work is done on the basis of the 'real' professional practice in architecture, which mostly involves the ability to sketch and to be confidential with examples and models.

Language and conversation play a decisive role both for architects when they construct projects, and for psychologists when they create tasks. For architects, it is a small step to concentration upon the final result, the actual product, rather than on the process. One may then think less about the conversation's significance than about the language of form which it conveys. Yet the path to the product is paved largely with layers of dialogue that merge into each other. For the psychologists, conversation makes up not only the phase of investigation but also those of advice and treatment. In this respect the psychologists are said to be an extreme case among the world's human-care professions. However, conversation occupies a very special position in all such professions and organizations.

Studies of professions at work often reveal a vast distance between formal education and the applied knowledge which working situations require. State control mainly concerns formal education, and this means that the professions' practice is very largely left to their own arbitrariness and discretionary power. In order to find points of contact between professionals' education, knowledge and work, one must use other concepts of knowledge – such as the reflective type of knowledge – which can better explain how professional proficiency is embedded in the practice itself, with the contextual conditions that are tied to specific situations.

> Formal knowledge is systematically transformed by professionals with differing perspectives created both by the particular demands of the work they do and by the demands of their particular clients. . . . (Knowledge) lives only through its agents, who themselves employ ideas and techniques selectively as their tasks and perspectives dictate. There is no assurance what knowledge will be used to guide the use of institutional power. No 'one best way' is predictable from the formal body of knowledge itself.[22]

The proficiency which then proves to be most central is bound up with experiences that often cannot be described verbally, and with the ability to chat and converse, persuade and convince – all traits that are associated with persons more than with organizations and professions.

Notes

1 Larson, 1977/1979; Johnson, 1982:189.

2 Roemer, 1982b; Wright, 1985, ch. 3 and pp. 148ff; Hoff, 1985:207–226; Blau, 1984:31.

3 Freidson, 1986, ch. 10.

4 Collins, 1979; Parkin, 1979, chs 4–6; Murphy, 1983:631–658; Bourdieu, 1981; Eyerman, Svensson and Söderquist, 1987.

5 Lundequist, 1984:58f, on the historical development of standards in construction; Franzen, 1977.

6 Larson, 1977/1979, ch. 7; Schön, 1983, part I; Disco, 1987.

7 Östnäs, 1984:197ff; Ödman, 1986:22; Lundequist, 1984:25; Blau, 1984:46ff.

8 Lundequist, 1984:58.

9 Åström, 1958.

10 Lundequist, 1984:39–40.

11 Schön, 1983:37.

12 Schön, 1983:43.

13 Östnäs and Svensson, 1986:52, 61; Schön, 1983:93ff.

14 Lundequist, 1984:38ff.

15 Schön, 1983:49.

16 Schön, 1983:69.

17 Schön, 1983:93–103.

18 Schön, 1983:116–127; Åström, 1958.

19 Schön, 1983:162.

20 Schön, 1983:221ff (on the conversational strategy of a town planner). Cf Forester, 1983.

21 Roemer, 1982b; Wright, 1985; Hoff, 1985.

22 Freidson, 1986:210, 217.

5

Proletarianization or bureaucratization: the fall of the professional?

Raymond Murphy

At the centre of the sociological study of the professions is 'the rise of occupations based on systematic or scientific knowledge, occupations with cultural rather than monetary capital'.[1] This cultural capital, or abstract utilitarian knowledge as it can more appropriately be called,[2] has been perceived by some as a resource of growing importance in the strategic struggle for rewards, status and power. Thus one of the major currents in sociology perceives the professions in particular and credentialled groups in general as a new governing class whose power is based on the control not of the means of production but of the means of knowing in a post-industrial system increasingly founded on science and technology.[3] The abstract utilitarian knowledge is seen as a potent resource which can be strategically mobilized and monopolized, regardless of whether the state is capitalist or socialist.

Marxists, realizing that such a thesis undermines the basic tenets of Marxism, have searched for arguments, evidence and illustrations to counter this new governing class thesis.[4] They have in addition proposed the antithesis – the proletarianization of professionals – derived from the class polarization postulate of Marxian theory. 'A structural analysis would suggest the prospect of assimilation to the working class as a more plausible consequence than the transformation of professionals into a new governing class'.[5] They view abstract utilitarian knowledge as a quickly eroding resource, an erosion which renders less and less effective professional strategies to acquire and/or maintain power, autonomy, rewards and status. Financial capital in pursuit of profit in the capitalist state is seen as either stripping professions of their cultural capital or rendering it impotent as an instrument in the deployment of professional strategies.

Since I have already argued against the new governing class thesis and suggested that credentials are best conceived of as derivative and contingent forms of closure subordinate to the principal forms based on private property and the Communist Party,[6] I will examine here the Marxian antithesis: the proletarianization of professionals.[7] The issues involved can be analysed by distinguishing two separate aspects: (1) whether the changing nature of the professions and credentialled groups is best conceived of in terms of proletarianization and assimilation to the working class; and (2) the reason for the changes which have occurred.

The proletarianization of the professional?

There is rough agreement concerning the changing nature of professions. A century ago professionals, unlike the working class, were largely self-employed and had an autonomous relation with clients protected by the state. Today the majority in almost all professions are salaried employees in organizations. Professionals are now submitted to a bureaucratic system of managerial control in formal organizations and have lost their traditional autonomy. Hence professionals express on surveys a degree of dissatisfaction concerning their work that has become more and more similar to that of other workers.[8] Their associations are increasingly using the tactics of, and forming alliances with, the labour movement.[9] These changes have been referred to as the 'fall of the professional'. Note that there has been no corresponding fall of 'professionalism'. As Larson has demonstrated, the ideology of professionalism is more prevalent than ever, but it has been transformed from an accurate portrayal of the autonomous working conditions of the professional to an illusion.[10]

The strong proletarianization hypothesis
At this point the agreement concerning both evidence and interpretation ends. It is necessary to distinguish two different Marxian hypotheses: a strong proletarianization hypothesis and a weak one. The first hypothesizes that professionals, like proletarians, have lost control of the overall goals and policy directions of their work *and* over their technical tasks and procedures.[11] Drawing an analogy with craft workers at an earlier stage in the development of capitalism, it claims that under monopoly capitalism professionals are sliding down the slope of de-skilling, degradation of work, and Taylorism depicted by Braverman for the working class and even to a slow degradation of status and rewards.[12] Thus illustrations have been searched for and found to show that computerized protocols have been used in an attempt to standardize work and relations with clients and diminish the discretion of professionals in social work,[13] architecture,[14] medicine[15] and science.[16] Even in the case of

the profession – medicine – usually used as the model for all the others, McKinlay and Arches 'believe that physicians are losing their monopoly control over strategic knowledge and will be gradually "deskilled" '.[17]

The strong proletarianization hypothesis can be logically derived from Marxian theory and consists of a coherent conception of proletarianization. The problem is, however, that the available evidence refutes it. Kornhauser, Larson, Freidson and Spangler and Lehman have found that the de-skilling described by Braverman has not been typical of any major professional group and that professionals in large, highly bureaucratized organizations continue to have technical authority and discretion.[18] Management has only been able to standardize complex, theoretically based scientific and professional labour to a very limited extent. Moreover, the strong proletarianization hypothesis has mistaken specialization (for example, of neurosurgeons) in the intensifying division of labour for de-skilling, thereby falsely equating the specialization of professionals in deepening niches of abstract utilitarian knowledge with the specialization of the proletariat in different segments of routine unskilled labour.[19] Many professionals may even be freed from mundane tasks by administrative and support personnel in order to pursue their esoteric interests, thereby enhancing their skills and autonomy.

> When the mechanization of labor robbed the skilled worker of his capacity to comprehend a whole process of production, his subordination to capital was, in fact, completed. Insofar as increasingly specialized professionals maintain, through overtraining, the 'intelligence of the whole', they escape the fate of most other specialized workers in our society. Overtraining appears, thus, as a specific attribute of *privileged* work.[20]

The reserve army of professionals created in some conjunctures by over-supply, although subjectively experienced by unemployed professionals as proletarianization, is fundamentally and structurally different from the reserve army of the proletariat: it is 'one in which unemployment and underemployment are not a consequence of deskilling, but of overtraining'.[21] Marxists are fond of extrapolating from the disappearance of craftsmen and guilds to a prediction of the same fate for professionals and their associations. An important difference is precisely that craftsmen became proletarians working under the same conditions and for the same rewards (salary, fringe benefits) as other workers when they were integrated into factories, whereas credentialled professionals and specialists in bureaucracies show no signs of working under the same conditions and for the same rewards as the proletariat.

Some Marxists now admit the absence of evidence that 'would support orthodox Marxist notions that professionals are slowly being assimilated to the working class in a society increasingly polarized between capital and labor'.[22] They have been forced to concede that

> professionals, unlike industrial workers, have salvaged from their new dependency the core of their self-respect and unique status: their technical skills and control of highly specialized knowledge. Professionals thus retain the anomalous authority of craft and expertise, envied and unattainable by all other employees. . . . In the new division of labor, professionals assume narrowed responsibilities and do a constricted range of tasks, but these are typically tasks demanding the most skill and discretion which only they have the knowledge to organize and perform.[23]

If professionals are undergoing proletarianization, it is a proletarianization very different from that of the proletariat: 'their [professionals] relative invulnerability to deskilling or knowledge erosion points to a subordination radically distinct from that of the industrial proletariat'.[24] Thus Derber concludes that 'professionals may be becoming workers, but in this period they appear to be a new type not adequately conceptualized in existing Marxist theory'.[25]

The weak proletarianization hypothesis

Faced with the problem of disconfirming evidence, some Marxists have now weakened their proletarianization hypothesis to the following: 'like industrial workers, their [professionals] labour is effectively subjected to the aims and controls of capitalist production'[26] through the use of management systems which control professionals without threatening their technical autonomy.[27] Thus Derber distinguishes between 'technical proletarianization', the loss of control over knowledge, technical job decisions, and the process of work, and 'ideological proletarianization . . . [the] loss of control over the goals and social purposes to which one's work is put. Elements of ideological proletarianization include powerlessness to choose or define the final product of one's work, its disposition in the market, its uses in the larger society, and the values or social policy of the organization which purchases one's labor.'[28] In organizations it is management, not professionals, that controls broad policy questions, the type of cases and clients, and standard procedures. Whereas the proletariat has suffered both technical and ideological proletarianization, professionals have experienced only the latter. The transition from free to salaried professionals has meant a loss of the freedom to define objectives but a maintenance of technical autonomy and status privileges.

Even this weakened proletarianization-of-professionals hypothesis is, however, fatally flawed. Professionals share with the proletariat non-ownership of the means of production and a dependence on bureaucratic organizations (capitalist enterprises, hospitals, schools, universities and so on) to provide the means to accomplish their labour. But professionals are unlike the proletariat in that they are controlled not so much by direct management commands as by socialization into the profession and by individual incentives: 'whether provided by a "free" professional entrepreneur or by a salaried professional worker, professional services are seldom subjected to the characteristic forms of discipline and control under which "ordinary" labor power is typically expended in capitalist societies'.[29] Furthermore, professionals, unlike the proletariat, typically control other workers and/or develop the technology that helps to do so. They often exercise an authority, delegated though it may be, over clients and over the working class (the latter frequently bearing the subordinate label 'support staff') which has no parallel among the proletariat. Professionals, unlike the proletariat, usually form the pool from which are drawn the high-level managers who shape the goals of the organization: 'top administrators (for example, hospital superintendents, medical directors and directors of health affairs) are almost exclusively recruited from the ranks of physicians'.[30] Moreover, 'the gap in competence between professionals and laymen, institutionalized by the monopolies of training and certification, ipso facto sets *every* professional apart: he belongs to a privileged society of "knowers", which the public tends to identify with its elite spokesmen'.[31] Proponents of the weak proletarianization hypothesis admit that 'even with an "integrative" professionalism, ideological proletarianization and the new labor system carry risks for management because they cede to professional employees a potential power, in their technical knowledge and "relative autonomy", far greater than that extended to other workers'.[32]

If professional employees are unlike the proletariat in such fundamental ways as their knowledge, skills, autonomy, control over the proletariat, potential power and the manner in which they are controlled, as well as their status rewards, privileged position in a system of material inequality and life chances, then the only reasonable conclusion to draw is that ideological proletarianization is not proletarianization. 'Ideological proletarianization' is a misnomer; it is in fact the bureaucratization of professionals – a system of organizing, controlling and rewarding the work of professionals quite distinct from that of the proletariat. Moreover, the evidence presented by the proponents of the 'ideological proletarianization' hypothesis does not support the contention of a structural tendency toward assimilation of the system of control of professionals with the system of control of the proletariat. Professionals and the proletariat are at present, and will according to the best available evidence remain in the foreseeable future, very different. The professions have become bureaucratized, but they have not become proletarianized. Any conception that mistakes the bureaucratization of professionals for their proletarianization obscures the fundamental differences between the two.

Credibility is often stretched to breaking point by attempts to marshal support for the hypothesis of the proletarianization of the professions. For example, Derber refers to Larson as a 'proletarianization theorist' even after Larson argued that '*professionalization appears as the other side of proletarianization* . . . the higher skills or knowledge of a minority of producers rest on the expropriation of skill or knowledge from the majority'.[33] Although one can question Larson's zero-sum assumption, it clearly does not allow both the degradation of proletarian labour and the proletarianization of professional work. Derber, Larson and Braverman make incompatible bedfellows. Larson conceives of professionals as 'the professional fraction of the bourgeoisie'.[34] Thus she argues that the parallels between professionals and the proletariat are 'striking, though superficial'.[35]

There is a tendency among proponents of the weak 'proletarianization of professionals' hypothesis to define proletarianization as work which does not involve ownership and is managed, thereby reducing proletarianization to an all-encompassing residual category that glosses over essential differences. 'A minimum definition of professional proletarianization would thus include a shift from self-employment to dependent employment, in which professionals' work also becomes effectively subject to management control.'[36] Since in a bureaucracy high managers are 'subject to management control' by even higher managers,[37] then corporate lawyers and chief accountants in capitalist enterprises, assistant deputy ministers in state apparatuses, generals in the military and the Politburo in the USSR are proletarianized by definitional fiat and there is nothing left to discuss or investigate. To state that 'the basic criterion of class position in capitalist society is not knowledge or skill but whether or not one is in a position of ownership and control over the means of one's production and labor' is to foreclose the issue a priori.[38] The question of whether knowledge or skill, even without ownership, affects one's control over the means of one's production and labour is best left an empirical and theoretical question that is not dogmatically prejudged. Larson concludes that for professionals

> the relevance and scarcity of the monopolized skill guarantee control at the level of execution and tend to push it 'upwards' – from the technical to the more visibly social level of work conditions and even, sometimes, policy decisions. Moreover, in the professions that control the production of their own knowledge, the accumulation of 'cultural property' or symbolic capital can be ordinarily translated into general social power.[39]

Since it forecloses these issues by definitional fiat, the weak theory of the proletarianization of professionals consists of the fall, not of the professional, but of sociology.

The control over the *general* ends and uses of work in monopoly capitalism and state socialism does seem to be concentrated in the apex of private and state bureaucratic hierarchies; neither proletarians nor professionals appear to have much control over those ends and uses (although even on this point there may be important differences between them, as the above quotation from Larson suggests). But that does not prove that professionals are in the process of becoming proletarianized any more than the fact that water shares with sand the quality of containing oxygen proves that water is turning into sand: the sandification of water. Professionals share with proletarians the lack of control over the general ends and uses of work under capitalism and socialism, but they differ so much in other important respects (control over knowledge and skills, over their work process, salary, status and so on) that any implication of the proletarianization of professionals is at best premature and more likely misleading.

Furthermore, it makes no sense to speak of 'ideological proletarianization' in a theory in which it is stated that professionalism provides 'professionals with a unique defense against corporatist or bureaucratic identities and ideologies'.[40] Professionals' abstract utilitarian knowledge on the technical level and their 'unique defense' – professionalism – on the ideological level distinguish them not only technically but also ideologically from the proletariat. For most professions and credentialled groups – those that were the offspring of bureaucratic organization – the 'loss of control over the ends and uses of one's work', that is, the defining feature of ideological proletarianization, never occurred because they never had such control.[41] The theory of 'ideological proletarianization' is a very misleading way to approach the question of the changing nature of the professions because the latter involves neither proletarianization nor loss.

One cannot conclude from the job dissatisfaction expressed by professionals that their objective working conditions have become similar to those of the proletariat. On the contrary, their dissatisfaction despite better working conditions probably reflects another difference that has been documented between professionals and the working class, namely the 'great expectations' of the former.[42] Their credentials lead professionals to a feeling of entitlement to a position of power and rewards and to a distinction between themselves and the proletariat. Frustrations resulting from great expectations only partly met must not be confused with an objective proletarian position. 'Surely, it is hard to consider the fate of an assistant professor who goes to a small town state college after Harvard or Berkeley as "proletarianization", although he or she may well see it as just such a loss'.[43]

Hence any analysis of the unionization of professionals must carefully distinguish, on the one hand, a tactical alliance of a professional association with a proletarian union to advance the entitlement interests of the professionals, from, on the other, a professional association becoming a proletarian union. Similarly, rare examples of radical caucuses of physicians,[44] lawyers,[45] social workers[46] and other professionals[47] must not be mistaken for a general movement toward 'deprofessionalization'.[48] Such an error makes no more sense than using the rare instances of capitalists supporting left-wing publications, conferences and parties to conclude that capitalists are becoming socialists. Proof by exceptional instances is inherently misleading. Whereas the rarity of radical caucuses of physicians makes their discovery all the more sensational, the difficulty in finding doctors to staff community health clinics (which give non-doctors more power over doctors) is not at all rare. Evidence of a growing movement of professionals becoming proletarian is lacking. Moreover, it is necessary to distinguish carefully the nature of professional demands. Doctors for peace, for disarmament and for the environment must not be mistaken for doctors in favour of sharing medical knowledge, power and rewards with the proletariat.

Union tactics, strikes and alliances with the organized fraction of the proletariat (the labour movement) are all strategic means that professional and credentialled groups may use in particular conjunctures to maintain, reinforce, or enhance their privileges, including their traditional advantages (working conditions, discretionary power, salary and fringe benefits) over the proletariat. These strategic means and alliances have little to do with the question of the proletarianization of professionals. A question which would address the attitudinal side of the issue is the following:

would professional and credentialled groups agree to eliminate their traditional advantages over the proletariat? There is no evidence of a tendency that would allow us to answer in the affirmative. On the contrary, professionals use even labour union tactics to maintain their advantages over the proletariat. For example, in Canada the nurses' association threatened strike action to maintain its traditional salary difference with nursing assistants who were awarded a substantial increase by the Human Rights Tribunal on the basis of equal pay for work of equal value between men and women. The strategic use by professionals of union tactics and alliances with the proletariat or its union to increase or maintain their power or rewards must not be mistaken for a willingness to share power and rewards with the proletariat.

Professionals are dissatisfied in bureaucracies not only because they are controlled by bureaucratic administrators and state regulations, but also because the proletariat and lower-ranking professionals, who were traditionally powerless, are attempting to usurp in the bureaucracy the power of higher-ranking professionals. 'Lower level educated workers may, for instance, cooperate with administrative efforts to curb the power of higher level professionals and to make the latter more accountable for their time and actions (such might be the case of nurses hoping to gain some autonomy from physicians)'.[49] Physicians' criticisms of the state and hospital bureaucracy involves dissatisfaction with giving outsiders to their profession more power, including not only hospital administrators but also representatives of elected officials, nurses, patients, citizen groups and so on. Teachers are dissatisfied when they feel that their credentials do not yield sufficient salary differential with less credentialled postal workers, police officers and others. Since the state bureaucracy is the immediate, transparent authority that caps professionals' great expectations, their dissatisfaction with the returns on credentials in terms of power and advantage over the proletariat is expressed as dissatisfaction with the state bureaucracy and its rules and power. Professionals' critique of the bureaucratic authority to whom aggrieved clients can appeal, described by Freidson in the case of physicians,[50] is in reality an attack by professionals on a resource that can be used by the 'demanding client' and the proletariat to defend themselves against a professional monopoly. Professionals' critique of the bureaucratic control over their work may be in part a critique by ricochet of the proletariat. It is naïve to assume that professionals' critique of bureaucracy is an egalitarian critique; it may well reflect their desire, not to eliminate inequality, but rather to maintain or improve their position relative to other groups, including the proletariat, in the structured system of inequality, monopolization and closure.

One characteristic which distinguishes professionals from the proletariat is that the former uses the ideology of service much more frequently and effectively than the latter to advance its interests. Physicians in Canada recently went on strike arguing that billing their clients for more than the government-paid rates (referred to in Canada as 'extra-billing') had nothing to do with money and only had to do with the quality of medical service. Their manifest target was the state bureaucracy which had stripped them of their autonomy and proletarianized them. The population was not, however, duped by this ideology and knew that they, the clients, were the real targets and that the issue was the autonomy to appropriate more money from clients. Similarly, when teachers, social workers, nurses and other professionals go on strike, they never admit that it is for money or benefits, they always claim that it is to improve or maintain quality of service. But quality of service is typically defined by the profession to suit its material interests: what is good for the profession is good for clients and the wider society.[51]

The Marxian theory of the proletarianization of the professional has a strong affinity with current ideologies used by the professions to combat threats to their monopoly position; it is in reality quite uncritical of professional monopolization. Schudson's critique of Larson applies with even greater force to Marxian proletarianization theorists:

> Where radical critics of professions attack the mammoth powers of the AMA [American Medical Association] or corporate lawyers, Sarfatti Larson emphasizes instead that most professions and professionals have very little power. . . . I believe she is at odds with most of the critics of professions who will be turning to her book for support. I do not think they will find comfort . . . most critics of professions emphasize the plight of the client in the face of professional power.[52]

Marxian theory runs the risk of being the opiate of the clients, tranquillizing resistance to and displacing it away from professional monopolization. For example, McKinlay and Arches condemn liberal and radical sociologists for ascribing responsibility to a villain – the physician – and for 'doctor bashing'.[53] They use the labour theory of value to portray physicians as greatly, and increasingly, exploited.[54] Derber and the authors in his reader are other clear examples of Marxian proletarianization theorists who have produced ideological weapons that are very useful to professionals in their struggle against the reduction of the social distance between themselves and the proletariat.[55] The Marxian thesis of the proletarianization of the professional confirms Bookchin's contention that

Marxism is 'the most subtle apologia' for hierarchy and domination and, if professionals can be considered a fraction of the bourgeoisie, as Larson suggests, refutes Mattick's negative response to the question forced on him by history: 'Marxism – last refuge of the bourgeoisie?'[56]

It is true that physicians, lawyers, accountants, engineers and others do not have the power to get everything they want, are dissatisfied and suffer stress from the worry that their entitlements may be usurped, but this is true of many capitalists as well. Professionals are not victims in the same sense that the proletariat is victimized. Professionals, like capitalists, profit from the bureaucratic and capitalist system in a way that is not true for the working class. It is necessary to develop a critical theory which is not merely the ideological expression of the interests of the professional class, a particularly challenging task for theorists, both Marxian and Weberian, who themselves belong to that class.

Both hypotheses of the proletarianization of professionals, the strong one and the weak one, tend to obscure the difference between professionals and the proletariat. Even the weak hypothesis leads to the conclusion

> that ideological proletarianization may be the foundation of a new post-industrial capitalism, in which professionals and other workers are managed through a system of 'relative autonomy' that does not threaten them with deskilling or loss of their technical knowledge and autonomy, but nonetheless effectively subordinates them to the imperatives of capitalist production.[57]

This mistakes what is peculiar to professionals for a structural development common to professionals and the proletariat (despite the admitted absence of confirming evidence in the case of the latter).

The process of formal rationalization can threaten some professions, just as it did craft workers and their guilds, but it also results in the creation of new professions. For example, accountants may be threatened to a certain degree by computerization, but the latter has also resulted in the creation of the new professions of microelectronic science and engineering and software design. Old professions fall and new ones rise, just as some old capitalists fall and new ones rise, but the professions as such are not eliminated.

Even the watered-down hypothesis of the proletarianization of professionals is unsustainable. We must be wary of the assumption that the only way to correct an error in one direction – professionals as the new governing class – is to commit an equally serious error in the opposite direction – the proletarianization of professionals.

Such an approach is not particularly satisfying when judged accord-ing to normal intellectual criteria. The problem is compounded because Marxists tend to conflate two distinct hypotheses: (1) pro-fessionals are being proletarianized; and (2) this is because of the development of capitalism. The second hypothesis is as simplistic as the first. There is a deeper phenomenon at work than capitalism; namely, the process of formal rationalization and bureau-cratization.

The basis of the changing nature of the professional: capitalism or formal rationalization?

Marxian theorists claim that the transformation from the self-employment of professionals to their salaried employment in organ-izations has resulted from the development of capitalism; in particu-lar, from the transformation of competitive capitalism into mon-opoly capitalism. 'Professionals are now slowly being integrated for the first time within capitalist relations of production. As for craft workers a century ago, the conditions favoring professional "pro-duction" outside the dominant capitalist enterprises are gradually eroding'.[58] The proletarianization of the professional has occurred 'because of changes in the structure of capitalist management' and control.[59] It is capitalism which is proletarianizing even the classical profession that is frequently used as a model for the others: medicine.

> Now, as a result of the bureaucratization which is being forced on
> medical practice as a consequence of the logic of capitalist expansion,
> physicians are slowly being reduced to a proletarian function, and their
> formerly self-interested activities subordinated to the broader require-
> ments of the capitalist control of highly profitable medical production'.[60]

Thus McKinlay and Arches claim that the proletarianization of physicians has resulted from the 'capitalist mode of medical care production'.[61]

The specific structural features of monopoly capitalism held responsible by proletarianization theorists for the increased pro-portion of professionals working for others are as follows.[62] First, technological developments have made professionals dependent on expensive and complicated machines that they can neither afford nor use individually, hence dependent on large-scale institutions. Second, the expansion of professional services requires centralized administrative mechanisms and organizational resources beyond the capacity of individual practitioners. Technical and administrat-ive economies of scale drive out self-employed professionals. Fur-thermore, state fiscal and regulative policy favour large-scale organization. Third, large-scale private and public capital has invaded the knowledge and service sectors as they expanded and became profitable, which has resulted in the swallowing up of self-employed professionals who subsequently become employed in private or public bureaucracies. This is referred to as the 'capitalization of mental labor and human services'.[63]

Similarly, proletarianization theorists contend that three new conditions are destroying professional monopolies.[64] First, microelectronics and computers are providing management with a technology for standardizing and controlling the work of professionals. Second, professionals are increasingly being managed by managers trained in management schools, whereas in the past they were managed by a member of their own community who acted as its defender. Third, austerity programmes in public spending, together with a weakening of the capacity of professional associations to restrict the number of their members, are resulting in a surplus rather than a scarcity of professionals.

The argument of proletarianization theorists – that the changing nature of the professional can be reduced to capitalism – is, however, unconvincing. The above structural factors and conditions are not peculiar to the pursuit of profit in the capitalist market. They are just as prevalent in the non-profit public sector and under state socialism. The employment of social workers, teachers and professors in social work agencies, schools and universities respectively cannot be reduced to the pursuit of profit by social work agencies, schools and universities in the same sense that private companies pursue profit. Physicians and nurses may be largely integrated into private, profit-seeking hospitals and insurance companies in countries without state medical care, such as the United States and Switzerland, but in countries with non-profit, state-run medical care, such as Canada and Britain, they are also integrated into bureaucratically organized (but non-profit) hospitals. In fact, much of the growth of salaried rather than self-employed credentialled groups, professions and semi-professions has occurred in the non-profit public sector. In state-socialist societies the profit motive, private property and the capitalist market have been abolished, yet there are no autonomous self-employed professions; instead, credentialled experts and their specific skills are subordinated to the central planning of bureaucratic organizations, and particularly to the bureaucratic Communist Party. The case that comes closest to the proletarianization of physicians is to be found, not under capitalism, but under bureaucratic state socialism in the Soviet Union.[65] State-socialist societies have amply demonstrated the spuriousness of the assumption of Marxian proletarianization theorists that 'bureaucratization can even be regarded as a manifestation of the presence of capitalist interests'.[66] The bureaucratic employment of professionals and the credentialled is based on a more profound and broader development than that of capitalism. The development of capitalism is but one element in a deeper and broader process of formal rationalization and bureaucratization.

Larson diminishes the value of her otherwise excellent study by attempting to force her analysis into a rigid Marxian framework.[67] For example, she writes: 'insofar as most professionals sell their labor power to an employer, they represent but a special case within the general pattern of labor organization in capitalist societies'.[68] But professionals also sell their labour power to an employer under state socialism, hence this represents a special case of labour organization in formally rational societies, not only capitalist but also socialist. Larson argues that 'as the gap between management and the working class and that between conception and execution becomes deeper, it also becomes permanent: as they grow, the superordinate functions of control, supervision, and planning are increasingly entrusted to college graduates', and she speaks of 'the characteristic polarization of skills in capitalist industry (i.e. the dual process which concentrates increasingly high levels of skill in a minority of producers as it degrades or eliminates skilled human interventions for the majority of workers at lower levels)'.[69] But such polarization of skills and monopolization by college graduates are no less characteristic of socialism as it exists than of capitalism. Just as it would be erroneous to attribute the polarization of skills, the monopolization by college graduates and the bureaucratization of the work setting of experts to something peculiarly American, since they have also occurred in Europe and Japan, so too it is erroneous to attribute them to something peculiarly capitalist, since they have also occurred under state socialism where the profit motive and the capitalist market have been eliminated. The common structural transformation, as opposed to the peculiarities of America, Europe, Japan and the USSR, can only be captured by a concept broader than that of America or capitalism. The most appropriate concept that encompasses the polarization of skills, the monopolization by college graduates, and the bureaucratization of the work setting of experts under both capitalism and socialism is formal rationalization, as I will argue below.

The problem inherent in capitalist and market reductionism can be illustrated by Larson's analysis of professional training.

> This training – or this passage – connects the sale of professional labor power with the educational system – that is to say, with the principal legitimator of social inequality in advanced industrial capitalism. . . . I

have emphasized the requirements imposed upon this project by the market orientation: the necessary homogenization of these intangible goods according to relatively universalistic standards could only be achieved at the level of training. . . . Homogenized years of schooling and standardized credentials provide a 'universalist equivalent' into which these exchange values can be translated and by which they can be measured. The monopoly of instruction and credentialing appears, thus, as the structural condition for the creation of 'professional exchange value'.[70]

But all this occurs under socialism too. Under socialism as it exists, the educational system is also a principal legitimator of social inequality, so much so that Roemer refers to inequality based on educational credentials as 'socialist exploitation'.[71] 'Homogenized years of schooling and standardized credentials' providing exchange values that can be measured – 'the structural condition for the creation of "professional exchange value" ' – are not requirements imposed by the market. They exist and are as much required under state socialism where the capitalist market has been abolished. They are the result, not of the narrow process of the development of capitalism and its market, but of the broader process of formal rationalization and bureaucratization.

The confusion arises because Larson conflates distinct meanings of 'exchange value'. Exchange value determined by the market and its search for private profit is peculiar to capitalism. This was the only meaning of exchange value known in Marx's time and is the usual sense of the term in Marxian theory. But the term can also be enlarged to include values that are exchanged in other contexts, in particular one unknown to Marx: state socialism. There too homogenization, universal equivalents and measurement are required for exchanges to occur, but they are imposed not by the market but by the central planning of a bureaucratic Communist Party. Thus three different meanings of exchange value should be distinguished. First, a general meaning of exchange value which exists in any society where individuals do not produce everything for themselves and where exchange goes beyond barter. Second, the sub-type, capitalist, exchange value where the terms of exchange are imposed by the market and its pursuit of private profit. Third, the sub-type, socialist, exchange value where the terms of exchange are imposed by the bureaucratic Communist Party. Thus under socialism there exists exchange value and even a market for expert services, but these are very different from those under capitalism. They are ruled not by the pursuit of private profit but by the central planning of the bureaucratic Communist Party. What is important to emphasize is that measurement by 'homogenized years of schooling and standardized credentials' are not only imposed by the requirements of capitalist exchange value, they are also imposed by the requirements of socialist exchange value. The 'monopoly of instruction and credentialing [that] appears . . . as the structural condition for the creation of "professional exchange value" ' exists under state socialism as well as under market capitalism, but it sows its seeds in a field dominated by the bureaucratic Communist Party rather than by the profit-seeking market and its private bureaucratic corporations. The effective dynamic of credential exclusion and bureaucratized professionalism cannot be reduced to the development of monopoly capitalism in its usual sense. It goes much deeper.

There is another reason why the Marxian conceptual framework is inappropriate for the analysis of the professions, even under capitalism.

> It is, however, inherently contradictory – as well as a departure from the strict commodity form – that the exchange value of professional skills should depend on cognitive and educational monopoly. This monopoly means that length of training can be arbitrarily determined. Taken together with the unquantifiable nature of intangible skills, the monopoly condition destroys the equivalence between length of professional training and a notion of the average labor time that is socially necessary for the production of a professional. Monopoly of training means, therefore, that the price of professional services is *not* the market expression of socially necessary length of training or average (educational) labor time.[72]

The only thing that is contradicted by this monopoly condition is Marxian theory – in particular, the labour theory of value. The exchange value and price of professional services are not determined by the socially necessary labour required to produce them – hence the inappropriateness of a Marxian theory of the professions – but by the relative power of the credentialled group (which depends on the structured cognitive, social, political and economic resources available to it) to carve out a situation of monopoly. The length of training can only be seen as 'arbitrarily determined' from the perspective of the arbitrary labour theory of value. It is not at all arbitrary from the perspective of a power theory of prices derived from Weberian closure theory. It is strictly determined by the relative market or bureaucratic power of the struggling groups under both capitalism and state socialism.

Thus Larson is correct in stating that the monopoly over training is 'a central condition for the effective creation of "professional exchange value" ', but is entirely wrong when she adds that this 'tends to place the price of professional "commodities" outside the realm of market determination'.[73] She confuses market determination based on the relative power of the struggling groups with labour determination based on the necessary labour content of the training and services rendered. Professional monopolies place the price of professional 'commodities' outside the realm of labour determination as seen from the point of view of the labour theory of value, but not outside the realm of market determination. Processes of monopolization are what markets are all about. 'Monopoly over training' is one of the specific means of monopolization used by professionals to influence the market determination of 'professional exchange value' in their favour, just as monopoly over capital is one of the specific means of monopolization used by capitalists to influence the market determination of the exchange value of their commodities in their favour. Under capitalism professional monopolization, far from being exceptional, fits into the pattern of market determination by processes of monopolization. One need only remove the blindfold of the labour theory of value to perceive this.[74]

Larson also states the following:

> I believe that the issue [of productive versus unproductive labour] becomes a matter of pure exegesis when (1) large proportions of heretofore 'unproductive' workers now sell their labor to capitalist firms; and when (2) the production and realization of surplus value increasingly depend on scientific and technological services, on the integration of distribution and supply with production, and also on a large range of governmental services.[75]

Well put. But this implies that the production and realization of surplus value now depend on the services of virtually all professionals, hence the distinction between productive and unproductive labour is of little help for the analysis of the professions. Even in the 'liberal' capitalism of the past, the quantity of surplus value appropriated depended on the 'personal' professions: physicians to reduce absenteeism of workers and lower re-training costs; lawyers to win legal battles with government, politicians, unions; and so on. The only way to 'use the terms "productive" and "unproductive" as symbolic references to the different kinds of link that different kinds of professional labor form with the production of surplus value' without entering *de facto* 'the controversy that exists in Marxist theory about which kinds of labor are productive or unproductive', as Larson seeks to do, would be to gloss over and fail to specify 'which kinds of labor are productive or unproductive', thereby resulting in vague concepts and a vacuous theory.[76] Larson cannot have it both ways: eating her symbolic cake without first having to make it.

Neither Larson nor Marxian proponents of the proletarianization of professionals hypothesis have come to grips with another important weakness of Marxian theory: its underlying assumption of the homogeneity of labour. 'The surplus-value theory of exploitation fails with heterogeneous labour, despite various attempts to save it'.[77] The assumption of the homogeneity of labour is particularly problematic when Marxian theory is being used to analyse professional labour and the labour of credentialled experts.

Throughout the Marxian theory of the proletarianization of professionals the claim is made that such proletarianization results from the pursuit of profit by private companies in the capitalist market – from, for example in the case of medicine, the 'requirements of the capitalist control of highly profitable medical production'.[78] Thus capitalism is implicitly defined in terms of the legal institution of private property and the attendant search for private profit in the market. According to this implicit definition state-socialist societies are not capitalist. But professional and credentialled groups have had no more control over the goals and uses to which their work is put in these societies than in capitalist societies, these goals and uses being determined by the bureaucratic Communist Party. Their lack of autonomous control results not from capitalism so defined but from something more fundamental – formal rationalization and bureaucratization – that is present under both capitalism and state socialism.

This Marxian quandary can be solved by definition, by defining capitalism to include state socialism: defining it in terms of the hierarchical control of the means of production and in terms of 'the system of wage labor in all its forms' rather than in terms of private property and the market.[79] Defining capitalism to include state socialism – usually referring to state socialism as state as opposed to private capitalism – has, however, very definite implications. It implies that capitalism is by definition just one component of bureaucracy – bureaucratic control of the means of production – other components being bureaucratic control of the means of destruction, the means of knowing and so on. It implies in addition that the bourgeois capitalist class is made up not only of the likes of Rockefeller and Dupont, but also of the likes of Lenin, Brezhnev, Gorbachov, Mao and Castro. It also implies that the elimination of the private profit motive is not what counts for solving the problems engendered by capitalism; what counts is eliminating the hierarchical control of the means of production and giving such control to workers rather than to an elite in the Communist Party acting in their name. It implies that the creation of a one-party state under the hegemony of the Communist Party to replace the legal institution of private property and the market is a pseudo-solution to the problems of capitalism and bureaucratization and may even worsen those problems. It implies that state socialism is merely a higher degree of monopolization than monopoly capitalism, where power is concentrated not in a small number of giant bureaucratic corporations, but in one colossal bureaucratic organization: the Communist Party. Replacing the pursuit of profit in the private property market by the pursuit of power in the state bureaucracy under the hegemony of the Communist Party merely changes the form, but not the fact, of bureaucratization, formal rationalization and closure. State socialism has yielded no reason to believe that credential barriers of exclusion and the bureaucratization of professionals and the credentialled will be eliminated with the abolition of private property, the profit motive and the market. They are the result of something much deeper that is more difficult to eliminate; namely, formal rationalization and bureaucratization. Defining capitalism to include state socialism so radically transforms Marxism that it becomes unrecognizable.

A major weakness in the Marxian theory of the proletarianization of professionals is that, although such proletarianization is attributed to capitalism, capitalism is never explicitly defined. There is a strong tendency in Marxian analyses to leave the definition of capitalism as vague as possible in order to slide between definitions to have the best of both worlds: to be able to blame the ills of society on the pursuit by private corporations of profit in the market; and yet, when pressed intellectually, to be able to hide behind an all-inclusive definition of capitalism that includes socialism as it exists (thereby contradicting the central importance of the pursuit of private profit in the market). There is no value in fusing capitalism and state socialism at the conceptual level under the term 'capitalism'. The fact that one has abolished private property and the market whereas the other is based on them, as well as the struggle between the two that this entails, have as a consequence that they are better conceived of as two generically different entities.

Although Marxian studies of the proletarianization of professionals routinely assert that the development of capitalism is the cause, the operative factor in their own explanations is almost invariably bureaucratization: 'we emphasize that proletarianization, as defined in this article, is occurring with respect to physicians principally *as a result of* the bureaucratization of medical care'.[80] Thus in Oppenheimer's, McKinlay's, McKinlay and Arches' and Haug's analyses the means by which professionals become proletarianized are those of bureaucratic organization: specialization, formal codification of procedures and power concentrated in hierarchical administrative elites.[81] Larson translates her analysis into a Marxian vocabulary in the final chapter of her book, even though she admits that the core of Marxian theory (the labour theory of value, productive versus unproductive work and so on) is inapplicable to professional services and training, as we have seen above.[82] Her excellent analysis, before being deformed by an inappropriate translation, is clearly founded on the process of bureaucratization.

> All professions are, today, bureaucratized to a greater or lesser extent. Organizational professions should not be seen, therefore, as sharply distinct from older and more independent professions, but as clearer manifestations of tendencies also contained within them. Organizational professions proper are *generated* by heteronomous bureaucracies, and primarily by the expansion of the bureaucratic apparatus of the state'.[83]

Moreover, the ideology of professionalism, as specified by Larson,[84] consists of elements based on the process of formal rationalization and are found not only under capitalism but also under state socialism where the pursuit of private profit in the capitalist market has been abolished.

Larson's Marxian translation of her implicitly Weberian analysis was a wrong turn that added nothing of value. The value was already there. Not only was Parkin correct when he stated, 'Inside every neo-Marxist there seems to be a Weberian struggling to get out',[85] but also in the seventies there were many neo-Weberians masquerading as neo-Marxists. 'I was too quick in my Marxist days in that I was so concerned with the proletarianization of the professions'.[86] The thesis of the proletarianization of the professions has had a very detrimental effect on the sociology of the professions by directing it into a descriptive and explanatory dead end.

Conclusion

I have argued previously against the new governing class thesis and suggested that formal educational credentials are best conceived of as derivative and contingent forms of closure subordinate to the principal forms based on private property and the Communist Party.[87] In this chapter I have demonstrated the deficiencies of both the strong and weak versions of the Marxian antithesis: the proletarianization of the professional. The response of Marxists to the falseness of the thesis of professionals as a new governing class has been to propose an equally false antithesis.[88] The use of a Marxian conceptual framework – centred on the appropriation of surplus labour by profit-seeking, private corporations – with which to analyse the bureaucratic control of professionals and experts results in a truncated, ill-founded approach which fails to compre-hend the depth and breadth of the matter, thereby condemning itself to mislead.[89]

The analysis of the development and change of the professions is better undertaken from a broader perspective which perceives the phenomena of credential exclusion, experts and professionals as based on the more general process of formal rationalization, whether it be of market capitalism or of state socialism. The syn-thesis of the thesis of professionals as the new governing class and the antithesis of professionals as proletarianized can, in this dialectical intellectual process, most logically and coherently be derived from the Weberian theories of formal rationalization and social closure. This synthesis goes beyond the thesis and the anti-thesis to a conception of professionals as having carved out on the basis of their formally rational knowledge and skills a distinct class position that is neither governing nor proletarianized.

Formal rationalization consists of three conceptually distinct but empirically interrelated processes, all of which are based on the pursuit of the means to control nature and other people: the devel-opment of the formal legal system, of bureaucratic organization and of the capitalist market. These developments have radically transformed the system of monopolization and exclusion, resulting in what I have referred to as the formal rationalization of closure.[90] They have given rise: (1) to a formal education system to certify the possession of the means of knowing how to control nature and others – hence to formal educational credentials as an important basis of monopolization and exclusion; (2) to the centralized and systematic search for new abstract utilitarian knowledge in insti-tutions such as the university; and (3) to a transformation of the professions and an increase in the number of professional specialities.

The development of capitalism was an important component of this transformation, but it was only one component. The early phase of formal rationalization gave rise to the liberal professions in private practice. The later phase of formal rationalization, in which bureaucratization was more advanced, drew even these pro-fessions into bureaucratic organizations and created new pro-fessions which were born into bureaucracy. Socialist revolution resulted in a new branch of formal rationalization, based not on market calculations in pursuit of power through profit, but on the central planning of the pursuit of power through the bureaucratic Communist Party. This too left its mark on credential exclusion and transformed the nature of the professions. Thus capitalism has historically been an important element in the origin of the professions, its early phase being essential for the autonomous liberal professions in private practice in the market. But now the bureaucratic control of professionals and experts has taken on a life of its own – with or without capitalism. A second-order monopolization has emerged in which the monopoly over abstract utilitarian knowledge by professionals and credentialled experts is in turn being monopolized by private bureaucratic corporations under capitalism and, under socialism as it exists, by the Communist Party bureaucracy. Groups of credentialled experts differ from the autonomous liberal professions in the early phase of formal rationalization in that they have increasingly come under bureaucratic control as the process of formal rationalization advanced.

The two branches of formal rationalization – capitalism and state socialism – have structural similarities based on the underlying process of formal rationalization, examples being the importance of bureaucratic organization, of formal educational credentials as a basis of social closure, and of scientific and technological expertise. But the fact that they consist of different branches has also resulted in structural differences; for example, in the specific nature of credentialled experts under each – stockbrokers and market analysts in one, Marxian central planners and theoreticians in the other; differential capacities to organize into 'professions'; differences in the power and rewards of the medical profession; and so on.

Even within the capitalist branch of formal rationalization, credential exclusion and the specific nature of the professions vary from state to state according to differences in the relationships among the capitalist market, the legal system and bureaucratic organization particularly of the state. For example, there are differences in the professions between the United States and Sweden as a result of the *laissez-faire* capitalist market system of the former as opposed to the legally based, welfare-state intervention of the latter.

The process of formal rationalization has resulted in specific resources which the credentialled mobilize and in opportunities which they seize in the structured system of closure and power of which they are a part. The development of abstract utilitarian knowledge and the centralization of its production in institutions, such as the university, which are also the training centres for the acquisition of credentials, have laid the basis for the creation of monopolistic niches by credentialled experts and professionals, even within formal organizations. The special relationship of credentialled experts and professionals to the process of formal rationalization – their monopoly over segments of abstract utilitarian knowledge – sets them apart from both the dominant class and the proletariat. Closure theory perceives professionals and credentialled groups as having carved out through the process of formal rationalization – of both capitalist society, dominated by the private property market, and socialist society, dominated by the bureaucratic Communist Party – a unique position based on their skills and credentials. Professionals and credentialled groups have forged their own original basis of power, rewards and privileges which distinguishes them from the proletariat, but that basis does not provide them with resources comparable to those of the dominant class. Furthermore, formal rationalization has resulted in the bureaucratic control of credentialled experts and professionals. Their special resources which distinguish them from the proletariat are embedded in a field of bureaucratic and/or market control. Professionals and credentialled groups cannot be characterized by either governance or proletarianization. They are not being assimilated to either the governing class or the proletariat. They have instead carved out specific niches of their own. And these niches are based not only on the development of capitalism, but also on the development of the formal legal system and bureaucratic organization; that is, on the more general process of formal rationalization. The latter is a deeper and broader force than capitalism, one that persists even where the pursuit of profit by private corporations and the capitalist market have been abolished and replaced by the central planning of the Communist Party.

This chapter has attempted to clarify the differences between a Marxian theory and a Weberian closure theory of credentials and the professions. They differ, in short, (1) in the effectiveness they perceive of abstract utilitarian knowledge as a resource in strategies of monopolization to form and/or maintain professions, and (2) in the role they perceive of bureaucratic capitalism and the bureaucratic state in setting the rules of the game within which these strategies are deployed. Hence Marxian theory and Weberian closure theory differ in their predictions concerning the fate of the professions and of credentialled groups.

Notes

1 Schudson, 1980:223.

2 See Murphy, 1988:174–175, 245–248.

3 Bell, 1976; Galbraith, 1967; Gouldner, 1978; Illich et al., 1977; Lasch, 1978; Steinfels, 1979.

4 Gorz, 1964; Mallet, 1975; Aronowitz, 1973; Oppenheimer, 1970, 1973, 1975:34–40; Derber, 1982; McKinlay, 1982.

5 Derber, 1982:5.

6 Murphy, 1984 and 1988.

7 Note that the title of this chapter refers not to 'professionalism' but to 'the professional', and that the chapter seeks to avoid the reduction of 'professions to professionalism, occupational roles or functions to the ideology about them' (Schudson, 1980:223).

8 Quinn and Staines, 1979; Wilson, 1979.

9 Tigar, 1961; McKinlay, 1982:58–60.

10 Larson, 1977/1979.

11 Aronowitz, 1973; Oppenheimer, 1970, 1975; McKinlay, 1982; McKinlay and Arches, 1985.

12 Braverman, 1974; Derber, 1982:168.

13 Patry, 1978; Cohen and Wagner, 1982.

14 Cooley, 1976.

15 McKinlay, 1982; McKinlay and Arches, 1985.

16 Rose and Rose, 1976.

17 McKinlay and Arches, 1985:180.

18 Kornhauser, 1963; Larson, 1977/1979, 1980; Freidson, 1970a, 1970b, 1973b; Spangler and Lehman, 1982.

19 Freidson, 1970b, 1973b.

20 Larson, 1977/1979:231.

21 Larson, 1980:149.

22 Derber, 1982:189.

23 Derber, 1982:173.

24 Derber, 1982:188.

25 Derber, 1982:195.

26 Derber, 1982:31.

27 Edwards, 1979; Burawoy, 1980.

28 Derber, 1982:169.

29 Larson, 1979:609.

30 McKinlay and Arches, 1985:184.

31 Larson, 1977/1979:231.

32 Derber, 1982:202.

33 Derber, 1982:199; Larson, 1979:623.

34 Larson, 1977/1979:222.

35 Larson, 1980:140.

36 Derber, 1982:29–30.

37 'Although their [professionals] activities are not prescribed, the organizational outcome to which they contribute is predetermined and they can but rarely change it. The same of course is also true of managers, even if they have access to high-level decision-making' (Larson, 1980:162).

38 Derber, 1982:206.

39 Larson, 1979:621.

40 Derber, 1982:189.

41 Derber, 1982:195.

42 Sarason, 1979; Yankelovich, 1974.

43 Larson, 1980:160.

44 Bloomfield and Levy, 1973; Ehrenreich and Ehrenreich, 1977a, 1977b.

45 Tigar, 1961; Ginger, 1973.

46 Galper, 1978:37–41; Bailey and Brake, 1976; Withorn, 1979.

47 Gross and Osterman, 1972.

48 Haug, 1973.
49 Larson, 1980:162–163.
50 Freidson, 1973a, 1975.
51 This is structurally similar to the argument of capitalists: what is good for capitalists (profit) is good for workers (jobs) and for consumers (choice of commodities).
52 Schudson, 1980:219.
53 McKinlay and Arches, 1985:162.
54 McKinlay and Arches, 1985:191.
55 Derber, 1982.
56 Bookchin, 1979:21; Larson, 1977/1979:222; Mattick, 1983.
57 Derber, 1982:200.
58 Derber, 1982:6.
59 Derber, 1982:10.
60 McKinlay and Arches, 1985:161.
61 McKinlay and Arches, 1985:188.
62 Derber, 1982:6–7.
63 Derber, 1982:7.
64 Derber, 1982:197–198.
65 Field, 1957; Brown, 1987.
66 McKinlay and Arches, 1985:163.
67 Larson, 1977/1979.
68 Larson, 1977/1979:210.
69 Larson, 1977/1979:623.
70 Larson, 1977/1979:210–211.
71 Roemer, 1982a.
72 Larson, 1977/1979:211–212.
73 Larson, 1977/1979:212.
74 I have argued in Murphy (1985, 1988) that the exchange value and price of commodities generally cannot be logically taken as the result of the socially necessary labour time to produce them, and hence that the Marxian labour theory of value should be replaced by a Weberian power theory of prices and profits. Larson's (1977/1979) long quotation above (p. 86) concerning professional services provides an unintended specific confirmation of my argument with respect to a particular type of commodity: professional services.
75 Larson, 1977/1979:291, n. 13.
76 Larson, 1977/1979:291, n. 13.
77 Roemer, 1982a:286.
78 McKinlay and Arches, 1985:161.
79 Poulantzas, 1978a; Bettelheim, 1974; Mattick, Jr, 1983:ix.
80 McKinlay and Arches, 1985:171.
81 Oppenheimer, 1973, 1975; McKinlay, 1982; McKinlay and Arches, 1985; Haug, 1973, 1975, 1977.
82 Larson, 1977/1979.
83 Larson, 1977/1979:179.
84 Larson, 1979:622.
85 Parkin, 1979:25.
86 Larson, 1986:10.
87 Murphy, 1984 and 1988.
88 See Derber, 1982:193.

89 Of course, market capitalism does result in specific features of credential closure, such as autonomous professions having a service ethic during the 'liberal' phase of capitalism, and an ideology of autonomous service as well as associational capacities under monopoly capitalism. But Marxian proletarianization theorists are not dealing with these peculiarities of capitalism. They are dealing with the larger question of the subordination of the credentialled (physicians, engineers, professors, architects, teachers, nurses and so on) in bureaucratic organizations and their lack of autonomy, phenomena which go deeper than and well beyond the pursuit of private profit in the capitalist market.

90 Murphy, 1988.

6

Escape from freedom? Reflections on German professionalization, 1870–1933

Charles E. McClelland

Did professionalization occur in Germany?

Erich Fromm's 1941 book, *Escape from Freedom*,[1] now remembered chiefly for its title, was then a widely discussed and bold exemplar of a certain type of social science in exile that, among other things, was to alter fundamentally the discourse about social science in the Anglo-American world. Today Fromm's book may appear rather naïve and in any case contrasts strongly with the more careful micro-analytic efforts of today, in which a constant guard is placed against untested assumptions.

But how effective is this guard? Looking at the sub-sub-field of recent historical research on modern professions in Germany, it would seem that the quality of micro-analyses improves all the time, yet untested assumptions and sometimes unwarranted conclusions can be found in otherwise admirable and exemplary scholarly works.

Particularly in studies of German professions and their representative organizations, Fromm's catchphrase 'escape from freedom' still seems to find an echo. Undeniably, the collapse of the German learned professions in the face of National Socialism and the well-documented fifth-column activities of some professionals, the craven acquiescence of others, and the opportunism of still others in the face of *Gleichschaltung* raise questions about the 'illiberalism' of the 'liberal professions' and a seeming penchant for authoritarian solutions to crises in the free market.[2]

A longer-term prefiguration of this 'escape' has been discerned in many works, dating back to the very origins of modern professions in Germany.[3] Some scholars suggest that fatalism, self-doubt and an underdeveloped sense of self-worth (all elements of masochism for Fromm) may have caused German professional groups to 'fail' in asserting themselves and wrenching autonomous control over the conditions of their professions from other social and political players.[4] By fearing the freedom and competition of the occupational market, by yearning for the protection of Father State, from which they had only recently been cast adrift, the nascent modern German professional groups (or at least some of them, or some factions within some of them) thus might be said to have botched the role assigned to them by those *ex-post-facto* playwrights of the drama of modern professionalization – Anglo-American sociologists of professions from the 1930s onward.

For, as these sociologists have usually argued, the central litmus test of 'successful' professionalization is domination of the conditions under which professionals exercise their occupations. Whether described as 'autonomy' or 'market monopolization', whether regarded as benign or malignant, the 'professionalizing project' (to use Larson's term)[5] must exhibit characteristics like those of the ruthless and almost unassailable American Medical Association to be deemed 'successful'. The limited usefulness of 'characteristics' of modern professions (or of 'essentialistic' taxonomies, to use terms employed elsewhere in these volumes) has long been conceded by most social scientists working on professions.[6] These consist of taxonomic lists of binary values. That is, if an occupational group exhibits autonomy, monopolization in the market for its services, demanding education and certification requirements, economic success, altruism and a code of ethics, or some mixture of these or yet other 'characteristics', it may arguably be called a profession. Failing to achieve a high enough score, however, it might be denied this ranking. The debate over which occupations were and were not 'professions' finally became so sterile as to provoke rejection by sociologists.

Nevertheless, reference to these characteristics is inevitable, if not as a whole, then in single dimensions. Here untested assumptions sometimes take the form of dwelling on one or two 'characteristics' and examining how well professions (or again more commonly one or two key professions) filled up the proper amount of content in those characteristics-tanks within a more or less extended historical frame.[7]

Such escapes from the aridity of a-historical schemata, welcome as they are, still resemble evasive action more than solutions. Another major difficulty with fixed taxonomic tables of characteristics is that if one applies them *all* over an historical spectrum, the variable-tanks do not fill up at similar rates, and indeed filling, leakage and inactivity appear to occur simultaneously.

These observations have been made by other recent researchers even of the Anglo-American world, but they also apply to the Central European experience, the central topic of this chapter.

Clearly, here Anglo-American conceptions (and presuppositions about those conceptions) are often out of place if one wishes to understand the ways in which professionalization actually happened. It may be more understandable than excusable for scholars steeped in the Anglo-American tradition (which still includes too often for complacency a learned helplessness about foreign languages) that they apply parochial measures to continental reality. But even continental social historians often do the same. As a result of many unanalysed presuppositions about professionalization in Germany, the process is sometimes described as either impossible or immoral, and by implication those who thought they were undertaking professionalization were held to be either fools or knaves.

For example, if German professional groups managed to score an occasional success in their struggle for control over the conditions of their occupational activity, they are often depicted in the light of anti-social selfishness, as when the medical profession used strike tactics to force reform of the medical insurance system before World War I. If they cooperated with state or other social forces, however, then they are often depicted as caving in to 'professionalization from above', which is presumably an inferior kind of professionalization, since what the state gives it can also take away. Or when the German chemical profession constantly pressed for higher educational and certification requirements, was it not only being 'elitist' (though why this was wrong is rarely made explicit) but simultaneously surrendering to a *Berufskonstruktion* from 'outside' the profession rather than developing in the good, healthy manner of 'professionalization from within', that is, in response to the membership's wishes?[8]

The 'outside' agent here was the chemical industry and its magnates, such people as Carl Duisberg of the Bayer concern. The fact that such magnates had often enough begun, at least until World War I, as working chemists, that traditionally a large part of the early membership of the Verein Deutscher Chemiker had been small-scale entrepreneurs, and that German chemists probably benefited more from the 'professionalizing' strategy of the VDC than from the 'union' model of such competitors as the Bund der technisch-industriellen Beamten (BUTIB) would seem unimportant compared to the fact that the richest and most powerful chemists dominated the VDC.

Such a pattern should not surprise anybody, since it largely holds true for most professional organizations, and not only in Germany. But somehow the notion that a professional association is a dangerous Trojan horse let loose on society *unless* it is controlled by its *Basis* has crept into the thinking of many German scholars since the late 1960s. They may indeed be correct, but their argument is based on implicit assumptions rather than explicit evidence.

To see occupations facing a choice between 'unionism' or 'professionalism' appears to be a temptation built into the choice of a single profession rather than the larger problem of professionalization, and of predominantly industrializable professions like chemistry and engineering at that. It suggests that employed professionals had to choose between 'professionalization', with its accompanying elitism, pro-capitalist attitudes, and acceptance of corporate conciliation and 'unionization' with its confrontational tactics, leadership from below and anti-industrial attitudes. 'Proletarianization' also has another meaning, which is really pauperization, a problem that seemed to worsen, especially for younger practitioners, after the turn of this century and, of course, during the economically unstable 1920s and 1930s. Unfortunately many historians of German professions tend to be specialists on either the nineteenth or the twentieth century, with corresponding weightings to perspectives.

Measures of professionalization in Germany to 1933

If we now turn to the actual goals and accomplishments of German learned professions from their beginnings as nationally organized bodies, applying some of the major indicators of professionalization, we may better be able to judge to what degree professionalization was possible under often quite differing circumstances from those obtaining in the Anglo-American world of experience.

A first question concerns the degree to which occupations became modern and professionalized in Germany. Certainly by one measurement, the creation of large and powerful professional organizations, the process began in the German states only shortly before the middle of the nineteenth century but, owing to persistent government mistrust, effectively only in the 1860s and 1870s. The early bureaucratization of so many occupations, not only in administration and justice, but in medicine, teaching and the clergy, was in some ways an alternative to modern independent professional organizations; certainly determining standards for recruitment and training were set principally by the state through its virtual monopoly over the educational system. Starting in the 1860s, however, a trend toward de-regulation of professions began as a part of the liberal era, making medicine, dentistry and lawyering into 'free' professions, and these quickly organized national associations around 1870, pre-dated chiefly by another 'free' and relatively new profession, engineering.

The modernity of these professions lay in their combination of rigorous and long-lasting education for a single, life-long occupation, less and less alloyed (as had been still common at the turn of the nineteenth century) with secondary or tertiary occupations.[9] With the rapid differentiation and growth of the professions (of course more rapid in some than others, and happening at different times), career ladders or stages also began to emerge, adding another characteristic of modernity. And the definitive acceptance of *Wissenschaft* as the basis of learned professions was a final factor in differentiating modern from earlier professional training.

That engineering, chemistry and teaching emerged as new 'professionalized' occupations had much to do with the process of scientification in the nineteenth century, a process that also affected such older learned professions as medicine and law. As knowledge and technique multiplied and came to be based more and more on abstractions, higher education came to play a more and more central role in the creation of professional cadres. It was no longer enough to be 'learned' in the classics to enter the 'learned professions', but it was now required to have a *wissenschaftlich* training. Themselves created through such training, followed by state examinations and certification, more and more professional men pressed their organizations to raise the scientific rigour (and by implication duration and cost) of qualifying education. In areas of curricular and licensing reform, modern professional organizations, with their high component of professorial members, collaborated with governments and the educational system to 'raise the standards of the profession', as the phrase went from the late nineteenth century onward. German professional organizations' record in achieving over the long run their educational and certification requests was a good one, even if one of the aims – to make the occupation more exclusive and thereby reduce competition – rarely was achieved.

Considering the fact that there was no genuine political structure one could even call 'Germany' before unification, the German professional organizations also carried out a large measure of standardization and nationalization of professional practice, even in cases where the federal states retained ultimate legal competence over their activities. This alone was no small achievement, considering the relative ease with which comparable professional organizations in France, Britain or the USA found a standard political framework in place for them to work with. The discussion of nationally applicable guidelines and their wide acceptance as goals by most professional organizations indicates that they were willing to work toward the elimination of widely differing standards that in effect protected the special rights of practitioners in this or that German state.

Thus most German professional organizations reacted to expanding competition with grudging acceptance and rarely, if ever, called for artificial limits on access to the education system (such as *numerus clausus*), except during the height of the Great Depression. In this sense modern German professional organizations might be accused of weakness, having failed to hammer through some mechanisms designed to foster market 'monopoly on services'. The squeeze of competition, however, appears to have affected mostly the youngest, less qualified and more marginal members of the professions, rather than the older, more established ones who tended to dominate professional associations (as with attempts to establish professional 'unions' after 1900).

Indeed, the creation of high educational and certification standards at the insistence of the leaders of Germany's major professional organizations should have guaranteed a measure of market control, if not monopoly, which has rarely been achieved in fact by any modern learned profession (including such organizations as the American Medical Association (AMA), frequently cited and even more frequently implicit in allusions to 'successful' professionalization). But the ironic fact of German educational history was that German higher education was more 'inclusive' in the late nineteenth and early twentieth centuries than that of most other countries.[10] Access to professional qualifications was cheaper than in Britain or America, for example, because of large state subsidies, and as long as Germany's economy was expanding rapidly, more and more professionals were needed. Thus any 'failure' to impose strict market monopoly by German professional groups should be blamed on their general satisfaction with the ones they were achieving. Over-supply and economic difficulties, as in the 1920s and early 1930s, were more signs of the weakness of the general economy (when professional study always appears more attractive) than of the professions.

By another traditional measure of professionalization, autonomy, German learned occupations surely achieved a high degree of success over the century leading up to the Hitler era, although it was neither universal nor even. Lawyers and doctors achieved their freedom from state control and their demands for self-governing disciplinary bodies (*Kammern*), and the national medical association (Deutscher Ärztevereinsbund or DÄV), combining with the economic pressure group known as the Hartmann League also won important victories in its struggle with insurance funds. Teachers achieved a different sort of autonomy – that is, from close or

arbitrary supervision by local church authorities or from interference by parents – even though such autonomy (again ironically)
had to be purchased with a higher degree of bureaucratization of
the profession. The creation of secure career ladders presumably
meant more to it than, for example, the 'freedom' of physicians
and lawyers: since education in Germany was overwhelmingly
public, and the teaching profession preferred it that way, autonomy
had to be found within the parameters of bureaucratic rights and
privileges (which of course also guaranteed a 'market monopoly').

The situation of such industrially oriented new professions as
engineering and chemistry appears not to have changed toward
more autonomy, at least not by the measurement of the percentage
of practitioners who worked for themselves. An irony in these
fields, but especially in engineering, lay in the parallel improvement
of higher educational qualifications along with the expansion of
employment positions for technical trainees emerging from secondary institutes. Attempts to create 'technicians' unions' (such as
BUTIB) before World War I reflected the resulting further division
of technically oriented occupations along such lines as higher or
secondary educational qualifications. The autonomy of engineers
and chemists (even those with the highest qualifications) was
undoubtedly restricted to some degree by the nature of 'practising'
in large corporations as employees (even when highly paid and
privileged). Nevertheless, such organizations of engineers and
chemists as the Verein Deutscher Ingenieure (VDI) and the Verein
Deutscher Chemiker (VDC) did manage to gain acceptance for
certain rights of professionals that had not existed before about
1900, as in the area of patents and *Karenz* (restrictions on job
mobility). The engineering profession, both much larger and more
variegated than that of chemistry, is difficult to generalize about.
The VDI down to the beginning of the Hitler period never achieved
the same standing as a *learned professional* organization as, for
example, the DÄV or even the VDC, because many of its members
were still self-taught engineers. The VDI, in other words, was as
much an *occupational* as a *professional* association, which muddies
the waters concerning the degree of autonomy of all its membership. A more exclusive professional engineering association such
as the Verein Deutscher Diplom-Ingenieure (VDDI) would be a
more likely exemplar for testing the question of autonomy, but not
enough is known about its success to make any safe hypotheses.
Other engineering-related breakaway groups, such as the steel-
industry-oriented Verein Deutscher Eisenhüttenleute (VDEh),
consisting of 80 per cent entrepreneurs, clearly had their own
financial interests in mind, rather than the professionalization of

the occupation. It remains difficult to exclude them from all scrutiny on this account, however, and that in turn shows the difficulty of empirical approaches to professional groups.

Aside from entrepreneurial groups, as they professionalized, did the German learned occupations grow wealthier? A privileged economic and social position is another of the often-proposed indices of the success of the 'professionalizing project'. The evidence points fairly clearly toward such success in the case of schoolteachers over the entire period under review. But it is more difficult to establish such a clear trend for most other professions taken as a whole. Certainly in the relatively backward and poor country that pre-industrial Germany was, and considering the catastrophic economic consequences of both World War I and the Great Depression, such a measurement might even be misleading as a sign of successful professionalization in this particular time-frame. The general prosperity enjoyed by professionals in the Federal Republic of Germany under what might be called 'normal conditions of comparativity' would argue strongly for the long-term success of professional organizations in establishing their members' rights to higher incomes and social respect than most other occupations. On some occasions, clearly, German professional organizations were able to improve their members' momentary economic position materially, as with the physicians' victory over the sickness funds prior to World War I.

In another sense, however, the measurement of economic privilege may also be misplaced in German society as it was constituted before 1933. This has something to do with the peculiarity of a 'corporate' social mentality, which will be discussed further below. Whatever the increasing role of money and wealth in twentieth-century social values, the earlier high value assigned to education (and the correspondingly low one to money) reinforced the prestige of professional expertise. This was undoubtedly one of the reasons German professional groups were so eager to tie qualifications to the *Abitur* and university-level education (for certainly less traditional methods of training were thinkable). In other words, if the professional class overlapped largely with the *Bildungsbürgertum*, then the professionalizing project had been largely achieved in terms of social standing, as membership in that social group was more highly prized than membership in the newly wealthy circles of industry and commerce.

As for altruism or a public-service ethic, as well as codes of ethics or other mechanisms for protecting that ethic, it is worth noting that most German professional organizations claimed such for themselves. It is also more likely that the *Kammern* set up for the legal, medical and other professions did more to regulate unfair competition than to protect the public. One is tempted to say that the controversy over altruism as central to professionalization is a false one. A service occupation, such as most professions are, must by definition serve the public, and whether it serves well or poorly is perhaps not provably a function of the 'good' or 'bad' intentions of its members.

Certainly, the history of modern German professions and their representative organizations shows that pure, high-minded altruism was never the main driving force behind organization and lobbying. Indeed, as we have seen, the tendency was for organizations to begin with declarations of high-minded ('scientific') purposes and, once established, to go over more and more openly to an everyday practice of 'interest politics'. But that same history also indicates that the favourite lever for 'raising the profession' was increasing educational and certification qualifications, which in turn produced an unarguably first-rate professional corps in all fields of service to the public by the beginning of this century. Thus, by heavily emphasizing one attribute of professionalization more than was historically common in the English-speaking world, German professional groups indirectly contributed to the public welfare.

Such a point must be considered when approaching critics of the 'functionalist' theory of professions, those who espouse a 'power' or 'critical' interpretation.[11] Power over the market in professional services – such as monopolization – is the presumed chief (and perhaps only) real goal of the 'professionalizing project'. Yet the German experience seems not to support this theory, which like so many suffers from its narrow origin in Anglo-American experience. German professional organizations did request that the state support higher standards of admission to the profession and in the long run received such state sanction – but the result was not to enhance the professionals' incomes vastly. (The German states were, by the way, carrying out their role as assigned in 'critical' models, that of protecting, not opposing, the professional drive toward monopoly.) Nor did German professional groups usually call for restrictions on numbers of people entering the occupation by restricting access, *as long as* those candidates met valid standards. Open market competition was chosen by most professions, although some (and parts of several others), such as teaching, actively promoted the bureaucratization of their careers, expecting improvements in working conditions and greater professional standards through that route. Thus by a 'functionalist' definition (validation of professions through expertise), German professions carried out a 'professionalizing project'; yet in their cooperation with the state, they were behaving according to a 'critical' definition; and with the result that they failed in their 'critical' mission, maximizing incomes by choking off 'production of producers' of professional services.

It would seem equally plausible to argue, from the German experience, that German professional groups did what they were supposed to do (at least in part) by both 'functionalist' and 'critical' definitions. If the qualification system appeared at times to 'produce too many producers', it may have been because there were too few consumers, or that they were not the right kind to fit Anglo-American models. The creation and expansion of mandatory health insurance after the 1880s, at first having little impact, came to create a whole new mass market for health-care services as well as lower per-capita fees for doctors. Yet the German medical profession did not oppose socialized medicine, only certain features regarded as unfair. By the standards of the AMA this may appear to be a total failure of the German profession's efficacy. But viewed in terms of the tradition of cooperation between state and profession in Germany, it does not appear as a form of de-professionalization, but as an opportunity to expand the market for medical services.

Just as there is nothing inevitable or irreversible about professionalization, one must accept the possibility of 'de-professionalization' as a natural part of the development of the service sector of the labour market. No doubt the rise of new classes of 'technicians' without higher educational qualifications (especially in engineering and applied technology fields) and working for less pay under less secure conditions may plausibly be viewed as a sign of de-professionalization in a given occupational area. Yet nobody would assert that the American medical or dental occupations have been de-professionalized because of the existence of paramedical personnel or dental technicians. Nor, comparing German and American engineering, can one say that either has been particularly successful in creating a monolithic professional organization capable of dominating the market for services. Indeed, organizational differentiation and competition on a *universal* level appear as much a part of the development of modern professions as the attenuation of rivalries among professionals on a *local* level. The multiplication of professional organizations, representing different specialities and differing levels of educational qualification (for example, 'academic' and 'technical' or 'shop' and 'school' orientations in engineering and applied science), do not appear to offer clear evidence of a failure of professionalization or of 'de-professionalization'. Instead, they merely show that growth in such occupations has been faster in occupational sectors of engineering and science that are not at the time able to follow the professionalization project as fully as members of the academically trained sectors. One might call these rapidly growing twentieth-century groups 'semi-professional' or 'proto-professional', but even these terms are of debatable use. Some authors argue that these cadres, though less well trained or paid, and more likely to be employees of large firms, are also products of a kind of professionalization.[12] They have also been more susceptible to unionization attempts, as was also true in the German case. But their existence would only be equatable to a 'de-professionalization' of an entire occupational category (such as engineering) if they undid or reversed the professionalizing achievements of the older or more academically oriented sub-groups within it.

Another threat perceived by some authors, particularly regarding the German experience, has been that posed to the autonomy of professions to create their own standards. As mentioned above, whether as 'professionalization from above' or as 'the construction of occupations' (*Berufskonstruktion*), German professions have sometimes been depicted as fundamentally different from Anglo-American ones because of the role of forces outside the occupational practitioners themselves in shaping the standards of the professional group.

The German states always had some direct or indirect hand in shaping the professions, even though they withdrew increasingly from regulation and unilateral impositions after the 1860s. But state power was never completely withdrawn from the realm of the professions, nor did the latter generally perceive such total withdrawal as being in their own interest. A state that was willing to subsidize professional education could hardly be asked to be indifferent to its structure. The same might be said of the private market for services. It was again the engineering and applied-science occupations in which the interests of the employers appear to have exerted considerable influence (for example, in the creation of the *Verbandsexamen* for chemists).[13] Yet on further reflection, the market for services usually has some impact on the shape of professionalization, even if it happens to be organized into capitalist industry. Similar influences might be discerned in the 'market' organized by the sickness funds. Did the funds (even before being checked by concerted action by the medical profession), however, 'construct' the medical profession or impose 'professionalization from above'? Only from a liberal-market perspective, in other words from a traditional Anglo-American bias, could one make the apposition of professionalization 'from within' (successful manipulation of the market by the group) and 'from above' (domination of forces external to the group). Unless German professionalization was not 'real', it must be seen as occurring on a field where negotiation with market forces, not a fantastic 'triumph' over them, represented historical facts (just as it often seems to have in Anglo-American facticity, if not in all theory). Momentary historical deviations from ideal-types should not be too worrisome to theorists, either, as long as theory can allow for the chance nature of all trends and shifts in the goals of professional groups over long periods of development (such as from 1850 to 1990). Thus, such theoretical attempts to differentiate German professional development from that of other countries based on 'occupation construction' or 'professionalization from above' really seem to reduce to statements that German professions were organized under different circumstances from those of some (if by no means all) other countries – a statement that requires little quibbling to agree with.

For it is precisely my premise that the rise of modern professions did take a different path in Germany from that in other, particularly more liberal-market, countries such as Britain, the United States or Switzerland, at least until after World War II. The reason for this was not so much because professions were 'weaker' or negligible'; or that the process of professionalization was stunted from birth or 'doomed'. Rather, it is because professionalization went on at a different (often, indeed, faster) pace, under clearly different social, economic and political conditions (not to mention attitudinal ones). Largely members of the *Bildungsbürgertum*, German professionals tended to share a social vision more attuned to corporatist, *ständisch* thought than the swiftly changing urban and industrial realities growing up around them. (As with so many other terms in German, *Stand* also failed to survive the Nazi period in professional use.) The mentality of the *Bildungsbürgertum*, not merely that of professionals, was conditioned by elite pride in being cultivated and knowledgeable, but also by an awareness of the need to cooperate with the state and its institutions, which provided the essential recognition and support for elite status. In other words, to fight successfully against 'state interference' in their autonomy (a part of the 'functionalist' view of the role of professions) or to 'capture the state' for their own use and manipulation (the role assigned in many 'power' analyses) would have neither been possible nor desirable for German professions. Interaction with the state, particularly with the educational system (many of whose leading figures also played important roles in professional organizations) was the modal German professionalizing strategy. (So as not to awaken echoes about 'special paths' in German history, let it be noted that it was also modal for many other societies, too.)

Modern German professions emerged not so much from a guild-based form of protectionism as a more recent bureaucratized form of both authority and protection. Medicine and the law, both arch-etypical 'free' professions in most Anglo-American models, were in fact subject to state regulation in most parts of Germany in the early nineteenth century. The guild tradition, in so far as it had survived or recovered slightly from the Smithian economic liberaliz-ation of the Napoleonic era, had long since ceased to have much relevance to the organizational forms of learned professions. Liber-ated from such strict regulation in the reforms of the 1860s and 1870s, German professional organizations began to develop more in parallel with their Anglo-American counterparts, but never without traces of their former close association with public authority. Nor did such 'new' professions as engineering and chemistry find any conflict in containing in their organizational ranks representatives of the very private authority (industry) that provided an increasing percentage of the employment for their members.

The civil service itself, having provided many models for the organization of professions, also broke out of the confines of pure 'professionalization from above' and began to organize its own lobbying organizations around the turn of the twentieth century. Nothing illustrates the mutability of 'professionalizing models' more than this emulation by the putative former 'model group' of the successful tactics of the so-called 'free' professions (as well as the successful tactics of such quasi-civil servants as schoolteachers). The weakness of such abstractions as 'professional groups' manipul-ating 'the state' for their own benefit becomes evident when one looks at the evolution of professional organizations of civil servants in Germany – they were the living incorporation of 'the state' and yet found it impossible to manipulate 'the state' to their satisfaction. Stepping into the 'private' sphere of lobbying seemed to many members of the upper civil service the only way to improve their professional position. Only members of the clergy and military officers, though both certainly professionalized 'from above' in that their training and certification requirements increased over the time period we have been examining, failed to lobby loudly and effec-tively for their professional self-improvement (although both groups had representative organizations by the 1920s). Perhaps rebellious priests and mutinous officers are harder to imagine in German history than self-assertive bureaucrats; but professional associations of military officers and clergy comparable to those in medicine or law have not been a notable feature of the history of professions in other countries, either.

The professionalization of clergy and the military through a chain of command or a hierarchy raises the question of elites within the professions. Just as synods, the Vatican or the general staff has more to say about the qualifications for entry into and careers within the priesthood or the officer corps, certain groups within each other profession exercised a disproportionate influence on its entry and career requirements. As we have seen, in the newer, applied-science professions such as chemistry and engineering, the elites tended to be drawn from successful practitioners in the private sector and higher education. Local elites in the medical profession tended to dominate the local medical associations, which in turn shaped the policies of the DÄV. In the national bar association, practitioners in the Reichsgericht or the Oberlandesgerichte tended to set the standards, rather than the attorneys practising in the lowest courts (for example, the Amtsgericht). The larger, better-organized and older a professional organization became, the less likely was full representation of the interests (particularly of the material interests) of the youngest, most vulnerable or least well-educated and certified members of the profession to dominate the concerns of the association.

Thus the rise of modern professions was also accompanied by the phenomenon of the elites in learned occupations attempting to impose discipline on those who would enter it – a function carried out by civil authorities under bureaucratic despotism or by guilds in local trades before the late nineteenth century. These same elites almost always pressed for increases in the educational and certification requirements for membership in the profession (arguably a self-serving goal for the members of the leadership, themselves active in higher educational establishments).

Yet there were limits to the justifiability of raising educational and certification requirements, and most professional associations (engineers and lower schoolteachers being exceptions) appear to have reached plateaux beyond which they did not push very much by the 1920s – precisely a time when the threat of overcrowding should logically have increased their agitation for raising standards.

This observation raises the problem of the role of education in professionalization: is its level of requirements set by the independent requirements of science or knowledge in the field, by the need for a determinable quantity and quality of advanced expertise? Or is the knowledge (or at least the certification of knowledge) for professions indeterminate, arbitrary and a function of struggles for power or social prestige? It is difficult to defend either of these extreme views on the basis of German professionalization. Clearly, the requirement to submit to some form of classical school education (to obtain the *Abitur*) was a residue of the traditional assignment of social status through the agency of an arcane (classics-oriented) and exclusive body of knowledge, without much convincing evidence that such pre-knowledge made for better or worse professional practitioners. The outcry among German physicians in the late nineteenth century concerning weakening the classics requirements for entry into medical study is a case in point. On the other hand, it is hard to deny that the revolution in science and the explosion of knowledge in general required a more complex, more rigorously organized and longer-lasting 'apprenticeship' for the modern professions than could be provided by traditional master–pupil relationships. Higher education and certification systems delivered this training more cheaply and efficiently. The fact that German learned professions and universities emerged in the modern form almost concurrently was also no coincidence.

The advantages of the German system of training members of the learned professions were clear enough to warrant considerable emulation abroad, even in the United States, where German methods had a particularly deep impact on legal, medical and engineering education. The close cooperation between the professoriate and the leading elites of German professions has been noted repeatedly in this work. The professoriate's influence doubtless had certain ineluctable shaping influences upon German professional development. Not only in the most obvious form of shaping curricula and helping determine examination standards, but in indirect ways, too, the interests of the professoriate ran counter to some of the 'natural' interests of the professional groups in which they served. For example, since a good part of the income of professors (particularly the more famous and influential ones) derived from student lecture fees (over and above their nominal salary), it lay in the economic self-interest of the professoriate to maximize the size of the student body, rather than to restrict the pool of future practitioners. By the same token, it was also in their interests to increase the number of recommended or required courses in each professional curriculum.

The effect of these self-interests was to make professional study more arduous, but also to make it relatively accessible to a growing percentage of the German population. Thus one factor of German professionalization – the mutual interest of the professoriate and professional leadership elites in higher educational standards for the professions – raised standards but did not make access more socially exclusive, rather the opposite. This is not to say that German professions were open to all strata of German society: very few children of peasants or labourers could afford the costs (including forgone income) of even subsidized education. But the children of the commercial and industrial classes increasingly could and did.

The increasingly critical 'over-supply' of professionals resulting at times in the twentieth century, whether in hard reality or in the fears of the professionals themselves, no doubt undermined the ability of many professional groups to achieve what they regarded as an adequate overall income or a strong negotiating position *vis-à-vis* clients and employers. But this problem seems to have been caused at least as much by the dislocations of the German economy (especially in the 1920s and 1930s) as by an absolute over-supply – far more professionals per capita have achieved satisfying incomes in the prosperous Federal Republic than the far fewer per capita were able to under the Weimar Republic.

In the last analysis, the problem does not appear to be that German learned occupations did not successfully undergo professionalization over the past century and a half; or that they cannot properly be called professions; or that they failed to overwhelm the authoritarian and bureaucratic traditions of the traditional German states (let alone stand up to the dynamics of the brief Hitler era); or that they were not in charge of the economic and social conditions that deprived their members of satisfying working conditions during certain phases of history. The problem rests principally with their history not conforming to that of the Anglo-American world, the experience of which has informed so much of the theory of modern professions and professionalization.

Their development was not unilinear or fore-ordained, although long-term trends can be perceived. The setback of the Hitler period (and of Soviet-model professions in the German Democratic Republic) show fully that no professionalization process is irresistible or even particularly powerful, but is rather dependent on the historical conditions of the moment. The German experience demonstrates the danger of thinking about professions in rigid categories. It seems to show that professionalization and bureaucratization can coexist (a lesson that other countries' histories also demonstrates), that professional autonomy and public control (such as the German medical insurance funds) are not mutually exclusive, and that professionalization and the public interest need not always be in conflict.

Notes

1 Fromm, 1941.
2 Cf. Jarausch, 1982; Jarausch, 1986a:136.
3 Kater, 1985:677, departs from the assumption of a linkage between the

'elements in their professional development' and the predisposition 'of the German physicians to fascistization [*sic*] in the twentieth century'.

4 The major theme of Gerd Hortleder's *Das Gesellschaftsbild des Ingenieurs* is the conscious evasion of responsibility of the VDI for the welfare of German engineers from its origins: 'It [the VDI] was useful to industry; it hardly helped engineers' (Hortleder, 1970:65).

5 Larson, 1977/1979.

6 In a recent trenchant critique, an eminent American sociologist described the condition of 'scholarship concerned with the professions' as 'an intellectual shambles' (Freidson, 1984:5).

7 For example, both Freidson and Larson, mentioned above, prefer to stress medicine as the significant profession and slightly different single characteristics of professionalization – autonomy and market monopolization, respectively – in the general observations. For traditional and obvious reasons, many historians have picked one profession to study and can be tempted into stressing intrinsic or extrinsic 'professionalizing factors' that may be almost unique to the studied group.

8 For a balanced discussion of this issue, see Burchardt, 1980:326–348; Johnson, 1987, distinguishes further between 'traditional' professional criteria like education and status and economic advancement, with the VDC doing well on the first but badly on the second, thanks to the presence of industrialists in its midst. For a discussion of 'professionalization from above' in the case of attorneys, see Siegrist, 1985:312, as well as Ledford, 1987.

9 For a fuller discussion of the concept of modern professions, see McClelland, forthcoming, chs 2–3; and for substantiating detail for the outline of professional development over the period 1800–1940, see ibid., chs 4–12.

10 See Ringer, 1979:152 and 229, for comparisons of percentages of youth cohorts entering German, French and British university-level institutions in the late nineteenth and early twentieth centuries.

11 For a discussion of these orientations, see Cullen, 1978:58.

12 Klegon, 1978:275.

13 For a discussion of this important professional certificate, see McClelland, forthcoming, ch. 7.

7

The welfare state, the professions and citizens

Margareta Bertilsson

What is the relation between the welfare state and the professions? This question is not sufficiently explored in the contemporary theories of the professions.[1] Here sociological attention primarily shows the monopoly of knowledge practices which the modern professions occupy and the various strategies that they pursue. The actor approach prevails while the social structural setting at large seems neglected. In this chapter I advance the thesis that the modern professions have a crucial role in the administration of the welfare state, especially within the frame of administering *citizens' rights*. One important collective actor in the modern nation-state is the *body of citizens* as it has become embodied in the policies of the welfare state. In this chapter I am thus seeking to develop the theory once formulated by Talcott Parsons, where he stated the following: 'Comparative study of the social structures of the most important civilizations shows that the professions occupy a position of importance in our society which is, in any comparable degree of development, unique in history.'[2]

In one respect I extend and develop Parsons' view much further than he himself did. His insistence on the essential role of the 'client' in understanding the 'professional complex' in modern society is in this chapter extended to cover the role of the (universal) citizen. This shift of attention permits us to locate the discussion of the modern professions in the midst of the social and political theory of the welfare state.

The chapter is structured as follows. First, I start out with a discussion on the difference between the 'liberal state' and the 'welfare state', because of the bearings that this distinction has on our understanding of the relation between the professions and social structure. Second, with the help of T.H. Marshall's schema, I outline the main stages in the development of modern citizenry and relate this discussion to the emergence of various professions. Third, I conclude with a discussion on the problem of professional representation and suggest a discursive model rather than the now prevailing symbolic one in current discussion.[3]

The liberal state and the welfare state

The distinction between the liberal state and the welfare state, seen here as ideal-typical models, has economic, political and legal consequences not only for how we view citizens but also for how we view the role of the modern professions. In the one (liberal) case we speak of professions regulating the market, and in turn being regulated by the market; and in the other (welfare) case we speak of professions regulating the law, and in turn being regulated by the law. In the first case, an important device to allocate social goods is by means of the supply and demand of the market, and in the other case by means of law. One could speak of these two mechanisms as *monetarization* and *juridification* respectively. Modern societies of course make use of *both* types of goods allocation. But for the purposes of illustration it is possible to imagine a continuum on which different states can be placed according to whether they predominantly make use of one or the other type. A study of professions in modern society must consider the socio-economic–political complex of which they are part and parcel. In a liberal state the realm of action freedom left to the professions presumably is much wider than in the 'juridified' welfare state. The 'free professions' are corollaries of the liberal state. But the welfare state to a very considerable extent depends on the professional judgements which it, paradoxically, seeks to control politically.

In the liberal state there is a set of elementary rights guarding the 'civil sphere' of individuals. The rise of the modern individual coincides with the rise of the liberal state itself. The maturation of the liberal state occurs when civil rights (freedom to hold and sell property, freedom of assembly and expression) are *universalized* and offered to all societal members (of a certain age and mental capacity).[4] In the USA the liberal state came to fruition in the 1960s when the civil rights movement extended citizenship to black people.

The welfare state differs from the liberal state in its expansion of the claims of rights of individuals. This means at the same time an expanded public sector financed by means of taxation. Individuals in the welfare state are citizens endowed with legally guaranteed social rights (with regard to health, pensions, child subsidies and so on) rather than customers/clients purchasing these goods on the market from diverse professional practitioners. The role of the professions is important in both types of structural goods allocation, but it differs considerably between them. The following examples from legal theory should reveal some poignant differences:

In the liberal state the typical structure of law takes the form of
'pure' legal propositions of the following type: 'if (x), then (y)' or
if the owner has acquired the merchandise through a lawful trans-
action (for example, a sale, gift or bequest), then he or she can
dispose of it at will lawfully. Such a legal system offers a set of
institutionally guaranteed rights to individuals, and gives them citizen status. These are negative rights; individuals are guaranteed
freedom from state intervention. As I shall elaborate later in the
text, an autonomous legal profession is essential for the upholding
of these rights.[5]

The negative rights are prototypical for the classical liberal state.
They are expressed legally as imperatives directed to the individuals
themselves. We speak in this case of a direct relation between the
state and the individuals, although in real life there are of course
mediating links in terms of administrative organs of various kinds.
Schematically it looks as shown in Figure 7.1. The courts intervene
when the rights of citizens are impeded. From the realist sociological perspective that I am advancing here as to a theory of rights,
the intervention of the legal profession guarantees and reproduces
the existence of these rights.

In political and legal language the classical rights of the liberal
state are *formal* rights. They grant, as Anatole France once put it,
the same right to both the rich and the poor to sleep under the
bridges.

The welfare state has as its primary aim to *materialize* the formal
rights of the classical period and extend them to cover a minimum
material standard of well-being for all citizens (and not only those
who can pay). New sets of rights are proposed which in the Swedish
case include the old-age pension, sick-leave pension, maternity and
parental leaves and allowances, and child allowances. More
recently claims of rights have been extended to 'consumers' rights',
'workers' rights, and 'patients' rights.

In the liberal state claims of rights are achieved by the market

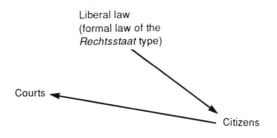

Figure 7.1   *The classical liberal state model*

mechanism, and may as such be equally extensive as citizens' rights in the welfare state, whereas in the welfare state they are achieved by means of law.[6] The role of the professions differs in each case: in the liberal state professional services are offered on the market; in the welfare state a set of 'material laws' make them available to the body of citizens. This distinction clarifies the difference between private customers/clients and citizens endowed with rights.

Of course, several mixtures are possible between the liberal state and the welfare state; individual work places in the liberal state may offer their employees extensive pension rights, or help purchase these at a reduced price. As is well known from the theory of marginal utility, the levelling out of differences that are too gross as to the life-chances of people is good for capital as well.

The schematized structure of material welfare laws differs from the classic liberal ones as shown in Figure 7.2. Welfare laws are of a 'compensatory' kind, and directly implicated in the re-distribution of social resources. They are positive rights; the state interferes with the lives of citizens in order to restitute their social life-chances. As administrators of welfare legislation, professional experts become the mediators between the state and the citizens. As seen in the schema, the relation between the state (polity) and the citizens is no longer of the direct (liberal) type. Some welfare rights, such as pensions rights, are offered directly to individuals once they fulfil certain criteria of age, pregnancy, ill health and so on, but professionals decide on the matter of candidacy. Other welfare rights embodied in general clauses are weak from a legal viewpoint: to offer an individual 'a right to gainful work, to clean air, to good health' lacks (legal) precision as to what constitutes 'gainful work', 'clean air', 'good health' and to whose duty it is to honour these rights in practice. Such promissory rights are seen rather as important social political directives, and form what T.H. Marshall has referred to as 'the legitimate expectations' of modern man. The welfare state is directly dependent on the competencies of various professionals to administer its wide extensions of rights. It is import-

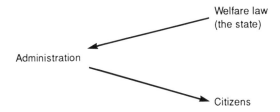

Figure 7.2 *Welfare state model*

ant for the credibility of a modern welfare polity to have access to professional expertise both in issuing and in executing rights.[7]

Professions are crucial in the running of both types of society, but their roles differ. A most challenging task for a theory of the professions must be to delineate differences and similarities in the structure of professional services between the two (ideal-typical) forms of modern societies. In the liberal society, the professions are client-constitutive, and in the other they are citizen-constitutive. In the welfare type of society professional practices are intimately woven into the political warp, and there is a 'politicization' of the professions, at the same time as political practice is being 'professionalized'.[8] In the one (liberal) type professional practices can help solidify the private well-being of (some) individuals, and thus put at risk the universal status of citizenry; and in the other type, professional practice can help strengthen state-administration, and thus 'colonize' the life-world of individuals and reduce their citizenships into mere state dependencies.[9] But in either case, the future of the individual as endowed with either client- or citizen-status is dependent on the extension and orientation of professional practices.

My theme in this chapter differs from many modern theories on the professions in that I suggest a constitutive link between the extension of professional services and the claims of the modern individual to possess either a client- or a citizen-status. Indeed, I think it is possible to extend this link to include even that of the individual; without professional services constructing 'needs' of individuals (often by means of an academic symbol system), they would be impoverished and pre-modern creatures, lacking subjectivity and individuality. The modern professional practitioners are constitutive of modern society and its individuals. It is this link between modern society, the individual and the professions which is at the centre of attention here. My essay is thus a contribution to the wider discussion on 'modernity' and an attempt to illuminate the role of the professions in processes of modernization. In order to reveal the different stages of this process, I shall draw on T.H. Marshall's schema on the making of modern citizenry.

A professional interest theory and the evolution of citizenship

In *Citizenship and Social Class* (1950), Marshall advances a developmental view of the modern citizenry and states (implicitly) the role of the modern professions in enabling citizenship.[10] The welfare state, he says, 'collectivizes the professions and professionalizes social services'. In the course of the evolution of the modern welfare state the once-free liberal professions lose their gentle social status and enter the middle of the social-political arena. Their services are becoming crucial political devices, and hence the professions themselves undergo a process of 'collectivization' (or socialization). New professions are being created in the process of expanding social services. In the following I shall explicate what a collectivization view of the modern professions means in more detail, especially in constituting modern citizenry. In developing T.H. Marshall's view of the rise of citizenship, I should like to stress the intrinsic, or what I call 'constitutive', relation between the various stages of citizenry and types of professional practices.

Marshall distinguishes three phases in the evolution of citizenship: (1) the civil citizenship starting to evolve in the eighteenth century; (2) the suffrage, or the political citizenship, evolving in the nineteenth century and coming to full fruition in our own century; and finally (3) the rise of the social citizenry clearly related to the emergence of the modern welfare state in our own century.

In this discussion I shall expound on a sociological and realist argument that the 'social rights' of modern man, as embodied in the modern welfare state, can exist only in so far as they are being 'guaranteed' by a public-professional social framework. The realist argument states that rights exist only to the extent to which they are being acted upon by special interest groups. From such a point of view the professions are crucial actors in the social struggle of just distribution. It is their business to administer as well as to legitimize the modern welfare state in its concern to extend citizen's rights via an abstract symbol system. Clearly, the professions occupy a similar role in the liberal state, although in this case they offer their services on the market.

Civil citizenship

As already suggested in the previous section on the liberal state, it is possible to trace the origin of modern society to the birth of the legal individual who can own and dispose of property, enter into contracts and express *his* own personal will (women had no legal status at the time). Locke's *Two Treatises of Government* (1689) stands out in the history of political philosophy as perhaps the first modern treatise. A civil space is carved out for the individual now given 'inalienable' natural rights. These rights include 'liberty of the person, freedom of speech, thought and faith, the right to own property and to conclude valid contracts'.[11] The civil space carved out for man meant an 'equal right to justice' for the bourgeois and the nobleman alike, and was in this sense a revolution of social forms (although most of the population without property were excluded from social participation). The emergence of the market and the nation-state demanded abstract social relations. The notion of citizen as an 'abstract individual' broke the boundaries of family, kinship and community. Social belongings were no longer decided by concrete and visible devices known to all concerned but by means of an abstract symbol system requiring verbal skills. Because of this structural transformation of social life, new professional groups trained in abstract thought became central to social administration. Previously the theologians had excelled in an abstract symbolic language, although in the service of the sacred rather than the profane.

According to the line of thought that I am following here, the legal profession was the first *modern* profession. Civil citizenship could come about only as a function of there coming into existence an independent order of courts free from the demands of both the church and the king. Max Weber saw in the rise of an independent law profession trained academically (at the new European universities) an important carrier of both formal and substantial rationalization of the social order.[12] A new abstract language of statehood and citizenship was needed to terminate the powers of the feudal lords. The king (at least if he was enlightened enough) needed citizens, initially only as his subjects, and he needed from them not only tax money but also their 'acceptance' of his rule. The legal profession was essential in the promulgation and articulation of the new social and political order, as only its members could generate the discursive base needed to legitimate the new rule.

There are different theories to account for the emergence of both citizens and their 'rights'. Instead of a natural law perspective I am here advancing a (realist) theory based on social interests in which, as we shall see, the modern professions occupy a central role. It is possible, as Ulrich Preuss has suggested in a much-discussed essay, to view the language of rights as discursive presentations of subjective interest on the level of action.[13] Professionals are powerful social actors in the wider structural articulation of human rights and human needs typical of the modern world order. The system of abstract symbols may very well conceal the subjective and particular interests of social groups. Nevertheless, it is the wider and perhaps unintended consequences of such a subjective interest theory that is of concern here.[14]

The linkage of interests and rights was to become powerful in modern history. For trade and industry to flourish subjective interests and individual rights were needed as 'motives' of action. The link between subjective interests and abstract rights turned out to be especially powerful when the interests of two collective actors could merge into a common destiny. The interests of the bourgeoisie coincided with those of an emergent law profession.[15] The latter profession gave, on the discursive level, and in a formal-rational manner, expression to the action interests of the bourgeoisie.[16] The affinity of interests between the bourgeoisie and the law profession led to an important structural, and perhaps pivotal, dimension in the formation of the new market society.

The emergence of a professional sphere with its own strong interests helped the new bourgeois class to state its interests *legally*. This is an important consideration, as it incorporated the birth of a new professional labour force trained academically, who were to formulate their interests around such 'universal' notions as 'citizen', 'mankind' and 'humanity'. The modern professions were important means of humanization of a secular social order.[17]

It is important to point out the shift in the loyalties of professions that occurred with the rise of the modern nation-state. Before the rise of the citizen-state professional practitioners were the servants of kings and masters, whose orders they had to obey. In the new industrialist society the rule shifted representational forms. The majestic appearances of the king as shown by spectacular displays of weapons and of armies were replaced by the (verbal) power of citizens-individuals: instead of spectacular physical displays the new forms of power took the shape of a neutral and abstract symbol system mediated by academically trained specialists. The professions – initially represented by the legal profession – were citizen-constitutive, for without the discourse that their members alone could offer no abstract citizen rights could have occurred. The power of the citizens had no other institutional backing than the one guaranteed by the 'power of speech'; for example, an abstract discourse, preserved 'legally' as the embedded interests of a special law profession. In the case of the imperial or feudal rules, the power was given by God often in combination with the army and preserved by extended family and kinship relations. It is a general characteristic of modern professions, however, that their role as 'power containers' resides primarily in a neutral and abstract symbol system, though often guarded by various ceremonial rituals. As discursive power it is as infinite and boundless as language itself permits and can easily be stretched to cover mankind as such. It is this rationalizing symbol system, earlier reserved for the celestial kingdom, that penetrated modern society thoroughly and whose bearers are found among the modern professions.[18]

The civil citizenship among men was soon to pave the road for even more radical demands: the rights of men to elect their own representatives of local and national government.

Political citizenship

In the nineteenth century, the process of individualization in the legal and the economic orders, perforated the organs of political power as well. As Marshall has put it, men demanded a 'right to participate in the exercise of political power', to be 'a member of a body invested with political authorities' and to become an 'elector of the members of such a body'.[19] The struggle for political rights, above all universal suffrage, resulted in the institutionalization of parliaments on a national level, and of community councils on a local level.

Poulantzas has well described the dual process in the emergence of state and citizenship.[20] He referred to it as the rise of 'body-politics'. The nation-state was the unity of now differentiated individuals. The new (democratic) rule needed new devices of power. Quantification became an important device of power where majority rule was accepted. What was 'typical' of a majority of men, either in terms of needs or opinions, was important to assess and to calculate. What was 'normal' among the population became a new legitimating base for power. The new political rule must 'represent' the population as a whole; 'body-politics' was to secure the majority interests of the population in getting a hearing in the newly installed parliament. In the wake of the new body-politics a whole cadre of new population experts such as statisticians and political scientists rose to social power. Modern democratic rule demanded new professional calculators in possession of neutral scientific statistical-social knowledge. New types of professional skills were needed by democratic forms of social power.

The institutional anchorage of the newly emergent political rights of the nineteenth century lay in the rise of a parliament with the diversity of political interests now represented as party politics. As a consequence of party politics and representative democracy, a new class of professionals entered the historical arena; the 'professional politicians'.[21] But as a rule politicians, whether they are laymen or professionals, did not (and still do not) speak in 'universal' categories. On the contrary, they have particular (party) interests to represent in parliament. In order to follow our line of thought we need to find new professional groups capable of expressing 'universal' interests. The question is which professional interests at the time were to further the political rights of men in the same way as the legal profession had helped in furthering the interests of the bourgeois?

Among the newly emergent professions of the nineteenth century were the educators and the journalists; namely, those encouraging man's mental capacity to reach above mental slavery. The reformers and the educators of the nineteenth century made up its vanguard strata. They nourished the hope that education could free man from his ancient tutelage. Certainly, these wide circles of educators and reformers could count as the (not yet specialized) forerunners of the modern social service professionals. The existence of these widely dispersed early 'professionals', whose mission it was to educate the masses (not least to avoid the communist menace), were sociological preconditions for the realization of political rights and political citizenship. Without men's ability to read and to write, modern democratic political culture would have been void of content. A prolonged process of political socialization was needed in order to form a mentality of independence and responsibility among men.

I am therefore suggesting that the widely dispersed educators and the reformers of the nineteenth century – such as teachers, ministers and journalists – took the same fostering role as had the legal profession in the previous century in strengthening and consolidating citizenship among the people. Thanks to their constitutive endeavours, both on the political and the symbolic level, an enlightened public could emerge where the germ of participatory democracy had taken hold. Nevertheless, the newly achieved formal rights of men could not long conceal the glaring inequalities inherent in the structure of social life itself.

Social citizenship

It is the third phase in the evolution of citizenship that is of pivotal interest for the theme that I seek to develop here. This is the phase when the previously free liberal professions enter into the centre of public power, and when new social service professions are created as well. This is also a phase when the professions become aware of their own role, and when the theories of professionalization start to flourish in the discipline of sociology.[22]

The social aspects of citizenship emerged in the twentieth century. The formal claim of equality among legal and political citizens revealed the social inequalities of men and women. Guarantees had to be made to eradicate these inequalities. This was (and is) a controversial stage as it required a redistribution of social resources, either by means of law (juridification) or the market (monetarization) or more often by a combination of the two. This required new institutional settings, either publicly or privately run. In any case extensive use of professional service was needed. The 'professionalization' of the social order formed the social structural context in terms of which the articulation of 'social rights' was made possible. The constitutive link between professional practice and citizen rights emerged in a new and politically explosive light.

The interference in men's natural-communal relations in order to re-distribute social resources is a double-edged process. It offers freedom to men and women in general (not only to those with property) but on the condition that they are severed from old traditions. This, as Adorno gloomily warns, is the rise of *'die verwaltete Welt'*. Old communal relations are replaced by social-administrative bonds requiring new types of abstract solidarities among men and women. This is also a process of extensive scientification of social life. In the realization of the modern welfare state political parties are dependent on modern social and economic science as mediated by the social service professions. The making of the welfare state draws upon intensified professional skills and practices. I think that it is indeed possible to claim that the welfare state is as much a professional as it is a political achievement. The social extension of citizenship requires the abstract reasoning and calculation of the modern professions trained scientifically in universal rather than particular categories.

Social rights differ considerably between countries and political cultures.[23] I cannot discuss here the controversial aspects as to the origin of social citizenry, although I wish to point out that it is by no means a clear-cut left–right issue.[24] What I want to stress rather is the fact that the professional action complex, as it specifically comes to emerge in modern society as a growing sector of its labour force, becomes the prime collective actor in the administration and legitimation of social rights and social citizenry. Whether ruled by left- or right-wing parties, the modern welfare state is anchored institutionally in the 'professional complex'. Hence, it is possible to claim that its stability resides in the strength of the professional ventures. The primacy of modern professional actors in reproducing the social rights of individuals is due to the fact that their diverse occupational *interests* are themselves at stake!

Let me illustrate some such social rights in the case of Sweden. This is not a complete list, but includes some of the more salient ones. In order to safeguard the individual from crises occurring both in his or her own individual life-cycle as well as those emanating from social life and the work place, social citizenry includes: old-age pensions; illness and disability pensions; paid maternity and parental leave; childhood allowances; student allowances and student loans both for the young and the adults who want to improve their professional lot; 'decent pay for decent work'; improvement in workers' participation in the running of the work setting; a better work place, equipment and environment; unemployment and work disability compensations; allowances for re-training and compensation for expenses in connection with occupational moves; and so on. It is part and parcel of both union and political-economic life to improve and extend this list continuously and to advise on possible means to effectuate and strengthen these diffuse and often controversial rights. Once rights have been achieved politically and codified legally and semi-legally, they become exceedingly difficult to abolish! Strategic social interests are at stake.

Nevertheless, unless these rights can become grounded in particular professional interests, they are likely to fade away from the public view. Professional agents administer these rights in daily practice; doctors, psychologists and social workers decide on the criteria of physical, mental and environmental health and whether a person can become a candidate for various types of allowances. The workers' rights to participate in the running of the work place (and not to interfere with the rights of any other); whether this or that clause is applicable in any particular case; or whether or not the correct procedures have been used, are decided by lawyers or by other professional representatives. The thesis that I am putting forward here is in accordance with the postulates of 'legal realism'; either professional actors have enough subjective interests at stake, collectively speaking, to administer and thus exercise these rights – or not. Social rights, and thus social citizenship, *exist* if, and only if, there are social actors in strategic representative locations, prepared to practise and to defend these rights when attacked by others.[25]

What I have been saying in the case of the welfare state and the role of the professions is of course equally applicable in the liberal state with its 'customers/clients'. The claims of the latter need professional representation, and professional interests need an expanding market of audiences.

Impact on professional life

In the process of this structural transformation of the social, political and economic life due to the rise of the welfare society, or in the case of the modern liberal state the rise of various customer-client organizations, the old professions of (for example) medicine and of law have changed considerably. They could hardly any longer be recognized as 'free, liberal professions' as they have become central agents in the administration of the modern state. The following quote from Michael Walzer's *Spheres of Justice* nicely illustrates what Marshall calls the 'collectivization' of the professions in today's society:

> In Europe during the Middle Ages, the cure of souls was public, the cure of bodies private. Today . . . the situation is reversed. . . . Among medieval Christians, eternity was a socially recognized need, and every effort was made to see that it was widely and equally distributed, that every Christian had an equal chance at salvation and eternal life: hence, a church in every parish, regular services, catechism for the young, compulsory communion, and so on. Among modern citizens, longevity is a socially recognized need; and increasingly every effort is made to see that it is widely and equally distributed, that every citizen has an equal chance at a long and healthy life: hence doctors and hospitals in every district, regular check-ups, health education for the young, compulsory vaccination, and so on.
>
> Parallel to the shift in attitudes, and following naturally from it, was a shift in institutions: from the church to the clinic and the hospital. . . . The licencing of physicians, the establishment of state medical schools and urban clinics, the filtering of tax money into the great voluntary hospitals: these measures involved, perhaps, only marginal interference with the profession – some of them, in fact, reinforced its guildlike character: but they already represent an important public commitment. Indeed, they represent a commitment that ultimately can be fulfilled only by turning physicians, or some substantial number of them, into public physicians . . . and by abolishing or constraining the market in medical care.[26]

This is the structural process of transformation that other commentators on modern professions call 'bureaucratization', 'proletarianization' or 'rationalization'.[29] But the 'bureaucratization' theme of previously free liberal professions corresponds only to the rise of the modern social citizen. 'Normalization' procedures are necessary in the running of modern body-politics! The theory that I advance here suggests quite frankly that the making of citizenship is intimately related to the rise of modern bureaucracy, and thus to the power of professional practices as devices of legitimation.

In the case of Sweden (as I suppose elsewhere) numerous examples could be provided of how the old gentleman-doctor or gentleman-judge became merely salaried, bureaucratized, state officials paid in accordance with union contracts with the state. This structural transformation was not won, and is not yet won, without resistance from the old professions, not even in an otherwise levelled-out society like Sweden. The medical profession certainly mobilized organized resistance against the attempts of the state to limit private practices among medical doctors in order to equalize medical practices across the country. Claims for equality of the various regions in Sweden demanded a much more controlled supply of medical practices. The state – that is, the association of abstract citizens – had at its disposal sanctions against the obstructions of an old and status-clad medical profession; no subsidies were provided from the state insurance, making consultation with a doctor a considerable expense. Such sanctions were and are efficient in the hands of the state (now representing citizens and thus abstract justice) to control the obstructions of private professions. Yet another example of resistance among a free profession was summoned in the case of the state organization of legal aid. The Association of Swedish Lawyers (Advokatsamfundet) mobilized resistance, as legal aid provided by the state threatened to 'bureaucratize' the free practice of law to state control. The legal aid programme, as opposed to the medical reforms of regional balance, has so far not been very successful, and is presently undergoing cuts.[28] These examples are provided so as not to give the reader the impression that Sweden would be a streamlined model of a well-organized welfare society of 'associated citizens' and of subjugated professions. In any society, including Sweden, there are resistances, deviations and resiliences. What I seek to outline here is rather a conceptual pattern of normative and analytical relevance for understanding current social developments.

It is not only the old professions in medicine and in law that have changed in character and identity in the course of the development of the modern welfare state. Most revealing in the changing structural profile of the modern professions is the explosion of new, so-called 'semi-professions'. The following statistics from Sweden (compiled according to union figures and therefore not complete) reveal the changing structural profile among the professions. A comparison across various academic professions reveals that the social workers have grown from ca. 3,000 in 1960 to an estimated but quite uncertain number of about 25,000 in 1987; the number of psychologists is today estimated at ca. 5,900, in 1960 they were ca. 260; the estimated number of professional economists in Sweden presently ranges somewhere in between 30,000 and 35,000, in 1960 a rough estimation of the economists amounts to ca. 5,000; the academic engineers are presently numbered at 49,500, whereas in 1950 they were no more than 5,000. In the period 1950–1987, the legal profession has grown 2.5 times; the engineers have in the same period grown 10 times. From 1960 to 1987 the social workers have grown at least 7 times; and the psychologists almost 23 times over!

The structure of growth among the Swedish professions over the last couple of decades certainly illustrates the growth of industry and of production, but also the expansion and institutionalization of 'social rights' socially and politically. An important question in this context is whether or not history can be turned back and if the welfare state is reversible. To the extent to which these professions, particularly those administering social and political life, have collective interests to defend and maintain against interferences from yet other group interests, one could expect the continuation of the welfare rights among modern citizens, even if there were to be a drastic change in governmental policies. Realistically speaking, any politically elected government must show restraints in dealing with well-organized professional (and corporate) interests. It would be costly, both economically and politically, to lay professionals off the labour market, and provide them with no substitute!

This is not a plea for the welfare state, as I can clearly visualize a better life, at least for some individuals, in their role as private client/customers. It is but an attempt to understand some important structural parameters of social justice and the role of the professions in the society which I myself inhabit.

The problem of professional representation

In many current writings on professionalism, there exists a clear tendency to view professional power from a cynical point of view, as 'symbolic capital', as 'monopolization of cultural resources', as 'credential politics' or the rise of the 'sinecure society'.[29] It is not my wish here to refute such views or even to dispute their value. It is my wish, however, to broaden our sociological vision and include into the theory of the professions a consideration of its correlate of the power of citizenry. The credential system in modern society bestowing upon the professions their 'sinecural locations' (Collins) allows them also to speak in universal categories, and thus make possible discursively the rise of universal men and women. Perhaps these practices are the unanticipated consequences of modern professional power, but a theory of the professions should also comprise such consequences. The correlate of the citizen allows us to take a different view of professional power and its accountability: to whom are the modern professionals accountable? whose interests do they represent?

In order to respond to these questions properly, we need to take a brief view on the problem of representation in social and political philosophy.[30] There are then two prototypical views illustrated by the descriptive and the symbolic theory of representation, respectively. First, descriptive representation features the relation between the representatives and those who are represented as primarily physical. It is desirable that members of different parliaments should resemble their electoral base in certain physical manners; for example, in age and genus, and in occupation and location. Important to note is that in this case the 'represented' individuals, the electorate, are somehow logically prior to their representatives, and because of this logical order control and accountability are made possible: the representatives can exercise power only as long as they serve the will of the people. The next election can dispose of them. Second, in the case of symbolic representation, however, the logical order between the representatives and their 'subjects' is reversed. The sovereign comes in this case prior to those he or she represents (as in the case of the British queen), and can affect those who are represented and shape their will accordingly. Symbolic representation has religious underpinnings, still exercised in the case of monarchy. In its secular version it becomes the fascist theory of representative power.[31] The question is which form of representation is applicable in the case of the professions.

It has been questioned whether it is at all fruitful to speak of representation, whether in a descriptive or a symbolic form, in the case of professional power.[32] The asymmetry in (for instance) the relation between a doctor and patients with regard to the possession of medical knowledge seems to rule out the concept of 'representation'. In the case of a lawyer, however, we speak of 'legal representation' as there is a supposed client prior to the representative act. The decisive question is thus whether or not there is a person prior to the act of representation capable of controlling its proceedings. In the context of professional powers it has been questioned whether there are prior wills to hold practitioners accountable because of the asymmetry in the relationships. Traditionally, the professional relationships were characterized as 'trust-relations'.[33] What other choices do we really have but to trust the competency of a doctor when he or she presents us with the diagnosis that we suffer from cancer, and that we are in need of a particular kind of therapy?

The traditional asymmetry with regard to the possession of knowledge between a professional practitioner and a client/patient certainly could mould professional power into the merely symbolic and representational kind. It is my belief, however, that modern society, whether in its welfare or liberal version, has gradually closed the gap in status and power that the old professions used to possess. Professions are today held accountable either by means of state control or by means of organizations of customers or clients, in particular by powerful insurance organizations in pursuit of malpractice. Although we do not insist that medical doctors should resemble the population in a descriptive sense (see above), there are certainly moves among both feminist women and various minority groups to make the profession better resemble the population as a whole with regard to sex and ethnic status. It is also of interest to note that the 'scientific base' of professional power in many instances no longer is sufficient, as science itself is a symbol system in need of justification.[34]

Whatever the future will be regarding the current moves on 'accountability' of both scientific and professional practices, the bases of professional powers are certainly coming under increasing attack due to the rise of various citizens' organizations and social movements. The results of these moves among groups of citizens and clients are likely to change the previous asymmetry and (unquestioned) trust that earlier characterized relations between professional practitioners and clients/patients. It is unlikely that professional representation would turn descriptive in the classical sense, but such powers will most likely have to deal with more or less organized 'interests' ready to question the mere symbolic content of professional power in the future, the justificatory bases of which are discursive; professional practitioners of various sorts will have to provide us with 'good reasons' for their diagnoses and treatments.

Seen from such a point of view it seems possible to advance a rational theory of professional power based on 'justifiable reasons' and on seeking to call out the personhood (that is, agency) in the clients/citizens. The point is that individuals as clients or as citizens are allowed to question the bases of expert power and seek to distinguish whether it is based on justificatory reasons or not. Professional representation can thus be seen from within the framework of the wider discursive culture which the professions themselves have helped to foster. The success of the professionalized society results paradoxically in the 'de-professionalization' of modern society; organizations among citizens and clients will force upon professional practitioners the necessity to review their own actions from the point of view of the larger citizenry and even of humanity as such.

In a society with a complex division of labour we need professional specialization and representation. It is not a practical and efficient state of affairs to let each individual be his or her own doctor, lawyer, accountant and so on. The point is not to let increasing specialization in knowledge and in practice lead to a state of affairs of ignorance and passivity, and thus alienation, among the citizenry at large. On the contrary, the promise of a modern, enlightened, professional culture lies in its discursive and justificatory bases of power. The menaces that confront us today are not the professions and their claim to power but blind faith, whatever its form of manifestation.

Conclusion

In this chapter I have stressed the intrinsic relationship between professional power and citizens' rights as constitutive of one another. I have not considered the controversial issue as to whether such links are best served by means of juridification or monetarization, by means of the welfare state or the liberal state with its market mechanisms. I have no answer to this question.

Instead, I focused on the strategic role of the professions in both types of social economies; in modern society they have become both client- and citizen-constitutive. But there is a contradiction inherent in the structural position of the modern professional, and perhaps the contradiction is more apparent in the case of the welfare state. In the (pure) liberal state a professional practitioner can perhaps claim that he or she *represents* the client only, rather than the abstract citizen body. Such a loyalty becomes more difficult in the welfare state where the medical doctor has to mediate between the concern for the patient and the abstract citizen body. What is good for all is not necessarily best for the individual. This is what I mean by the duality of the modern professional practice finding itself torn between the body-citizen (the state) and the individual person. The fusion of universal and particular interests, of state and individual representation, is likely to elicit role conflicts in the professional practitioner. Such role conflicts are really individual embodiments of what Habermas has spoken of as the 'crises of legitimation' of the modern state.[35] There is a cleavage in the 'legitimate expectations' (to use Marshall's term) of an individual and that which can be provided by state means. It is this kind of crisis symptoms that perhaps torment the modern (welfare) professions. It is not easy to be an executor of legitimate power and at the same time serve those who are the subjects of that same power.

Our social citizenship and the rights that it bestows upon us are said to be much more resilient and perhaps negotiable than the more consolidated civil rights of an earlier epoch. To work out the negotiable status of our social citizenship by means of an interest theory of the professions would be the ultimate theoretical *and* political test of the thesis that I have suggested in this chapter. There is no room, however, to develop that theme here.

Notes

1 Larson, 1977/1979; Collins, 1979; Parkin, 1979; Murphy, 1988; Selander, 1989; Brante, 1988a:119.

2 Parsons, 1949:34.

3 Collins, 1979, is the best-known spokesman for the symbolic power of professional representation; see note 1.

4 The German equivalent to the English term 'liberal state' is *Rechtsstaat*. It is generally understood as a nineteenth-century notion; it was in the last century that the Rechtsstaat became institutionalized, and extended to the population as a whole. There is a difference in the Anglo-Saxon and German conception that is akin to the differences in the status of the professions in the two areas. The Anglo-Saxon 'liberal state' carries with it the strong connotation of a civil sphere of the individual guaranteed by constitutional law. In a like manner, the 'liberal' professions have been phenomena primarily in the Anglo-Saxon context. On the Continent of Europe and in Scandinavia the professions have been understood as *Beamten* rather, as servants of the state. The *Rechtsstaat* conception stands for a political power that 'binds' itself differently from that of the liberal state – it promises regularity and predictability, whereas the liberal state guarantees freedom and rights from state interference. See Slagstad, 1987.

5 Weber, 1978:775; for a legal realist perspective on rights, see Ross, 1953.

6 See Korpi, 1988:3–34.

7 In social science literature, the implications of the 'intellectuals/professionals' in state power is a popular theme. *The Intellectuals on the Road to Class Power* by Konrad and Szeleny, 1979, was a recently widely read book in which warnings were given against the alliance between state power and intellectuals in the case of the socialist regimes in Eastern Europe. The same theme is found in Foucault, 1978; Poulantzas, 1978b; and more recently in the popular book by Beck, 1986.

8 In Sweden the members of both parliament and local councils are predominantly 'professionals' employed in the public sector. Social workers, for instance, have a very high degree of political representation.

9 Habermas, 1981.

10 Marshall, 1950.

11 Marshall, 1950:10.

12 Weber, 1978:809–831.

13 Preuss, 1986.

14 Weber, 1978:422–439.

15 Anners, 1974/1980.

16 Weber, 1978:871–875.

17 From a Foucaultian point of view, the humanized order of modernity very well may mean a social order of increasing surveillance and discipline. See Foucault, 1978.

18 It is possible as Parsons has also pointed out that the law profession had an exceptional status in ancient Rome, where the legal notion of 'persona' was first formulated. Nevertheless, the former had priority over the latter, and Caesar or the priests thus could change legal judgments should they conflict with the divine order. See Parsons, 1977.

19 Marshall, 1950:10.

20 Poulantzas, 1978b.

21 Weber, 1977:40–95 (the callings of politics).

22 Carr-Saunders and Wilson, 1933; Parsons, 1939:457–467.

23 Korpi, 1988; see note 6.

24 Bismarck is often referred to as the first leading politician who by means of law institutionalized some elementary social rights for the German workers in order to undermine from within the socialist menace. See Therborn, 1986:131–164.

25 A realist and sociological theory of human rights would suggest that without the existence of an autonomous legal profession and its self-interests to uphold specific symbol systems embodying constitutional law and universal citizenship, there would be no such rights – and thus no individuals in a modern sense. It is to be noted that legal realism has a proud and long-standing tradition within the Scandinavian juridical community. A classic reference is found in Ross, 1953.

26 Walzer, 1983:212–213.

27 Murphy, 1988.

28 Modéer, 1987; Jon Johnson, 1987.

29 Bourdieu, 1977; Collins, 1979; Parkin, 1979; Freidson, 1986.

30 Pitkin, 1967.

31 The descriptive mode is rational in the extent to which the represented can exercise control over their representatives by means of electorate policies. The symbolic mode is considered a non-rational form of representation, as it does not allow the 'subjects' to control the representative powers. From the viewpoint of social methodology the difference between the two modes of representation amounts to the difference between 'reason' and 'causes' of action.

32 Pitkin, 1967:135.

33 Parsons, 1939, 1949.

34 Rorty, 1979; see also Beck, 1986.

35 Habermas, 1973.

8

Professional education in a comparative context

Tony Becher

A study of the characteristics of professional training offers a particular perspective on the sociology of professions. Britain has had a tradition of strong professional bodies, directly responsible for providing their own qualifications. That tradition of independence from the established academic system has gradually given place to a transfer of training responsibilities from practitioners to academics: a shift which, in the case of relatively low-status 'minor professions',[1] is reinforced by the expectation that graduate-level qualifications will enhance their standing in society.

The resulting distinctions – between those who induct new recruits into the profession and those who practise it from day to day – pose questions about the nature of the relevant knowledge base. This chapter seeks to explore such questions through a comparative study of three so-called 'caring professions': pharmacy, nursing and teaching. It provides an analysis of certain key aspects of the graduate programmes for each, in the particular setting of British higher education.

The argument has an empirical base, in that it rests on the findings of a relatively small-scale research project, further details of which are given in the Appendix. At this point, it is perhaps sufficient to say two things. First, the study involved interviews, predominantly with academic staff, but also with senior academic administrators, members of staff of validation agencies and experienced practitioners in the professions concerned. The focus of these interviews was on the various activities and problems associated with the provision of a professional qualification at graduate level. Second, the study was carried out in close partnership between three people – Ronald Barnett, Morwenna Cork and myself.[2] My intellectual debt to my two colleagues is considerable: although I am here presenting my own version of the findings, I have drawn very heavily on our collective data and discussions.

In what follows, I shall give particular emphasis to three sets of distinctions. One focuses on the institutional status of the professional schools in question. Another concerns an indirectly connected issue, the nature of the relationship between academics and practitioners in each professional field. The last is to do with the familiar problem of the relationship between theory and practice in education for the professions, and with the light that throws on the nature of professional knowledge.[3]

Institutional status

In Britain, those schools of pharmacy – six out of sixteen – which are in polytechnics enjoy a generally high reputation and standing (one interviewee described them as 'the jewels in the crown').[4] For those located in universities the situation is more ambiguous. The pharmacists 'have to fight their corner': there tends to be a lingering feeling that 'pharmacy isn't a proper degree subject'. It is a matter for rueful comment that, on the wider scene, there have never been any Fellows of the Royal Society in pharmacy. One or two pharmacologists have been so honoured: but theirs is felt somehow to be a more patrician discipline ('it's even taught at Oxbridge').

As in any other sphere of academic life, departmental reputations wax and wane – the changes often coinciding with changes in academic leadership. However, the overall 'pecking order' between pharmacy schools remains relatively stable, favouring the schools based in the longer-established university institutions.

The struggle for reputation, though, is hardly a crucial one: nearly all schools have an abundance of well-qualified applicants, with formal entry qualifications comparable with those for medicine, and an enviable record of virtually 100 per cent graduate employment.[5] Most also have a respectable pattern of research, with sizeable grant earnings. By a number of the current criteria for academic merit, pharmacy departments therefore come off well.

In some institutions, there is a fair amount of interchange between the pharmacists and other academic groups, particularly in the form of service teaching. This traffic goes both ways, helping to enhance the comparability of academic status between pharmacy and other science departments. But this very need to maintain the image of a 'hard science' – to keep up with the biochemists and the microbiologists – builds up the pressure for an academicized curriculum, and (as we shall see later) creates problems by downplaying the vocational elements.[6]

Departments of nursing are in a different situation. They start with a number of disadvantages as compared with the pharmacists. First, graduate nursing is a more recent arrival on the academic scene:[7] it has not yet fully established its currency.[8] Even the more senior members of staff tend to lack familiarity with, or skill at, the subtleties of institutional politics. Second, although pharmacy has a high intake of women students (now running at some 60 per cent), nursing is even more predominantly female – a fact which sets it apart from most academic subjects. Third, the status of the nursing profession itself – in terms of salary, working conditions and degree of autonomy (as against its favourable public image) – is not particularly high, and this reflects back on the academic standing of departments of nurse education. Where such departments are located in a faculty of medicine, their plight is even more dismal, yielding as they must to the traditional snobbery of the medics about their paramedical co-workers. Fourth, the amount of research funding available is substantially less than that which comes the way of the pharmacists.

There are, however, some positive features which help to raise the political profile of nursing departments. As in the case of pharmacy, there is an abundance of highly qualified applicants for nursing degree courses, and school-leaving examination scores for successful entrants are invariably high. Subsequent employment rates, too, are good by any standard. Particularly in polytechnics where such departments have a working relationship with a prestigious teaching hispital, their standing tends to be further enhanced.

On the whole, graduate schools of nursing are largely self-contained for teaching purposes. Where it occurs, service teaching is a one-way process, enabling specialist knowledge to be bestowed by departments of physiology, psychology and the like: the nursing faculty are not seen to have much to offer in return. But the occasional outside contacts are welcomed, because they help to demonstrate to others the intellectual quality of the students, and thus to legitimate nursing as an academic discipline.[9]

The staff members, anxious to ensure their parity with other academics, experience a strong pressure to match community norms. In university departments, many of them strive to complete doctorates, to publish and to undertake funded research. These tasks are made more difficult because of the heavy time demands of clinical teaching, for which the institution normally gives no credit.

Teacher education is a more familiar part of the academic scene than nursing, though it has experienced a number of dramatic changes over the past decade. The effect of these changes has been, on the whole, to raise its status – which has never been high – at the expense of closing down many of the smaller and less prestigious institutions.[10] The main factors making for improvement in the reputation of education departments have been the generally stable recruitment record, the high figures for graduate employment (which are less impressive, however, than those for pharmacy and graduate nursing), and the steadily increasing volume of funded research.

Lecturers in education, like those in departments of graduate nursing, tend to seek academic respectability through the completion of doctoral research and through scholarly publication. These are indeed seen as the main criteria for promotion and for professional advancement in university departments, though administrative ability is an added consideration in polytechnics and colleges. Educationists also have additional, and institutionally unrewarded, demands for involvement in professional practice, but they are considerably lighter than those for academic nurses. Perhaps partly for this reason, academics in education appear to be more taken up with institutional activities – which in turn serves to increase their visibility and their claim to a legitimate place in the scholarly domain.

Relationships with the wider profession

Academic pharmacists, as has already been implied, pattern themselves closely on other academic groups in science faculties. Thus it is not surprising that their method of recruitment is very largely through the doctoral route. The standard pattern is for an aspiring lecturer to complete his or her pre-registration year in a hospital or community pharmacy, so gaining the key professional qualification, Membership of the Pharmaceutical Society, before embarking on a doctorate. Because of the current shortage of jobs in both universities and polytechnics, it is usually necessary then to undertake one or perhaps two post-doctoral assignments before gaining an established academic post.

Because of the highly competitive nature of a research-oriented career, many pharmacists have scant time and energy for more widely professional concerns – their peer networks will often comprise specialists in particular branches of the biological or physical sciences, rather than their fellow pharmacists. Academics who follow this career line may therefore have virtually no contact with practitioners in any of the three main categories – industrial, hospital or community pharmacy.

Other members of staff, less oriented towards pure science, may involve themselves in the type of applied investigation which brings contact with practitioners in drug companies and hospitals, but less commonly with community pharmacists (who account for some 70 per cent of the profession). There are also some academics who have a strong professional loyalty (inevitably, given the time constraints, at the expense of more conventionally academic pursuits). Some of them – though a decreasing number, as pressure for academic productivity mounts – own, manage or work as locums in retail pharmacies as a side activity. Some take a leading part in the work of the Pharmaceutical Society, both nationally and regionally, running and teaching on updating courses for practitioners.[11] The society is in fact particularly active in maintaining intra-professional links, through its series of regular conferences and through *The Pharmaceutical Journal*.

Yet, despite the fact that pharmacy is 'a close-knit profession – everybody more or less knows everybody else', there is a clearly discernible antipathy between academic and community pharmacists in particular. The latter recognize their academic colleagues as important sources of new knowledge, but complain that they are for the most part haughty and stand-offish: their heads are too often in the clouds and their feet too seldom on the ground. The academics in their turn are embarrassed by the 'small businessman' image associated with neighbourhood chemists, and consider that their emphasis on 'selling cosmetics, contraceptives, hot water bottles and sunglasses' damages the serious professional image which most of them consider every pharmacist should cultivate.

The gulf between academics and pharmacists working in hospitals and in industry is negligible in comparison. The former are indeed cited with particular approval, having now achieved a responsible place as specialists in prescribing drugs and monitoring therapy within the medical consultant's team. It is perhaps a mark of this parity of esteem that a number of joint appointments have recently been established between hospitals and pharmacy schools (though there are still problems here about the definition of roles); and that part-time visiting appointments are occasionally offered to distinguished pharmacists in industrial firms.

However, the embarrassing fact remains that industry only takes on some fifty to sixty pharmacists a year, and that hospital pharmacy is chronically under-subscribed, and recruits very poorly, because of its unfavourable salary structure. So the large majority of the thousand-odd students who complete their qualifications each year end up in community pharmacy, as what one interviewee unkindly (and inaccurately) described as 'graduate grocers'.

The pattern of academic–practitioner relationships in nursing is different in a number of respects. In the first place, academic nurses are expected to have had a significant period of experience as practitioners before they can be considered for appointment. That

is to say, recruitment does not follow the doctoral route characteristic of pharmacy, but adopts a professional pattern more characteristic of, for example, mechanical engineering. In the early years of
graduate nursing, some otherwise well-qualified applicants were
appointed without degrees, but the norm now is to have at least
a first degree in a relevant subject (not necessarily nursing) and
preferably a master's degree as well. As noted earlier, the pressure
to take a doctorate usually comes after a lectureship appointment
has been made.

Nursing departments, though some of them are under the shadow
of medical faculties, do not closely follow the patterns of behaviour
of medicine or science. Lecturers' attendance at academic conferences is more limited, and their peer network tends to be mainly
confined to nursing, with relatively less contact with cognate disciplines. In Gouldner's terms pharmacists are cosmopolitan in contrast with the localism of nurses.[12] Although many lecturers in
nursing see their prime loyalty as being to academic values, they
nevertheless retain a strong sense of professional identity. They are
thus inclined to be ambivalent about the direction in which their
energies should be channelled, and are liable to end up attempting
to satisfy both academic and professional demands at a level which
outsiders might consider unrealistic.

Their clinical teaching commitments, referred to earlier,
reinforce their links with the world of nursing practice, and encourage calls for their services on the part of the profession at large.[13]
Establishment figures in academic nursing thus find themselves
caught up in the work of the National Board, the Royal College
of Nursing and other professional bodies; in committees and commissions of inquiry; in publishing ventures; in programmes of continuing professional education; and in a variety of lecturing, examining and refereeing activities. The same, it might be remarked, is
true of other disciplinary groups as well: but the small size of the
academic community exacerbates the problem here, concentrating
the burdens on a limited number of people already struggling to
make research and teaching ends meet.

The degree of academic nurses' commitment to professional practice, then, is manifested in the time which they devote outside
accredited teaching hours (and indeed a fair amount of it during
academic vacations) to clinical teaching, and also in the degree to
which many of them are involved with activities in the nursing
world at large. It does not follow, however, that the relationships
between academics and practitioners are either close or reciprocal.

There is a considerable respect on the part of the professional
community for the range of contributions made by staff in depart-

ments of graduate nursing.[14] Such departments are regarded as a major resource on which the profession is able to draw for new ideas and sound judgements, but they are at the same time seen as distant, aloof and elite. So too, academic nurses, despite their professional commitment, experience a distance between themselves and the rest of the profession. The establishment of a very limited number of joint appointments between hospitals and schools of graduate nursing has not done much to close the gap. The appointees tend to be seen as second-class academics on the one side and as 'not proper nurses' on the other. As in pharmacy, their roles are inadequately defined and their contributions problematic. In spite of such attempts at mediation, the academics disapprove, some quite strongly, of current professional practice. They consider the majority of practising nurses to be under-qualified, inadequately informed and insufficiently professional in their approach. One might almost portray the lecturers as colonialists, regarding the native population with some contempt, seeking to take over the established institutions and endeavouring to superimpose their own norms and values.

In teacher education, the current pattern of staff recruitment is closer to that in nursing than to that in pharmacy. There was a stage, particularly in the late sixties and early seventies, when graduates with higher degrees in subjects such as psychology and sociology might be offered posts in teacher education without a requirement for professional experience. But that reflected a particular view of the curriculum for intending teachers which enjoyed only a brief spell in fashion. It is now quite rare for anyone to be appointed to a department of education without a substantial body of practical experience as a class teacher. A successful applicant would also be expected to have a master's degree – though a doctoral qualification is not unusual.

In terms of identity and allegiance, lecturers in education fall somewhere between pharmacists and nurses. They are neither so powerfully identified as pharmacy teachers with conventional academic norms, nor so strongly geared as graduate nursing faculty to the demands of professional practice. Some continue to attend conferences, read and contribute to journals, and subscribe to learned societies in their own parent disciplines (history, modern languages and the like); but the majority see their first allegiance as being to one or more explicitly educationist networks, which commonly include practitioners as well as academics.

While education lecturers maintain contact by these means with colleagues in other academic institutions and in the school world, many of them are also engaged in research. The pattern here is closer to pharmacy than to nursing, in that projects are often team-based rather than individual, and may involve substantial outside funding. As in most vocationally oriented departments, research is applied rather than pure in its emphasis, seeking results which have some relevance to practice. The active participation of school staff in such research is a recent, and growing, phenomenon.

The idea of joint appointments does not appear to have been taken up as extensively in education as it has in pharmacy and nursing. There is, however, some staff interchange, in that education lecturers are now required, as part of the process of course accreditation, to update their practical experience every four or five years by a temporary spell of school teaching, while an increasing number of practitioners are invited to contribute to aspects of initial teacher education courses.

But perhaps the most significant form of contact between teachers and teacher educators is through in-service activities. The provision of mid-career courses, whether full-time or part-time, whether leading to a qualification or non-award-bearing, is on a much more substantial scale than it was a decade ago – and greatly in excess of that available for nurses or community pharmacists. As a result, many practitioners will have had some recent contact with fellow professionals in universities, polytechnics and colleges; and virtually all academics in education will have had a chance to teach, or to teach alongside, their school-based colleagues.

In such circumstances, it is almost inevitable that the social and intellectual distance between lecturers and practitioners should be substantially reduced.[15] In the relatively recent past, the antipathy between the two was comparable with that already noted between staff in pharmacy schools and those working in retail pharmacies. Schoolteachers complained that education lecturers dealt in airy-fairy and irrelevant theories and were totally out of touch with the harsh realities of classroom life; lecturers despised teachers as intellectually illiterate and given to peddling out-of-date and educationally unacceptable practice. These attitudes seem quite rapidly to have been displaced by a general sense of mutual respect, and indeed of equality between professional counterparts. The change has had important repercussions for the nature of the teacher education curriculum, setting it apart from those for pharmacy and graduate nursing.[16]

Links between theory and practice

The brief accounts already given of institutional status and academic–practitioner relationships in pharmacy, graduate nursing and education have a direct bearing on how theory and practice are interrelated in each of the three domains. It is a common and difficult problem in any professional induction programme to determine how best to equip students with an appropriate background of theory and an armoury of relevant practical skills, while also demonstrating the relevance of each to the other. The three case studies examined in this chapter suggest that the solution is determined as much by social and political as by intellectual and pedagogic considerations.

As has already been noted, academic pharmacists are recruited in much the same way as members of pure science departments, and identify strongly with scientific norms. It is not altogether surprising, therefore, that they see the undergraduate curriculum as 'a fundamental education rather than a training course'. Their task, as they see it, is to equip intending practitioners with all they are likely to need in the way of a sound and comprehensive basis of scientific knowledge. Since the curriculum does not differentiate between industrial, hospital and community pharmacy, the coverage tends to be very wide. There is never enough time to fit everything in: so although there are growing pressures – not least from the students themselves – for a more strongly vocational emphasis, changes in the direction of vocationalism take place at the margins. For the most part, students are expected to acquire the necessary practical skills and know-how during their pre-registration year, when they have completed their degree course and are working as probationers in an appropriate professional setting.[17]

During their undergraduate years, pharmacy students have heavier workloads than most of their contemporaries. One member of faculty acknowledged this as 'a terrible problem – first year students are timetabled for practicals and lectures all day'. A critical outsider observed that 'they are regimented like A-level candidates – the course is deadening because it is so exam-oriented. There is much unnecessary material. There are few tutorials; students don't know how to use the library, and are unprepared to talk in seminars.' A thoughtful insider echoed these sentiments: 'It's generally acknowledged that the students are over-taught. There's a lot of repetition in the curriculum, but it's hard to know where to cut. Maybe we shouldn't fill the students so full of knowledge, and throw them into the labs to do even more titrations. And maybe we should try to replace some of our lectures with small group teaching.'

The students, highly selected as they are, have also to be highly motivated and hard-working to survive. Perhaps it is because they have a clear sense of identity, a strong vocational commitment and a powerful incentive in the form of a virtually guaranteed job at the end of the course that the drop-out and failure rate is relatively small. In almost direct contradiction to those who teach them, they show 'a strong preference for the patient-oriented aspects'. As the course goes on, they become increasingly dissatisfied with the theoretical elements, regarding anything which is not practically related as a diversion. All in all, as one academic pharmacist wanly remarked, 'they seem to regard the scientific stuff as what you have to go through to be a professional'.

The relationship between theory and practice in the pharmacy curriculum is at best, therefore, a distant one. With relatively few exceptions, there are only tenuous connections between the background scientific knowledge acquired during the undergraduate course and the practical capabilities developed mainly after graduation.[18] The links, in the words of the hard-worn academic cliché, are forged in the student's mind. It is not altogether fanciful, perhaps, to see this distance between theory and practice as a reflection not only of the strongly scientific orientation of the academic staff, but also of the social and intellectual distance between academics and community pharmacists. Whatever happens, the course 'must be about more than selling shampoo'. The risk of its becoming 'purely vocational' is that it might then end up as a sub-degree qualification – 'you could teach people to work in a shop in much less than three years'.

Although relationships between academics and practitioners in nursing are not significantly more comfortable, the approach to the theory–practice divide is different from that adopted in pharmacy.[19] The latter profession has opted for a simple territorial and temporal division – students learn theory from academics, then become apprentices who learn practice from practitioners. The teachers of nursing at degree level have preferred a more ambitious programme of territorial annexation. That is to say, academic nurses see their role as encompassing – in so far as it is possible – a total responsibility for the coverage of both theory and practice, thus reducing the practitioners' role to a minimum.

The reasons for this choice of strategy seem likely to include the strong residual sense of professional identity of academic nurses, together with their generally poor opinion of practitioners. It was observed earlier that recruitment to departments of nursing almost invariably followed a professional, rather than a doctoral, route. In consequence, most of those appointed are confident about their own skills as practitioners, and knowledgeable about the demands of professional practice. Unlike their counterparts in pharmacy departments, they do not see themselves as having to subscribe to the values of academic science; the status of their discipline is too marginal to make this a strong imperative. Instead, they have preferred to build up a corpus of 'nursing knowledge', based largely on empirical studies of ward practice, hospital management and community nursing.[20] Round this as yet limited, but growing, body of material central to the graduate nursing curriculum are clustered topics drawn from such disciplines as psychology and sociology on the one hand, and physiology and anatomy on the other.

The theoretical component of the degree course is complemented by a very substantial practical element.[21] Students are required to carry out a systematic programme of work placements in a variety of contexts, including psychiatric and geriatric wards as well as more routine hospital and community settings. This programme, alongside its academic counterpart, is enormously demanding in time, and undergraduate nurses are therefore allowed much shorter vacation periods than most other students.

With some exceptions, the relevance of theory to practice is clearly brought out. The relationships are developed in two main ways. First, the theoretical components of the curriculum are matched, in so far as it is possible to do so, against the sequence of work placements (for example, the lecture series on developmental psychology helps to introduce the placement in a paediatric ward). Second, it is the members of staff involved with professional topics in the core curriculum who normally accompany students into their practical settings, and are thus able on a day-to-day basis to identify significant connections between experiential and conceptual learning.[22]

However, it has to be acknowledged that this apparently close symbiosis between the worlds of the academic and the practitioner is not without its problems.[23] They stem mainly from the disjunction in values between academic and hospital nurses. The former tend to see the essence of nursing as patient-oriented, and to base their teaching strongly on the related ideology of 'the nursing process'.[24] The latter, ground down by the economic realities of the National Health Service while attempting to introduce new procedures, are forced to adopt a more narrowly task-oriented approach. The distinction is analogous with that of a progressive primary teacher, concerned with 'the whole child', as against a traditional teacher focused narrowly on the three Rs: a patient-oriented ward seeks to respond to people's personal and individual needs, while a task-oriented one focuses on routine tasks, treating all patients as largely depersonalized. Thus the degree students in nursing are strongly inculcated with a set of norms which are at odds with the established practices of the large majority of the profession.

It would seem that the theory–practice gap is closed, in this case, by creating an unrealistic image of practice which closely conforms to the academics' preferred theoretical values. None the less, because of the human limits of lecturers' supervision, there are times when the students are exposed to nursing practice as it is, rather than as their teachers maintain that it ought to be: that is, their experiences as surrogate apprentices under surrogate practitioners are compensated in part by their having to work as actual apprentices under actual practitioners.[25] Even so, it is interesting to note that, according to recent studies, many graduate nurses end up in psychiatric or community appointments, where their degree of autonomy is greater and their ability to treat 'the whole patient' is enhanced.

Teachers in departments of education, as we have seen, like lecturers in nursing, are recruited in the main through the professional as against the doctoral route. However, they retain a closer affinity with practitioners than do their counterparts in either nursing or pharmacy. This is partly a consequence of their applied research and consultancy activities, which quite commonly involve them in the day-to-day activities of schools; and partly a result of their role in post-experience training, which brings them into regular contact with a wide range of serving teachers.

The links between theory and practice, here as elsewhere, tend to mirror the relationships between theorists and practitioners. In teacher education they have become, over the years, increasingly close.[26] As in the case of nursing, and in contrast with pharmacy, lecturers have begun to establish a body of professionally based knowledge to replace the former reliance on 'the basic disciplines of education' (philosophy, psychology and sociology, perhaps with a sprinkling of history).[27] The more that theory is identified by its derivation from, or relevance to, the key issues of practice, the easier it becomes to bridge the gap between the two. At the same time, the cooperation of practitioners has been sought, and has generally been offered, in relation to various aspects of professional training. There are now several degree courses in which appropriately experienced school staff interview applicants, monitor teaching practice and assess students' teaching competence; and some in which they go beyond this to supply key elements of tuition. With a parallel programme of school placements run largely by practitioners and university activities run largely by academics, the need for close liaison between the two becomes obvious. The logical consequence is a practice-led programme in which the theoretical elements are for the most part determined by the demands of the students' practical experience.

The growing emphasis on professional practice, illuminated as it needs to be by theory, is underlined in the case of teaching by a requirement similar to that of the intending pharmacist – namely, a probationary year spent in a supervised work placement between graduation and the award of the professional qualification itself. Nurses – perhaps because of their exceptionally heavy undergraduate involvement in professional activities – are spared this extra requirement.

Figure 8.1 summarizes briefly the differing relationships which have been identified between theory and practice in the three professions, in terms of the respective roles of teacher and student, practitioner and apprentice.

Implications for the professional knowledge base

The analysis in the preceding pages underlines the contention that, although trainers and practitioners necessarily share a substantial area of professional knowledge, the relative emphases they place on its theoretical and practical elements are predictably dissimilar. As they progress through their courses, the students identify themselves increasingly as apprentice practitioners, and become less receptive to activities which are not clearly related to practice. Their responses serve to mark the contrasts between acquiring a conceptual framework relevant to the profession (the main desideratum of the trainers) and learning how to perform like a professional (the main desideratum of the practitioners).

In all three of the fields in question, the shared area of knowledge is thus seen from distinct perspectives by those whose prime task it is to inculcate it and by those mainly concerned to apply it in their daily lives. The divergence here is not an irremediable one, as the possibility of interchange or merger of roles between the two groups makes plain. None the less, the connections between the theory and practice of a profession, to which the distinction relates, would seem to merit some further scrutiny.

It is perhaps less fruitful to explore these connections in general terms than to examine their manifestation in particular occupational settings. The way in which the theory–practice distinction reveals itself is interestingly different in the cases of pharmacy, nursing and teaching. The comparisons between the three can be linked with the nature of the social relationships between trainers and practitioners; they may also help to throw some light on the types of theory prevalent in each field.

As we have seen, the practical knowledge of the professionals is played down by academic pharmacists; revised and reinterpreted by nurse tutors; and afforded a measure of legitimacy by teacher

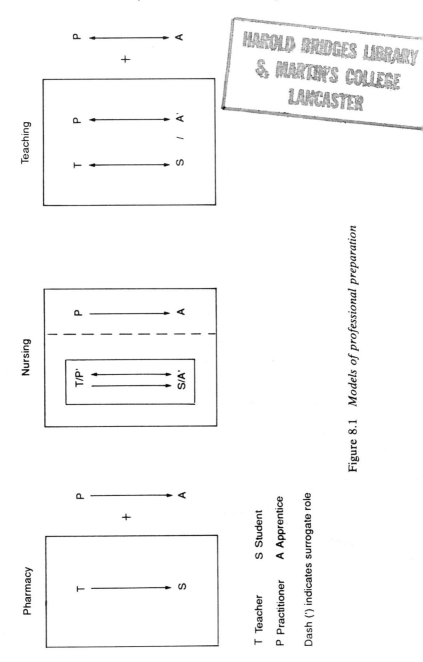

Figure 8.1 *Models of professional preparation*

educators. Theoretical knowledge, on the other hand, is heavily emphasized but not clearly related to practice in pharmacy courses; practice-oriented in nursing degree programmes but unshared with hospital nurses; and shared in some measure between lecturers and practitioners in the teaching profession.

The main orientations of the trainers themselves echo these distinctions. By and large, the staff of pharmacy schools classify themselves primarily as academics, maintaining some distance from community pharmacists. Those who hold posts in nursing schools are liable to categorize themselves less clearly as members of the academic world: they are in general more strongly identified with their fellow professionals, though holding themselves in some sense superior to them. Teacher trainers tend to occupy the middle ground, seeking to maintain a dual role as practically oriented academics and as academically oriented practitioners.

These relationships may arguably be reflected in the epistemological status of theory in each field. It can be held that professional knowledge does not directly depend on high-level general theories, such as may be discerned in some 'pure' academic disciplines. In pharmacy, the theoretical component is derived mainly from what Merton identified as 'theories of the middle range' in other relevant disciplines – notably chemistry, pharmacology and a number of specialisms in the biological sciences.[28] Nursing theories, in contrast, would appear to comprise mainly low-level generalizations – models, taxonomies and procedural rules – derived from practice. In teacher education, the pattern has shifted over the past decade or so from a dependence on theories drawn from diverse disciplinary bases – as in pharmacy – to a greater reliance on theories stemming from reflective practice – as in nursing. The level of educational theorizing none the less tends to be nearer to the middle range characteristic of pharmacy than to the limited empirical generalization which typifies nursing.

Such arguments have been developed more fully in another context.[29] However, in summarizing the main themes of this chapter, it may be fruitful to characterize the differing models of professional preparation that have emerged from the three case studies in terms of partition, patronage and partnership.

Pharmacy education offers a classic case of role differentiation. Pharmacy lectures are predominantly concerned with the scientific aspects of the field. Their courses are designed primarily to contribute to the formation of knowledgeable professionals, as against the development of effective practitioners. The latter task is relegated largely to the pre-registration year, for which the schools of pharmacy assume no responsibility. Much of the material taught is seen by students, as well as by practising community pharmacists, as irrelevant to operational needs. The partition between practice and theory results in limited institutional – and sometimes little personal – contact between academics and professionals.

In nursing, the trainers tend to maintain a tight control over both practice and theory: the role of the practitioners is marginal and incidental. The frequent assertion is that 'there are few good role models among practising nurses': the common attempt is to generate better ones. The consequence of this patronizing attitude is that, although practice and theory are closely intertwined, the practice is the practice of an idealized professional world, rather than one attuned to the exigencies of the average hospital ward.

The preparation of teachers involves a closer approximation to full partnership between trainers and practising professionals. The model here rests on a relationship of complementarity rather than duplication, but also calls for a close and regular interchange between the partners, involving a shared set of values and a reduction in the social distance found in many professional fields between the two. From the point of view of the students – those aspiring to the necessary licence to practise – this seems likely to offer the least unsatisfactory means of providing a sound professional knowledge base.

Appendix: nature of the research study

The research project on which the major part of this chapter has drawn was funded by the Department of Education and Science. It involved a study of the relevant literature, together with 102 semi-structured interviews (averaging 1½ hours in length).

The interviews were mainly with academic staff in the three subject fields in questions: eighteen divided between two pharmacy departments (one university, one polytechnic); twenty-two divided among three nursing departments (two university, one polytechnic); and twenty-eight divided among four teacher education departments (two university, one polytechnic, one college of higher education). The remaining interviews were with senior academic administrators in the institutions concerned, members of staff of relevant validating agencies, and practitioners in the three professions. In the cases of nursing and teacher education, interviewer bias was checked by using two interviewers working independently. In pharmacy, the overall findings were checked independently by five of the interviewees.

Themes for exploration included the nature of the discipline; research and research funding; modes of communication (networks, conferences, journals and so on); teaching issues; academic career patterns; roles of professional bodies; relationship of department with institution; issues of status; ethical and value questions.

The research team (working part-time for an equivalent of 150 person-days in all) comprised Dr R.A. Barnett, Assistant Registrar, Council for National Academic Awards; Professor R.A. Becher, Chairman of Education, University of Sussex; and Miss N.M. Cork, Senior Lecturer in Health Studies, Brighton Polytechnic. The work was completed between April and December 1985.

Notes

1 Glaser, 1979.
2 Barnett et al., 1986.
3 Blume, 1977.
4 Pharmaceutical Society, 1985.
5 Pharmaceutical Society, n.d.
6 Manasse and Groves, 1985.
7 Marsh, 1978; Owen, 1984.
8 Hayward, 1982.
9 Sheahan, 1980.
10 Taylor, 1981.
11 Mottram, 1985.
12 Gouldner, 1957.
13 Hunt, 1981.
14 Hunt, 1981.
15 Eraut, 1985.
16 CNAA, 1983, 1984; HMI, 1983.
17 Pharmaceutical Society, 1984.
18 Pharmaceutical Society, 1980.
19 English National Board, 1985.
20 McGlynn, 1984; Roberts, 1985; Smith, 1983.
21 Quinn, 1980.
22 House, 1977.
23 Wood, 1985.
24 Yura and Walsh, 1978.
25 Marson, 1982.
26 Barnett, 1987.
27 Hirst, 1983.
28 Merton, 1967.
29 Becher, 1989.

9

The knowledge aspect of professionalization: the case of science-based nursing education in Sweden

Aant Elzinga

Professional groups look to academic research for the theoretical core needed to validate their knowledge, and obtain official recognition through the institution of degree programmes. It is a sign of a coming of age when they can point to the beginnings of a production of Masters and Ph.D. students, professorial appointments and other research positions and tasks in 'their area'. The scientification of the knowledge core has two important functions. For one it sets up a demarcation *vis-à-vis* an earlier phase when this knowledge was largely tacit, non-formalized and transmitted by an apprenticeship tradition. Second, it is meant to distinguish an occupational group from its neighbours in the same arena.

In a modern hospital, for example, we meet a wide range of occupational groups today that make independent claims to professionalism. Physicians enjoy a long-standing recognition of their professional status, and they still monopolize the market of medical knowledge. As an occupational group they also dominate the power structures of hospitals and health care and defend that position by reference to their special expertise. However they are now being joined by nurses, laboratory and X-ray technicians, physiotherapists, occupational therapists and others who are also making use of science to exercise their skills. These groups are now defining parts of their knowledge in terms of scientific specialities, and seek recognition and more leverage at their places of work by pressing for new arrangements whereby some of them can go on to training for research.

In this chapter I consider nurses. This is an occupational group that has expanded very rapidly since the 1960s in most countries. A characteristic feature of Scandinavia is that since 1945 the growth of the public sector has been heavily skewed in favour of the health and care system, and this has brought women into the labour market. In this context it might be said that nursing belongs to the welfare occupations which have grown with the development of the welfare state. The focus in this chapter is on the Swedish situation, where nurses' training was brought into the higher educational system through a university and college reform of 1977 which requires all higher vocational studies to have a scientific knowledge base.

The structure of the chapter is as follows: nursing is first considered in an historical perspective, in Sweden and then more generally. This is followed by a brief sketch of the problem of defining a unique identity for a new scientific discipline like nursing research. In general terms the problem is posed as one of developing social and cognitive legitimation strategies for a new discipline – 'social' in the sense of pointing to important social groups which can be said to be beneficiaries of the new scientific field; 'cognitive' in the sense of developing arguments that motivate the need of a new kind of research and delineate its character and content compared to other academic disciplines. In the case of nursing, the welfare state is seen to be an important source of legitimation for a new academic niche, at least in the Swedish situation. Nursing is understood as a welfare occupation, and its attachment to research is seen to be politically mandated on the highest levels of decision-making.

After the foregoing review of some problems relating to the emergence of professionalization and a new discipline of nursing science, the chapter turns more explicitly to the Swedish higher educational reform of 1977, which led to the creation of special chairs in 'nursing care research' at several – especially the newer – universities. It is found that the conflicts and legitimatory discourses that evolved around these events may be mapped out in terms of social and cognitive legitimation strategies for professionalization. At the same time, conflicts and tensions also reveal a deeper dimension, where one finds that professionalization is only one of two over-arching strategies used by nurses to advance their aims. The other strategy used is trade-union struggle, and in some parts of the nursing community it seems to be preferred over professionalization. The latter, it is feared, may just turn out to be a new form of bureaucratization.

Nursing – an expanding welfare occupation

In absolute numbers, nurses in Sweden have increased roughly fourfold during the past couple of decades (Table 9.1).[1] This rapid increase should be seen within the context of the Swedish welfare state. Today the number of nurses is in the order of 100,000.

Table 9.1 *Expansion of nursing*

	Nurses (no.)
1962	21,000
1970	34,000
1979	65,000[a]
1984	85,000

[a] For 17,000 physicians

The steady increase in the numbers of nurses follows a general trend of expansion in the welfare state. From 1965 to 1975 the number of persons employed in the public sector and services in Sweden nearly doubled. On the average, the increase was in the order of 50,000 persons per year during the period 1970–1975, with a peak figure nearer to 60,000 for 1974 and 1975, about 17,000 of these being in the hospital, health care and social work areas. More recent figures give an increase of numbers employed in lower-status jobs in the hospital and health-care sector, from 49,000 in 1958 to 203,000 in 1982. This gives an indication of the rapid growth of only one part of the general sphere of social reproduction represented by schools, social services and health care.[2]

A recent survey reveals that in Sweden, health-care workers trained in university programmes are to a much greater extent recruited from the working classes than is the case for physicians, lawyers or, for that matter, architects, engineers and journalists. The higher professional categories are dominated by persons coming from the homes of academics. About half of those who were accepted for Ph.D. studies in Sweden during the years 1965–1976 came from the homes of academics and higher managerial cadres.[3] According to a report from the Swedish Central Bureau of Statistics cited here, a rough estimate is that 80 per cent of children from academic homes begin university and college studies, while the corresponding number from working-class homes is about 10 per cent.

In their ambitions to professionalize, nurses thus find themselves entering an academic world where the middle classes and middle-class values dominate. This provides special difficulties for those who elect to go into research, and it tends to differentiate them from the main body of nurses, who for the most part come from working-class homes – including rural families and those employed in services. It also means that a majority of nurses may find other strategies more appropriate than professionalization when it comes to advancing their aims. For example, will professionalization facilitate research based on a caring perspective, or will it contribute to

an assimilation of mainstream scientific norms and criteria, leading
to a separation of the new discipline of nursing science from its
practical underpinnings in the real world of bedside care in modern
mechanized hospitals? This is a question that comes up, and in this
chapter we cannot give any definite answer.

Another aspect that must be taken into account, but which is not
developed at length here, is the fact that nursing is a semi-profession dominated by women. What does this mean for the agenda
of nursing research, and does it provide special difficulties in a
health- and hospital-care system in which professionalization comes
into conflict with a hierarchy that is dominated by physicians, the
majority of whom (in Sweden almost 70 per cent) are men?

During the past decade this issue has been brought forward in
feminist literature. There is considerable controversy as to the
extent to which health care and hospitals, or, for that matter,
research, would become more 'caring' and less bureaucratic-mech-
anical, if the medical profession was dominated by women. Some
sociologists have assumed that, as more and more women become
physicians, they will change the hierarchical structures, while others
firmly maintain that they will instead assimilate the dominant attitudes in their profession, much the same as seems to occur in
science.[4]

Nursing from a craft to science

In Sweden, as in some other countries, although nursing is still
basically a craft comparable to, say, carpentry or plumbing, like
these it has gone a long way from its original character in order to
adapt to the conditions of the modern industrial era. Originally it
was regarded as a calling – the Florence Nightingale image of
the middle-class woman devoted to her duty is the classical one.
Nightingale herself, in her book *Notes on Nursing* refers to nursing
care as an art which, if it is to maintain that character, requires
absolute devotion and careful training, just as much as in the case
of an artist or sculptor. In this sense it is a calling of the same kind
one finds among craftsmen – what drives the cobbler to make shoes,
the carpenter to make cabinets, and so on is a satisfaction of
craftsmanship, and pride in work well done. In the case of nursing,
Nightingale says, it is not dead clay or cold marble, but living
bodies that one has to deal with.

In 1860 Florence Nightingale founded the first school to train
nurses, at St Thomas's Hospital in London. Pupils who went
through it received a certificate, usually after a year. Today a
nursing education takes several years, and its knowledge core

includes elements from many different disciplines, while the human being is sometimes rather abstractly defined in terms of a holistic system comprising physical, social and psychological sub-systems.

The industrialization of the knowledge-producing process makes itself felt in nursing also in the practical activity of nurses and other health workers, and in their ideology and demands. Nurses have moved towards a professional self-conception, and their tasks include highly specialized interventions using the most advanced medical technology. The rapid development of medical technology itself has become a problem. In Sweden, for example, during the years 1977–1983 there were 410 reports of accidents and short-comings in the application of modern equipment, costing twenty-nine patients their lives and causing 212 injuries.[5] In four out of five cases this was a result of technical failures or malconstruction, and in the remainder a question of improper handling due to a lack of knowledge or misunderstanding. In some cases nurses have been personally charged and brought to court, which has prompted a review of medical technical safety rules and systems of responsi-bility at the work place. The mechanization of hospitals and hospital care has been a strong driving force in the transformation of nursing as a job. Centralization of hospital care and its integration into national welfare schemes is another. More recently there has been a move toward decentralization and putting the onus on self-care as far as possible.

In general one may sketch the course of development in nursing in four stages:

1   a *calling* followed by middle-class women who built up a fund of practical knowledge permeated with specific values peculiar to their background;

2   *semi-professionalization*; or the organization of nurses into a semi-profession with its own traditions, formalized qualification criteria and career patterns, as well as associated values on the part of some to seek status and strive for professional acknowl-edgement. At the same time, expansion of numbers brought in women from working-class homes, who gradually came to make up a majority. This second phase seems to have been sped up with the centralization of hospital care, a certain specialization of functions, and an expansion of tasks requiring additional skills and knowledge;

3   the '*scientification*' and 'technification' of nursing care, in the sense of, on the one hand, basing the knowledge core on modern science, and on the other, a further formalization of task division associated with administrative and technological

changes in the health- and hospital-care systems. This third phase may be identified by the wide-ranging discussion and debate which is often associated with it, relating to the 'scientific' character of the emerging discipline, its proper contents, methodology and relationship to other disciplines within the same general area, which includes medicine. In some countries there have been academic programmes for BNSc and MNSc for many years, but it is interesting to note that these are frequently situated in the Faculty of Applied Science rather than in the Faculty of Medical Science. Integration of nurse training programmes into the academic system is preparatory to the fourth phase, professionalization;

4   *professionalization*, characterized by the establishment of an independent research capability that is associated with nursing, the introduction of special university chairs and Ph.D. programmes, as well as new career patterns partly based on research or research training. In this fourth phase the complex interplay of 'internal' and 'external' factors continues, and the search for interdisciplinarity to bridge the disintegrative tendency of specialization is also evident.

Changes in the hospital-care system

Parallel to the development that has been sketched here, with a focus on the emerging profession as such, trends or changes in the health- and hospital-care system must also be considered. The environment in which the professionals work and seek to make their mark provides at one and the same time constraining and enabling determinants. There are degrees of specialization, task differentiation, hierarchy in levels of authority, as well as the need to further develop skills and specialist knowledge.

In their on-the-job situation nurses and other health-care workers are responsible for the daily functioning of the ward, while physicians and medical specialists are responsible for diagnosis and treatment of patients. There is a division between caring and curing, a basic differentiation that continues even when nurses increasingly acquire supervisory roles. This latter trend is closely associated with the increasing complexity of modern hospital and health care. Historically one can identify four phases of development. In each of these 'care' is given a different focus and meaning. Maj-Len Sundin, Head Nurse at Oslo City Hospital, in charge of 3,000 of the 4,500 employees there, has described the four phases in the evolution of nursing care as follows.[6]

The *pre-scientific* period which came around 1860 involved 'care' as an act of devotion, not subject to special demands;

– thereafter came a period dominated by *medicine*, which began around 1920, when 'care' was identified with practical medicine; nurses assisted physicians and became low level apprentices; patients' recovery and further needs were exclusively discussed by the physicians themselves, without nurses being present;

– a third period, beginning around 1950, was marked by a focus on *interdisciplinarity*, as nursing care became a kind of technology, but not yet a science in its own right. Here one can speak of a 'technification', requiring knowledge from different disciplines in the natural and social sciences. It was a period marked by a dissolution of the traditional identity of nursing as a calling, but still no replacement by a new identity that might receive its definition through a recognition of a unique and independent form of specialist knowledge.

– the *scientific* period began around 1970, when the new form of specialist knowledge itself began to be recognized as a form of science in its own right; this was the beginning of the exploration of boundaries to define an independent scientific field with its own theoretical development and functional specificity; at the same time in this fourth phase one witnesses a return to the original notion of nursing as a calling, which is now grafted onto a scientific core with the help of a philosophical discourse and the incorporation of humanistic studies which hopefully would contribute to an holistic perspective and attention to quality of life. Thus the aspect of a 'calling' assumes an ideological role, and other forms of academic knowledge are introduced in order to professionalize what previously was an unquestionable part of the tacit knowledge of the craft.

It is interesting to note here in the fourth phase a recognition of the tension between tacit and professional knowledge, and the attempt to use studies in the humanities and social sciences as a means to counteract the fragmentation that came with centralization and rationalization of the hospital system in the previous phase. At this point there also emerges a latent ambivalence with respect to professionalization itself, since this process is embedded in and depends on the transformation of a hierarchical and differentiated work-place structure. On the one hand, the centralization of the hospital- and health-care system is a precondition for and tends to reinforce professional career and status ambitions of nurses, affording a social and material basis for task differentiation and specialist knowledge. On the other hand, the present trend of scientification, preparing the way for professionalization, is itself a continuation of a rationalization process with extreme functional differentiation in the labour process, perpetuating social differences in status between male- and female-dominated occupations, and between high and low wage groups in society as a whole.

Nursing care: science or ideology?

In the previous section it was noted how professionalization implies a significant degree of specialization. The emergence of nursing-care research as a new speciality can be seen both as a continuation of this specialization, and as the expression of the search for a professional identity. In both cases the focus on interdisciplinarity and the renaissance of the idea of nursing as a calling signifies a reaction to certain aspects of specialization, and an attempt to overcome the disparities of the mechanized hospital where the patient is reduced to a number, a variety of organs, a piece of luggage on an assembly line, or a statistical budgetary figure. The ideology at present surrounding nursing-care research is not only internally generated; it is at the same time a reflection of the changing politics and ideology of health and hospital care in society. The present ideology with its emphasis on holism, putting the patient back in the centre, when seen in a wider perspective, is a manifestation of a movement away from the previous emphasis on medical, technical and organizational aspects of health and hospital care. Corresponding roughly to the different phases in nursing described above, there are three distinct orientations in the approach to patients. At the outset nursing care was something to be carried out at home: it was home-based. With the expansion of medicine and the emphasis on hospitals, technification of care brought with it a certain reification of the patient. Now we see an attempt to decentralize, in some cases linked to a re-privatization of medical care within the welfare state. The notion of putting the patient back into the centre, and promoting self-care and coping systems, which are reflected in modern theories of nursing and patient care, is thus generated externally in society as a new ideology, internalized at the same time as part of the process by which nursing is being provided with a scientific basis in its theoretical core.

Translated into the discourse of nursing-care research, the move away from technification and towards a more holistic approach takes on philosophical overtones. There have been several conscious efforts in the nursing science literature to introduce holistic perspectives with a base either in natural science or the humanities. At an early stage in the scientification phase, systems theory was introduced as a way of connecting the great variety of aspects and 'systems' studied. This, however, carried an ideological tone, where human individuals are reified. Later, and this has been especially prominent in Scandinavia, there was an anti-positivist debate, and attempts were made to attach consciously to alternative theories of science, such as 'hermeneutics', which might help legitimate a break with a scientification in a positivist sense. This move also involved a demarcation and declaration of independence at the level of philosophy of science *vis-à-vis* what was considered to be the dominant (positivist) ideal in medicine. To be sure, there is still contention around the very concept and implications of scientification and nursing-care research. Its very legitimacy and possibility is sometimes questioned, not only by the medical profession but also by the rank and file of nursing, where trade-unionist strategies are favoured. In the eyes of both these categories, nursing-care research may well smack more of ideology than science. As ideology, 'nursing-care research' corresponds to the ethos generated as part of a professionalization strategy. As science, it corresponds to skills needed in the performance of supervisory and caring functions in the modern health- and hospital-care system.

Rival philosophical standpoints thus seem to have counterparts in the politics of knowledge in modern society. In the Swedish case the problem of transition from vocational, crafts-based knowledge to scientific knowledge became particularly clear when a major university reform of 1977 began to be implemented, bringing all higher vocational studies, including those that lead to certificates in nursing, into the academic system. The different viewpoints on what was to be meant by scientification, and which of the rival philosophies of science within the academic system one should lean upon, developed at a time when there already existed a more general polarization in science. In the wake of the oil crisis, the student protest movement and science criticism in various contexts like environmentalism, women's studies and the labour movement, there existed a strong tension between philosophies of professional science and those of the so-called alternative movements. Nurses in search of a scientific identity were also influenced by this.

A particular impulse that has in some cases affected both the perspective and theoretical content of nursing science literature is the feminist movement. Women's studies, and discussions relating to feminist epistemology in particular, have given rise to a notion of gender bias in science. In this context men are associated with 'macho' approaches, typified by technocracy and manipulative or intrusive techniques, while the female gender is held to represent and promote a 'caring' rationality, totally different from the cold instrumentality of means–ends rationality of established institutions. Even if there is considerable disagreement as to the ultimate underpinnings of this caring anti-technocratic attitude and how it is generated – by specific female qualities or by selective social structures and mechanisms that draw women into caring occupations – there is no doubt that this discussion has influenced nurses and the understanding of nursing-care research. Some professors of nursing science today openly advocate feminist perspectives in their research, and this may already have had some impact on theories of nursing.

Social and cognitive legitimation strategies

When a new scientific discipline is to be developed, its advocates have to bring forward arguments relating both to its relevance and specific scientific status. This is also the case when nursing is brought into the academic sphere. There are many who at the outset will ask, 'Is this really "science"?' Others will ask, 'What is it good for?' Arguments aimed at answering such questions are in practice often intertwined, but in some cases they may be teased out and reconstructed as the manifestation of cognitive and social legitimation strategies.[7] The cognitive strategy deals with the question of locating a new research speciality on the map of science; therefore it will have to employ arguments and definitions that, on the one hand, distinguish the new area from the crafts-based know-how from which it emerges, and, on the other hand, boundaries have to be marked off *vis-à-vis* existing disciplines with different traditions. The social legitimation strategy which runs parallel to this has to be able to point to the utility of the new discipline, and thus references will be made to various beneficiaries for whom it is or should be relevant and important.

An example of such legitimation strategies may be found in the history of ecology as a discipline. At an early stage ecology did not exist as an independent, university-based discipline. Elements of theory could be found in a number of biological subjects, while ecological practice existed in various traditional forms of agriculture, fishing and forestry. It was not until much later that all of these were brought together. Certainly, ecology as a theoretical field was gradually established, but it did not win force until arguments for it were combined with a social legitimation strategy, in which the discipline's role for understanding and protecting a threatened and polluted environment could be demonstrated.

Social legitimation strategies maintain an element of ideology, while cognitive legitimation strategies have to distinguish science from ideology. The element of ideology is important when it comes to appealing to a specific social group, to politicians, clients or members of an occupation. In this case references to special codes of ethics are also important. In the case of nursing research, its social significance may be claimed by referring to the need for more efficient and highly qualified care in hospitals, or to the expanding numbers of nurses who need a scientific knowledge base. Welfare benefits to a larger population are also significant, and the idea of nursing as a calling may be given a new interpretation. In some cases a social movement connection – say, to feminism – may also be invoked as an argument in favour of the new science.

Reconstructing cognitive legitimation strategies is more difficult. By and large they can be taken to involve three steps. In the first the advocates of a new discipline point to the lack of a particular sort of specialist knowledge. A 'territory' on the map of science is found to be uncharted, and arguments are put forward in favour of filling this gap in our scientific knowledge. The second step of the strategy is to demarcate the subject matter of the new speciality, distinguishing it from other, neighbouring and already established older areas of scientific enquiry. This may be called the step of 'disciplinary demarcation', a form of closure at the cognitive level.

The third step in a cognitive legitimation strategy is to go further and sketch something of the positive contents of the new speciality.

Altogether, the three steps in the cognitive part of a strategy for legitimation serve to point to specifics of the new discipline, establish its scientific credentials, and show how it fits in *vis-à-vis* other disciplines in the academic system. From the vantage point of the theory of science one might speak of the strategy as stipulating an ontology and a methodology. That is, it delineates a specific object of knowledge, and how one should proceed to acquire scientific knowledge of it.

It should be evident that the three steps alluded to do not in fact appear as clearly and distinctly as they have been reconstructed here in this very general way. In actual practice the 'steps' are more like elements in a discourse of legitimation. Of course there is a kind of progression in the way in which these elements are unfolded, and frequently the chronological chain of events is marked by the emergence of controversy at specific points. Thus the postulation of a need for new scientific knowledge and the demarcation *vis-à-vis* established disciplines will evoke criticism from those who see their stakeholder interests in existing disciplines threatened, or their cognitive monopoly challenged. When it comes to filling in the new field with positive content, differences also arise within the community which has been formed around the new subject – differences regarding the proper orientation, methodologies and research priorities.

Legitimation through welfare

Nursing belongs to a category of welfare state occupations or, in short, 'welfare occupations'. These derive their social legitimacy from their function in the welfare state, and this carries over into the legitimation of new areas for research.

A characteristic feature of welfare occupations is that their members are delegated to discharge various obligations that the welfare state has *vis-à-vis* its citizens. In exchange for this they are authorized by the state to perform particular tasks, and the state helps implement certain social and cognitive closure mechanisms, in part based on higher educational credentials. The knowledge and skills required are conditioned by the fact that members of these occupations deal with people, ideally in a direct face-to-face relationship. For this reason they are sometimes referred to as 'soft' occupations or semi-professions, as distinct from the 'hard' professions which deal with material things (cf. Inga Hellberg in this volume).

For the most part the practice of such occupational groups today is institutionalized in the public sector, or in forms of self-regulated voluntary activities that receive subsidies from the public purse.

Members of welfare occupations, when they formulate a set of ideal norms, develop a perspective on how to steer their interactions with those they 'treat'; and this treatment then has to proceed in accordance with professional goals and norms. When they articulate a conception of their own role in society, which is important in outlining social and cognitive legitimation strategies for research, members of such occupations usually invoke three important premises:[8]

1 they ideally provide help or deliver services in a face-to-face contact situation with their clients (patients, students, welfare recipients);
2 their services are regarded as essential, not only by welfare recipients, but also for the well-being of society as a whole;
3 ideally, welfare occupations are founded on humanitarian and non-commercial values.

The third point implies that when a 'research attachment' is sought in the academic system, elements of the humanities and social sciences become important for these occupational groups, even though this may not lend them the same scientific status that engineers receive from the natural sciences and physicians from medicine. All three points figure centrally in legitimation discourses surrounding professionalization strategies in nursing.

Apart from nursing there are several other occupations where one can see the same premises invoked in arguments for professional status – for example, in the case of day-care personnel, kindergarten teachers, social workers, teachers of many kinds, those who provide services for the elderly, vocational guidance counsellors and many other groups that would fit in under the general definition of welfare occupations. The demand for research is an old one in some cases (school research in the case of teachers), and in others it is just beginning to be articulated (for example, vocational guidance counselling research is a novelty in Sweden). In some respects physicians, forming a well-established welfare profession with strong scientific bonds and a clear-cut ethical code, seem to serve as an ideal-type for some of the semi-professions that have been boosted by the expansion of the welfare state. At the same time it becomes important to specify ways in which there are differences compared to the older professions, including the medical one.

In the case of nurses the concept of 'care' is frequently evoked in order to point to something unique in their area of endeavour, something going back to the old notion of a calling, which is being overlaid by references to specialist knowledge and its independent links to science. As we have already noted, this means that legitimatory discourses both for nursing science and professionalization easily take on ideological overtones. In practice, one of the difficult things has been to try to unpack the concept of 'care' in order to translate it into a discourse of science.

One thing that welfare occupations have in common is a stakeholder interest in the way the state and agencies at other (municipal and county) levels distribute and use resources paid out from the taxpayers' purse. They have a symbiotic relationship with the welfare institutions that maintain them, and thus their own existence contributes to the legitimation of this very system in modern society from which they in turn derive much of their own special legitimation and claim to professionality.

'Women's work' – a delegitimizing factor?

While the connection to welfare and welfare machinery constitutes a basis for legitimatory claims, a semi-profession like nursing is also beset by definite constraints which are shared by many other welfare occupations. The fact is that many welfare occupations are dominated by women, which in present-day society functions as a delegitimating factor, if not in theory at least in practice. In other words, the members of these occupations, both by virtue of the work they do and the fact that a majority of them are women, face special difficulties in their pursuit of professionalization. The world of higher-status professions and the social and cognitive hierarchies of science and the traditional academic system, as well as hospital- and health-care institutions, tend to be dominated by men, male attitudes and male perspectives. Three particular aspects of this problem may be noted.

First of all, welfare work tends easily to become equated with 'women's work'. Women are supposed to have innate 'caring' abilities, and their march into this part of the labour market may be seen as an extension of task repertoires that they have traditionally had in the home. In the history of nursing, before the focus turned on hospitals, care was also mainly provided in the home, and the notion of nursing as a calling still carries overtones that go back to this situation. 'Society has been reluctant to be serious about academic education for nurses because nurses do in the hospital (bathe, feed, comfort, soothe, discipline) what all women do at home'.[9] Also there is the matter of wage scales – women's work is not as highly valued in economic terms as the kinds of activities carried out by men or male-dominated professions.

Second, there is the fact that the boards of trustees, hospital administrations, top decision-making bodies in universities and so on are predominantly made up of males. In hospitals, even if the domain of nurses expands with the institution of a cadre of supervisory nurses, these are still dependent on decisions made higher up in the hierarchy, by physicians and administrators, who are often men. The paradox is that the welfare state on the one hand gives nurses greater responsibilities and encourages independent thought. On the other hand, new health- and hospital-care legislation introduced in Sweden reaffirms the physicians' total decision-making power and overall responsibility for the whole ward. Against this some spokespersons for nursing science have argued for a de-institutionalization which would involve a form of organization in which nurses, physicians and patients can meet on equal terms and plan together. This may be seen at one and the same time as a manifestation of both a democratic and professional demand on behalf of nurses.[10]

Third, at a more general level there is a segregation of the labour market which cuts across professions, with men tending to cluster more heavily in the private sector which pays more, and women in the same occupation more apt to appear in the public domain with less pay. This is a structural inequality that runs through society as a whole (cf., further, Inga Hellberg in this volume).

Higher education and the establishment of linkages with and inroads into research are important for professionalization, but they do not in themselves break the barriers that meet professional aspirations of women in the welfare occupations. Therefore social and cognitive legitimation strategies for professionalization in these cases may be heavily overlaid with broader strategies and discourses referring to equality and democracy. Given that most of the women who go into nursing now come from the working classes, and will for the most part maintain their strongest ties there, the differentiation introduced by the introduction of research opportunities can be seen not only as a promotion of professional aspirations. It also represents the breakaway of a small elite who are successful in finding their way into the academic research system and with it into what Poulantzas has called a petty bourgeoisie of a new type, based on the rationalization of modern society and an expansion of specialist knowledge-related functions.

Given the various double bonds and double loyalties of members of the welfare occupations, it is not surprising to find professionalization strategies, including the introduction of new scientific specialities, generating conflicts and tensions. These conflicts also appear in the legitimatory discourses surrounding the emergence of nursing research in Sweden. There we find conflicts at the social level – for example, between nurses and physicians – translated into conflicts over knowledge, methodology and ideals of science. As I shall try to indicate in a later section, debate over philosophy of science within the hospital- and health-care system recapitulates tensions over power and authority.

The institutional situation of nursing research

A common development of nursing research in North America has been to go through three stages. First, there is the institutionalization of university-based nursing schools. Second, research-based education was introduced in the form of MNSc programmes, aimed at research utilization in the nursing sector. A third phase has been the introduction finally of Ph.D. programmes in order to create a cadre of researchers with nursing as a speciality.

In Sweden the field has been going through the same phases, only in ultra-rapid sequence. This is largely due to the university reform of 1977, whereby nursing education was incorporated into the academic system across the whole country. Now teaching has to be founded on a cognitive basis in science. Nursing has to have its own characteristic 'discipline', and a research potential has to be built up.

The first professorship in nursing research was created at Umeå University and the second is located at the new Health University in Linköping. At the Tema University in Linköping, the Health 'tema' has introduced a professorship specifically oriented to 'the internal work of the ward, its theory and ethics'.

It is interesting to note these first institutional settings. Umeå is a very young university, created in the 1960s. The Health University in Linköping is a completely new venture (1986), merging the faculty of medicine of the university with the 'ward' College of Östergötland County. It also boasts a unique approach to curricula, providing some courses where nurses, medical students and physiotherapists can all study together. Lena Lundh, interim rector at the time, hoped this experiment in breaking disciplinary and social barriers would in the long term help change the health-care system: 'Today doctors do not know what nursing care is, and nurses do not know what occupational and physiotherapists can do. It is too prestige-filled, one plays out the other and the doctor's treatment goes before everything else'.[11]

It is interesting to see too how county authorities responsible for hospital and health care in their regions are pushing for nursing research, while the older universities have been more hesitant. However, in all the major universities moves are now afoot to create special professorships or some form of coordinated research capability of a permanent kind in the area of nursing. As one informant we interviewed put it, the medical people are starting to move, and once they do, they tend to do so quickly. Whether it is out of concern or because they want to have the new discipline under control is an open question.

What we see are three different institution-building strategies: (1) to create an institution first and let a person grow with the task (Umeå); (2) to wait until there are a greater number of competent researchers around before introducing a professorship competition (Uppsala and Gothenburg); (3) to rely on foreign expertise until the field has been well established in Sweden (Lund).

Already there are networks and many projects in the new field throughout Sweden. According to the first professor, Astrid Norberg (Umeå), 'the field is becoming increasingly recognized, and there are now more than 50 researchers working on dissertations in nursing science. There is even a tendency toward male interest in what has understandably (95 per cent of Sweden's nurses are women) been a female dominated field'.[12] This statement was made a few years ago, and today the number of doctoral students has almost doubled since then.

Under the surface, however, there is still tension, with rival views regarding the focal points of the new area of science. To understand the background it is useful to go back to the late 1960s when nursing was just beginning to be earmarked for science. At that time when nurses made research demands they pointed to three main areas that have since come to play an important role in the cognitive legitimation strategy. One is the labour process in the ward (sociology), another is curricular planning and teaching (pedagogy) and a third area concerns administrative and organizational questions. Later (1968) the World Health Organization (WHO) adopted the latter two in its documents, and added 'nursing practice'. This definition of *nursing education*, *nursing service* and *nursing practice* as three 'territories' for a nursing science discipline was also adopted in Sweden when the National Board of Universities and Colleges prepared a review.[13] However, there was no clear conception as to the inner connections between the three territories, and soon conflicts developed. The main point of the early discussions and reviews, however, was to point to the need for a special kind of research that was not adequately covered by existing disciplines. This is the first step of a cognitive legitimation strategy.

Conflicts and problems of demarcation

Most of the projects started in 1974–1978, it was found, were carried out by researchers without a background in nursing. As nurses were brought in to define research topics and perspectives it became evident that the concept of nursing was very diffuse, and hence it was difficult to point to the theoretical core of nursing research as a new discipline.

Hereupon soon followed the step in which the main focus of the strategy became to distinguish 'nursing care' and nursing-care research from clinical medical practice. In this connection the concept of 'clinical nursing-care research' was introduced. This marked the development of tensions between nurses and other groups, medical practitioners, but also physiotherapists. The latter, because their activities involve physical rehabilitation of patients, tend more naturally to assume a natural scientific perspective, which also dominates in the medical profession. In order to distinguish themselves, nurses began to invoke concepts from the philosophy of science, creating controversy and a polarization around two major orientations. The one, the ideal of science subscribed to by the medical profession, was now described as 'positivist', while some of the new nurse researchers advocated a 'hermeneutic' approach for their own speciality, thus emphasizing a methodology where the medical faculty cannot make any claims to priority.

Those researchers who advocated a hermeneutic approach wished to stress the communicative understanding dimension in nursing, contrasting it to the cold objectifying and analytical methodology of clinical and medical research. Another way of developing the same point was to distinguish 'caring' from 'curing', and to build claims on the unique way in which nurses deal with the 'whole' person. However, this was to ride more on the rhetorical and ideological connotation and less on the scientific definition of the term. The latter also became increasingly difficult as other groups like physiotherapists, occupational therapists, and laboratory technicians began to do research and refused to be classed outside the umbrella of nursing research on this basis.

Clearly, it became important for nurses to develop special niches for research, and it was valuable if these had an impact on their professional aspirations. This is clear from the point made by one spokesperson when she noted how 'previously education taught submission and it [the new Health University in Linköping] can certainly help create nurses that are a bit tougher. The new professorship in nursing research also provides an opportunity to develop our profession'.[14] Pedagogy and organizational studies relating to nursing education and the caring system respectively are two obvious niches, but they give no unique claim to a clear identity since such research may also be done within order disciplines. The more difficult aspect has been to give a positive, scientifically sound content to the term 'caring'. One approach has been to distinguish 'caring' and 'nursing', where the former depicts a wider territory and the latter a narrower one. The narrower definition refers to tasks that are normally carried out by nurses, while the wider one also includes parts of physical therapy and occupational therapy.

A working group for nursing research at the new Health University in Linköping, led by Rector Henny Olsson, has noted how definitions have been strongly influenced by social and medical developments.

> Theories from social and behavioural as well as medical sciences may be distinguished. Despite the hospital system's disease and task-centered thought model, the point of departure for nursing care research has been the human being as a physical, psychological and social whole and part of his/her environment and culture.[15]

In their review, the working group found that central to most definitions of the field are such concepts as: 'man'/individual; environment/society; health/lack of health – illness; ward activities/-nursing. The official definition for the professorship in Linköping speaks of the subject area of nursing-care research as covering studies of the system in which care is provided (*vård*) and the act of caring (*omsorg*). The area also covers development of methods relating to these aspects.[16] Astrid Norberg in Umeå states, for her part, that 'nursing science deals with methods and techniques of caring for the aged and infirm, who unlike young and healthy individuals cannot carry out the simplest tasks'.[17] Kerstin Andersson, who has written a small book on the emergence of nursing science in Sweden, emphasizes how the new discipline is concerned 'with the human being's total life, the total interaction to sickness and health. Nursing is based on a holistic view of man and focuses on the entire life cycle.'[18]

Systems theory as philosophical and social legitimation

A common feature in most of the foregoing definitions of nursing research is the implicit demarcation that advocates are trying to make *vis-à-vis* medicine, which is purported to deal with limited aspects of the human body. However, in the further delineation of perspectives and approaches in the new field this is not sufficient. Clear boundaries have to be staked out internally as well, in order to point to specific problems for research and methodologies for solving them. In this third phase of cognitive legitimation, systems theory is sometimes employed. It provides a way of sorting out different levels of competence in the hospital system, at the same time thus affording a further means of legitimating demands for professionalism. This is explicitly clear in the writings of early advocates of nursing research in North America; in Scandinavia where nursing research was introduced at a later stage it has become less clear, since systems theory has been associated with a technocratic ideology in some cases, and because the emphasis on hermeneutics as opposed to positivist methodologies dominated the debate.

Martha Rogers in the United States wrote early on: 'refusal to state frankly a clear differentiation of levels of nursing constitutes one of the most significant problems facing nurses today . . . the further the development of professional education demands such a differentiation'.[19] This statement is significant in that it goes some way to explaining the preoccupation nurses often have had with systems theory and their attempts to promote it as a kind of general philosophy and guideline in designing curricula and defining research interests.

Systems theory as a general philosophy can have a legitimatory function by lending a profession a certain 'scientificity' in its identity. This was particularly striking in the early stages when rationalist planning theory still dominated and went hand in hand with the centralization and mechanization of hospital care. Systems theory was used to *differentiate* different kinds of *tasks and rules* within the health- and hospital-care system, physicians' tasks, nursing tasks and delegated tasks. This is said to have helped reduce some of the friction between nurses and doctors, since it clarified areas of responsibility and task structures.

The arguments against a systems-theoretical perspective in nursing science are of two kinds. One is that it tends to reduce sensitivity to power relationships, thus leaving the physician's claim to cognitive and social monopoly in the hospital undisturbed. The other argument is more philosophical, pointing to the technocratic flavour of systems theory, which stands in strong contrast to the need for a humanistically oriented theoretical basis of the kind provided by hermeneutics. Thus one gets back to the older tension between positivism and anti-positivism. This tension continues, even though the debate over ideals of science has ebbed somewhat during the last few years. One of our informants referred to the present situation as one of 'peaceful coexistence'. However, a recent motion to parliament calls for the introduction of a professorship in nursing-care research in Stockholm to compensate for the one in gerontology which 'has gotten too much of a medical-natural scientific orientation'.

As for social legitimation, there is no lack of groups and tasks that may be invoked. For Astrid Norberg, 'research in nursing science is aimed at determining the needs of the various patient categories – as well as of those responsible for caring for them – and deciding how these needs are best met'.[20] Kerstin Andersson in her study cites Hinshaw in the United States, who points to the importance of upgrading the knowledge of health-care workers so as to improve service to patients. 'Just as the profession and its professionals have a responsibility to society for the delivery of health care, nursing researchers are accountable to the profession for generating and testing knowledge as part of the developing body of nursing science'.[21] Even doctors are seen as a target group, but generally the claims staked emphasize the importance to the clients, the patients.

As indicated before, the welfare system comprises means whereby economic security, physical and mental as well as cultural well-being are facilitated for individuals in society. Rules and regulations are needed to spell out the tasks of welfare occupations, as for those responsible for delivering the goods of social and economic security and those responsible for health care and medicine. In the case of nursing, systems theory may provide one means of teasing out what falls under 'nursing care'. At the same time it permits definition of the social relations of skill monopolization and resource mobilization in the larger framework.

Professionalization: another form of bureaucratization?

The development of links with science is an important step in professionalization strategies. Science is meant to help define territories for exclusive control. However, in the case of nursing, this is no easy task, neither cognitively nor socially. There is no easy one-to-one relationship between nursing practice and a specific field in academic science. The concept of 'care', often used to claim uniqueness, is vague, and several occupational groups can make counter-claims under the same heading. Neither are there clear-cut criteria of 'scientificity' to which nurse researchers can appeal, since science itself is in constant flux, and even in established fields there are controversies around rival theories and contending images and ideals of science. Nurses become caught between the hard criteria of the medical faculty and the softer ones of some of the social sciences. 'Positivism' and 'hermeneutics' are the terms used in a debate which at another level has much more to do with power struggles between nurses and physicians, nurses and therapists, nurses and laboratory technicians, and so on. If nothing else, the study of philosophy of science may help provide nurses with insights into the dynamics of the growth of science and therewith not only a resource in formulating cognitive, legitimating strategies but also in critical appraisal of methodologies borrowed from older sciences.

The plurality of philosophies and concepts in nursing research is a reflection of task uncertainty, theoretically as well as on a more practical level. A major concern that has been raised is the tendency to 'academic drift'; that is, a tendency in the name of science to cut off research from its necessary base in daily practice on the ward and from the tacit knowledge of the craft of nursing which is still borne up by its older practitioners. Certainly, the links with science have increased the visibility and status of certain groups within nursing, at least in the eyes of higher educational authorities and high-level decision-makers in the welfare state. However, it has not yet been demonstrated that nursing research will make for a more 'caring' science. Also, research is only one means of gaining recognition. Others are trade-union action, tighter controls over recruitment and certification, more influence in decision-making and so forth.

In view of the uncertainty of nursing research and its appeal only to a minority of nurses who might aspire to bootstrap themselves up into the petty bourgeoisie with academic status, many health-care workers, including nurses, seem to prefer trade-union strategies as a means to improve their working conditions, salaries and status in society. In the broader perspective it is not clear that the creation of new research fields like nursing science will immediately (if at all) benefit the majority of the welfare occupation considered. It is also dubious to what extent research can enhance the image of nursing in the eyes of the clientele, many of whom still seem to prefer the older, more experienced nurses who possess a lifetime of tacit knowledge.

Thus, although nurses as an occupational group have some common interests, it is not definite that professionalization strategies and the linkages to science are the way to consolidate these interests. There are at the same time conflicts and tensions that run right through nurses as a group, some displaying stronger loyalties with the welfare and rationalization process that lends them higher status, others opposing this process on the grounds of the gender and technocratic bias found in the hierarchical structure and power relations of the health- and hospital-care system. The conflicts between doctors, nurses, nurses' aides, occupational therapists, laboratory and X-ray technicians and other categories of health professionals have their basis in objective factors like wage differences and gender relations as well as differences relating to knowledge traditions and occupational roles.

At a general level professionalization of nurses and their linkages with science coincides with a bureaucratic process which itself does not fundamentally change the more basic tensions, but may just as well tend to aggravate them. In this respect there seem to exist two different types of logic. There are those who apply a capitalist logic and see efficiency as the primary aspect, and others who would postulate welfare as being more fundamental, something that must ultimately be defined in terms not of bureaucratization but of democratization. In terms of strategy this would mean a focus on decentralization of decision-making, employee control and better wages and working conditions, placing this above any strategy for professionalization. Whereas a professionalization strategy leans heavily on the scientification of nursing knowledge, this alternative – trade-union activism – as a strategy seeks to put research in perspective, noting that it sometimes serves as an alibi for inaction when it comes really to changing power relations.

Notes

1 Figures from Swedish statistical year-books.

2 This refers to the sphere of activities that is necessary as a precondition for the maintenance of the social sphere of production, labour and the regeneration of modern society.

3 SCB, 1977.

4 Riska and Wegar, 1988.

5 Vårdfacket, 1988:3.
6 Vårdfacket, 1988:32–34.
7 Brante, 1988a:30–60.
8 Rogoff Ramsöy and Kölsröd, 1985.
9 McCloskey, 1981:40–47.
10 Andersson, 1984.
11 Vårdfacket, 1986:24.
12 Norberg, 1984.
13 UHÄ report, 1978:14.
14 Vårdfacket, 1986:24.
15 Internal document received in a personal communication from Henny Olsson, who is herewith at the same time thanked for her interest and the information provided on different occasions; representatives from other nursing colleges have also been helpful with basic factual information as to the developments in various locations in Sweden. No one but myself, however, is held responsible for the interpretation put forth here.
16 Nordiska Hälsovårdshögskolan, 1987.
17 Norberg, 1984.
18 Andersson, 1984.
19 Rogers, 1961:4.
20 Norberg, 1984.
21 Andersson, 1984:52.

10

The Swedish veterinary profession and the Swedish state

Inga Hellberg

Since the early nineteenth century, Swedish veterinarians have striven to create and maintain two monopolies – one of knowledge and the other of positions in the labour market – in order to close the field of veterinary medicine and to maximize their control over that field.[1] For the creation and maintenance of these monopolies the veterinarians turned to the state. The relation to the state is therefore a central theme throughout the history of the professionalization of veterinarians and is the main subject of this study.

The veterinarians and the state are not, however, the only actors in the professionalization process. The heart of this process is the interaction of the veterinarians with those who give them legitimacy and those who contest their legitimacy. Clients, competing occupational groups and citizens in general all have interests to protect and have all played a part. Sometimes their interests have coincided with those of the veterinarians, sometimes they have conflicted. These interests appear to be differently articulated over time, and these shifting patterns of interests are in the end attributable to the actors' position in the social division of labour and ultimately to the conditions of production in society.

The example of veterinary medicine in Sweden shows the critical role of the state in the professionalization process – the veterinarians seeking to persuade the state, as the ultimate guarantor of a knowledge and occupational monopoly, that it should allow the veterinarians to protect vital social interests. In the eighteenth century those interests concerned military defence, in the nineteenth, the primary production (namely, agriculture) and towards the end of this century, they have concerned both the economic and preventive health aspects of animal food production.

I shall examine veterinary medicine during three time periods which describe distinct and contrasting settings of interaction. The periodization is based on changing relations to and structure of veterinarians' clients. The first period starts in the mid-eighteenth century, the second in the mid-nineteenth and the third one starts in the last half of the twentieth century. My purpose is to describe ways in which different interests revolving around veterinary medicine work together and in opposition, as well as practice of veterinary medicine under different conditions of production.

The development of the veterinary profession[2]

The horse doctor period, 1760–1860
Around the mid-eighteenth century veterinary medicine was first proclaimed necessary by the state through the Collegium Medicum. This came about due to recurrent epidemics of *epizooti*, as well as the calvary's need for horse doctors, particularly in the royal horse stalls. This need stretched beyond the limitations of the smithies and farriers under employment. In farming, however, animal husbandry was low and greater emphasis was given to cultivation, so farmers demonstrated less interest in veterinary medicine. *Epizooti* control was the responsibility of the community at large and not of individual farmers. The vast majority of farmers turned to wise old women for treatment of their livestock, which were few.

Human medicine was ensconced in the universities, far from veterinary medicine. However, Carl von Linné, one of the most prominent scientists of Uppsala University, agitated for the recognition of veterinary medicine at university level. He sent, in 1762, one of his best students, Peter Hernqvist, to the newly opened veterinary school in Lyon in France. Hernqvist left with a promise from the Collegium Medicum to establish veterinary medical training in Sweden upon his return. Back in Stockholm he successfully stopped an outbreak of *epizooti* at the royal stud farm, Strömsholm, but he was less successful in getting resources from the state to open a veterinary school. He probably never dreamed that the parsimonious Swedish state would come to restrict his veterinary teaching to a lectureship in mathematics at a high school in Skara, a small town 250 kilometres away from the capital city, Stockholm.

Apart from insufficient funds offered by the state, it was difficult for Hernqvist to recruit students; treating sick animals was generally looked upon as a job for citizens on the lowest rungs of the social ladder. Entrance requirements had to be set low: only reading and writing abilities were demanded by Hernqvist. Even those were probably in the beginning hard to follow, as Hernqvist gave lessons in reading and writing besides the lessons in theoretical and practical medicine, mathematics, natural history, economy and religion.

The pupils also had lessons in singing so that they could work as parish clerks in addition to their veterinary practice. The position of parish clerk was high in esteem at that time in the countryside. Combining this position and veterinary medicine, Hernqvist thought, was a way to make the veterinary profession respectable in the eyes of the farmers and of the general public.

As an individual representative of veterinary medicine, Peter Hernqvist agitated for organized veterinary training and spent the rest of his life trying to influence the Collegium Medicum and other state representatives, but without success. He died in 1808, and the veterinary school in Skara closed down, to be opened five years later by one of his students, Sven Adolf Norling.

The question of organized veterinary training came up in parliament (the Riksdagen) in 1810 when a representative of the noble estates proposed that veterinary science should be made 'available' and that veterinary medicine should be included as an essential part of medical and surgical training. This proposal met with strong opposition from the medical faculties in the two universities in Sweden, Uppsala and Lund. It was not only opposed but also ridiculed. The Uppsala faculty said, for example, that the doctor 'could not, without losing the esteem upon which he endeavours to stand, appear to order and treat simultaneously the farmer, his horse, his wife and cow, his child and pig'.

The discussion continued in parliament. In 1818 the four estates in parliament proposed that the king, Carl XIV Johan, should support veterinary medicine, with reference to the high death-rate among horses in Stockholm. A committee was appointed which eventually led to the proposal for a veterinary institution in Stockholm. One opinion is that Hernqvist's work at the royal stud farm, Strömsholm, was as decisive in establishing the Skara school as was Nordling's in establishing the veterinary institution in Stockholm. This institution gained about the same status as a handicraft school. To house veterinary medicine within the gates of the university was unthinkable to the powerful human medicine faculties. Professor Sönnerberg in Lund, for example, held that,

> The university does not have a menagerie in its possession, does not even own a single horse whose health is its responsibility, cannot and need not appoint any scientific assistant from the veterinary institution, just as the veterinary students, the farriers, neither need nor are capable of receiving university education, of which it is clear that there is no exchange possible between the university and the institution in question.

In summary, this initial stage in the history of veterinary medicine can be characterized by the direct although not permanent interest of the central state powers in supporting certain veterinary activities; by *epizooti* control mainly in the military sector; and by activities carried forward by a handful of enthusiasts. It was too early for veterinary medicine to gain wider support; few farmers had animals. As late as the mid-nineteenth century the ratio between draught animals, horses and oxen, and cattle, was 1:2, and this ratio has been estimated to be even more disproportionate to the advantage of draught animals a hundred years earlier. Only a few members of the upper echelons of society, the nobility foremost, had valuable horses and therefore economic interest in veterinary medicine. To reach the position of parish clerk was one way to seek recognition of veterinary medicine and was a first step to close an occupational territory, just as the opening of the two handicraft schools were the first steps to institutionalize knowledge of veterinary medicine.

During this period the veterinarians' struggle for educational institutions was most strongly opposed by practitioners of established human medicine; medical doctors dominated and controlled the Collegium Medicum. The active resistance from human medicine could be analysed in terms of a closure strategy, and as such, an answer to, as they saw it, the veterinarians' usurpation strategy. The usurpation did not mean that the position of human medicine was threatened but rather that a socially subordinated occupational group demanded equal status to that of human medicine.[3]

The animal doctor period, 1860–1970
Our next time segment starts in the mid-nineteenth century. At this time the question of the profitability of livestock production in farming comes up increasingly at the farmers' yearly agricultural meetings. Before investing in animal husbandry, farmers demanded an organized and regulated veterinary service. At this time there were a hundred practising veterinarians, educated at the veterinary institutions in Skara and Stockholm. The majority of these were military veterinarians. Supported by the articulate interest of the farmers, veterinarians founded the Swedish Society of Veterinary Surgeons in 1860. Their objective was to place veterinary medicine on the same level as human medicine; to establish national county and regional veterinary stations (the equivalent of county and district medical officers); to have their education acknowledged at the university level; and to establish a veterinary central authority (instead of answering to the Board of Health, Sundhetskollegium). In other words, their objective was to establish a clearly defined monopoly of knowledge and to monopolize positions in the labour market. Strong support from farmers and weakened opposition

from doctors of human medicine influenced the state. All these objectives and demands were finally met. The Royal Veterinary College of Sweden was opened in 1914, district veterinary services were nationalized in 1934, and the crowning success came in 1947 when the National Swedish Veterinary Board was set up.

At the beginning of this period two educational institutions existed, both handicraft schools, one in Skara and one in Stockholm. By that time higher entrance requirements were demanded in Stockholm and only those educated in the Stockholm school were accepted in state employment. A distinction was made between veterinarians of first and second rank. By the end of the century the Skara school closed down and the school continued as a school for training farriers in civil and military employment. The Stockholm school gradually became an academic institution and received the same formal status as that of the medical faculties in the university. The Royal Veterinary College was opened in 1914. According to the statutes, the training of veterinarians was to be based on scientific grounds.

The number of veterinarians steadily increased; there were no longer any problems in recruiting students. At the end of the nineteenth century there were 300 practising veterinarians, and by the middle of the twentieth, 675. Military veterinary service declined, eventually to become negligible, and animal husbandry grew to make the greatest demands on veterinarians. The parish clerk veterinarians faded away; the last of them were active up to the turn of this century. By this time both the state and the municipalities had set up positions not only for animal health care but also for preventive veterinary services. Completed veterinary training in Stockholm and legitimation issued by the National Board of Health gave access to these positions. In 1934 the district veterinary service was nationalized; more than 300 veterinary stations were set up, and covered all Sweden.

As a homogeneous profession was formed regarding knowledge and positions, veterinarians strove for full control of their occupational domain. Even when the regional and district veterinarian positions were set up, the veterinarians still had to report to the National Board of Health dominated by medical doctors. In the 1890s the head of the veterinary school acted as a rapporteur to the board in veterinary matters, a function which became a permanent position in 1900. Soon after, a special bureau for veterinary medicine was set up which came to work parallel with, rather than subordinated to, the medical bureaux. Thirteen veterinarians were employed, when the veterinarians' own National Board was created in 1947. Few veterinarians were really interested in it but it was carried through for reasons of prestige. By then most veterinarians thought they could benefit from close cooperation with the medical doctors. The old inferiority had given way to more of an equal footing as regards social status.

What had been the struggle of a few men was replaced by the purposeful efforts of an organized profession. The first veterinarians practised in isolation from one another and furthered their own interests without mutual cooperation. By the mid-nineteenth century their activities became organized collectively, and the 'profession in itself' became the 'profession for itself'. The advantages of acting collectively and the disadvantages of acting individually became clear once the professionals were defined as a 'profession for others'; namely, by the farmers.[4] A great number of farmers, who also had political clout, became interested in veterinary medicine around the mid-nineteenth century because of an increasing profitability in livestock production, mainly as a result of landowning reforms.

Their definition as not only an important but also an indispensable group for agriculture led to conscious, organized efforts from the Society of Veterinarians. With support from farmers, the veterinarians could actively call on state authorities, like the National Board of Health, the Ministry of Education and the Ministry of Agriculture, for increased resources and legal protection of their occupational activities. Agriculture was the primary source of production in society, and the state became more and more conscious of the need to control and protect societal interests in this sector. The veterinarians received this mandate, and the three cornerstones in the professional project – namely, monopoly of knowledge, monopoly of positions and professional discretion – were met. In order to form a homogeneous profession and to increase their status, the veterinarians excluded the less-educated Skara veterinarians and only one type of education was established.

The modern veterinarian – health and animal production in the 1970s

Our third period begins in the 1970s, by which time there were more than a thousand practising veterinarians, a third of them working with animal production as district veterinary officers. Animal husbandry became animal production. During the 1970s the overall trend was a rapid decline in the number of dairy farmers (from 83,500 to 44,200); while the proportion of large herd-owners doubled, the number of small herds decreased even more rapidly than the overall declining trend.[5] Thus, food production has become increasingly industrialized in the form of large-scale production. New problems, stock problems and general preventive veterinary medicine gain importance in relation to the previously predominant problems of curing individual animals. Fewer, although stronger, animal producers make demands on veterinary medicine and the role of the state becomes more critical.

Compared with previous years, veterinarians' line of work has increasingly come closer to new professions in agriculture and forestry (with the National Swedish Board of Agriculture as the responsible government authority). Veterinarians are also expected to work in the field of preventive medicine not covered by their legitimation. Veterinary training now takes place at the College of Agriculture and Forestry in Uppsala. More than half of the new students are women (in 1986 76 per cent), and the proportion of women to men in veterinary medicine is continuously increasing. In 1987 one-third of practising veterinarians were women.[6]

Their clients are large-scale animal producers, an increasing number of pet owners (the number of dogs, for example, grew by 60 per cent in the 1970s), but also the general public place demands on the veterinary profession's role and responsibility in animal and food production. Recent public criticism has been aimed at what veterinarians do not do rather than what they do, and touches on problems brought about by market conditions, problems which are difficult for veterinarians alone to master and solve. Critical comments have been made in the mass media by journalists and authors well known to and popular with the Swedish public.

During the seventies a wave of labour legislation was introduced; laws were enacted which are difficult to apply to traditional district veterinary services with working hours extending to day and night and to shifting work places. Male district veterinarians who could depend on their wives to help are on the way out. Younger veterinarians and particularly female veterinarians demand working conditions equivalent to those to which other government employees are entitled. Working conditions for district veterinarians became more and more criticized during the seventies, and later in the decade a government committee was set up to investigate animal health and medical care.

The committee presented its report in 1981.[7] One of its duties was to revise the organization and financing of animal health and medical care. The committee's proposal should, according to directive, be capable of being put into effect within a framework of unchanged resources. The committee's general point of departure was that the state has an overall responsibility for animal health and medical care; in addition, the state has particular responsibility for the care of animals in production, combating contagious diseases of domestic animals, and for satisfactory veterinary service to animal owners at reasonable cost, not only in farming regions but also in areas with low animal populations. District veterinarians, under state leadership, are responsible for animal production. Pets are not the direct responsibility of district veterinarians, but limits of responsibility are difficult to maintain and are not desirable in areas with few animals. Employment conditions of district veterinarians are partly based on fixed government wages and partly on fees paid by animal owners fixed by the National Board of Agriculture.

The committee concluded that the district veterinary organization must be increased from 310 positions to 390, so that the state obligations to both animal owners and veterinarians could be satisfactorily met. This increase in volume was to a large extent based on veterinarians' demands that laws regulating working hours and conditions be followed. Since the committee's proposal was not to increase costs at state level, according to directive, financing became a vital and much-debated question. If the state could not absorb these costs, who then would pay? The committee discussed four alternatives in which animal owners, individually or collectively, would accept the extra costs. For veterinarians the alternatives meant completely new employment and work conditions. State appointment would be a consequence of one alternative, that animal owners pay fees for animal care through central revenue collection. Another alternative was that veterinarians' fixed government wages would be lowered and compensated through increased fees from clients, but this would imply economic dependency on animal owners and, thus, increased wage differences could be expected between veterinarians in rich and poor regions. In a third alternative the division between fixed salary and fees for services would remain and would be combined with an extra state fee paid for each veterinary visit, the 'revenue' alternative. A drawback of this alternative was increased administration for individual veterinarians. A fourth alternative was that the agricultural cooperative would collectively make payments directly to the state in order to cover increased costs, and the individual veterinarians would not be directly affected.

The Swedish Veterinary Society preferred the third alternative if the state could not absorb the increased costs, and this was clearly felt to be the best solution.[8] The remaining alternatives were criticized by the society as devastating, not only for veterinarians' working conditions but also for animal health and medical care. The different alternatives implying that individual animal owners would bear financial burdens for veterinary care would also mean increased competition between private veterinarians (as fees for treating pets were not affected), and increased dependency on animal owners, which would lead to a decrease in preventive veterinary medicine. In the long run these alternatives would lead to private district veterinary practice, and private practice in this field, according to veterinarians, would mean that it would be difficult to meet community and societal needs. In addition, veterinarians would face greater differences in subsistance levels if they accepted work in regions with low animal populations. The alternative involving 'tax enforcement' while giving medical attention was considered humiliating, and veterinarians feared that in the long run the tax would become disproportionately large in relation to the actual medical fee.

The agricultural cooperative opposed the idea that it should collectively pay for increased costs. The best alternative for the state was for the veterinarian to collect fees. Administratively this was the simplest solution, and it also permitted the state to maintain its interest in animal care. Despite lobbying by the veterinarian union and support from all parties in parliament, except the Social Democrats, the 'revenue' alternative was passed in parliament with a Social Democratic majority.

Thus veterinarians neither wanted to be solely government servants nor did they want to be totally steered by the animal owners' interest. Public and private interest were seen as best looked after under the prevailing form which had been followed for nearly fifty years. This gave some protection against the profit interests of the animal producers. Veterinarians thus felt that demands on reasonable working environments and working hours were the responsibility of the state, as an employer, but the extra cost involved in implementing these changes should not necessarily affect the free part of professional practice.

Dynamics of discretion

In literature on professions the most common motives explaining why professionals use strategies to close a knowledge and occupational area are status, material rewards, prestige and power. However, the history of Swedish veterinarians suggests another base of great significance for closure strategies; that is, the professional community's ambition for discretion, or the ambition to control the work by means of the monopoly. The greater the power of action, or leeway for autonomous assessment, the greater the liberty and power of deciding and acting without other control than one's own judgement. The means used in achieving discretion appear differently in relation to different social interests and vary at different points in time. Space for autonomous assessment must be appropriated and defended in relation to competing professional communities, clients, the state and citizens in general. For Swedish veterinarians, educational institutions and a central administration of veterinary services were the means to free themselves from the supervision of medical doctors and thereby reach full control over their work. Legal protection of veterinarians' positions was not only a means to exclude less-educated veterinarians and others, but also a means to claim discretion in relation to powerful clients.

This struggle for discretion is an ongoing 'tug-of-war' between professional interests and other, organized or unorganized, interests in society. The three chosen periods show how the veterinarians, at different times, found themselves in different fields of interest and power. Their actions and reactions were not only dependent on external structural changes but also on changes within the profession. These external and internal changes lead to new demands and relationships between the profession, their clients, other professions and citizens in general.

The state has thus been the main target in the veterinarians' professional project. This has been based on the claim that veterinary medicine is not only necessary but indispensable for protecting vital interests of the state; in the eighteenth century these interests were mainly related to military defence, in the nineteenth to the development of a productive agricultural sector, and in the twentieth century to the preventive aspects of veterinary services in animal production and food hygiene.

The activities of the state have not only been dependent on the activities of the veterinarians but also on its relation to other actors involved in the professionalization process. These interrelations have varied over time and been decisive for the actions and reactions of the actors. The clients, competing professions and citizens in general have been close to the state in different ways, and their political potential and influence has varied over the centuries.

In the first period the state itself was the client, specifically military institutions. The initiative to establish veterinary medicine came from a respected, far-sighted person, Carl von Linné, the professor of medicine who had great influence on the National Board of Health; the influence he brought to bear his pupil and Sweden's first veterinarian Peter Hernqvist lacked, and was never able to gain when he was sent to a small town far from Stockholm. Also representatives of the politically strong nobility now and then supported the idea of a veterinary profession. The National Board of Health was dominated by opposing medical doctors, and after the death of Linné and Hernqvist veterinarians widely scattered across the countryside could only respond to the irregular demands of the state for their services. The constellations of actors involved led to an active but not permanent interest by the state in protecting and legitimizing veterinary activities.

It was at the beginning of the second period that the farmers entered the scene. The farmers were already the dominant political influence as representatives of the primary production sector of the time, and this influence increased. Their active support had an effect on the professionalization process in two decisive ways: the veterinarians organized themselves, and as an organization the professional project could be more effectively carried through; the state had to listen to the farmers and take a more permanent interest in veterinary medicine through mandating and legitimizing the veterinary profession to protect vital societal interests. Through the activities of the Veterinary Society the veterinarians gained respect, among the clients, the general public and certainly also among their earlier strongest opponents, the medical doctors.

Although an established profession, the veterinarians in the 1970s were questioned both by the state and also by representatives of the general public. Strong economic pressure from one client group, large-scale specialized farmers, is tending to threaten the authority and discretion of the district veterinarians. In order to maintain their authority and discretion the veterinarians demanded improved working conditions and continued legal protection from the state.

Differentiation and specialization within the veterinary profession has divided the practitioners by segment of the labour market and by client category. Veterinarians' clinical work is now found both in the sector under state control, animal production, and in the private pet sector. Veterinarians also work in the food industry as well as in the public regulation of this industry, a field not altogether covered by the state legitimation. Specialization leads to different types of control over working conditions, and the example of veterinarian history shows that the need for legal protection is even more crucial the more specialized the profession becomes.

Notes

1 For analysis of the professional strategy as a special case in closure theory, see Murphy, 1988.

2 The first two periods in veterinary history are covered in Hellberg, 1978.

3 Discussions on the two closure strategies are in Parkin, 1979.

4 The concepts 'profession in itself', 'profession for others', 'profession for itself' are analogues to the general discussion on group and class formation in Elster, 1974.

5 SOU, 1981:57.

6 *Swedish Statistical Yearbook 1988.*

7 SOU, 1981:57.

8 The attitudes and actions of the veterinarians have been published in their monthly journal, *Svensk Veterinärtidning*.

11

Technical and political knowledge: the relationship of lawyers and other legal professions to the market and the state

Lucien Karpik

How can one explain the contours and the contents of the types of knowledge used by French lawyers? How is it that the legal domain covered by lawyers in America, for example, is divided, in France, among several professions? The first obstacle to an understanding of this phenomenon is the definition of 'professional knowledge'. The ambiguity of this notion stems more from the first word than from the second. Today it is accepted that 'knowledge' refers not only to the symbolic reality transmitted by the university, but to that combination of abstract knowledge and practical application that appears in the form of books, legal codes and procedures, in the practices of organizations and institutions, in oral transmission and tradition, all of which are used daily. Although historical documentation is not the way to reconstruct such a reality, something which only a quasi-ethnographic approach could do in detail, the overall goal is not really in question. In the present case, we shall be referring to concrete activities and functions in order to identify the specific type of knowledge associated with each.

Disagreements as to the nature of this knowledge are not so easy to resolve, however, as they are rooted in two different interpretations of the profession: skills recognized by some are not recognized by others. On this question, which is central, since it bears upon the limits of the object of our study, I intend to defend the thesis that French lawyers have long tended to combine what Anglo-Saxon sociologists persist in keeping separate: technical and political knowledge. I shall trace the genealogy of these two types using changes in the activities and functions of a number of legal professions, and fluctuations in the influence of the state, the market and the public. This socio-historical approach makes it possible to identify major transformations occurring alongside a stable tradition dating from not just the past, but the very distant past. At the end of this twofold journey, I show that the unique character of the French system is inseparable from the central position occupied by the state, which is scarcely surprising. But far from being exceptional, the French case is only an extreme example of the evolution of the profession in other countries; it is therefore part of a more general interpretation, presented here somewhat schematically, of the forces that determine the unity or duality of professional knowledge.

Technical knowledge

The technical knowledge of today's French lawyer has been handed down from the very first legal order, formed at the end of the Middle Ages, and has since undergone two major transformations: a split between lawyers and the state in the sixteenth and seventeenth centuries, and the refusal to enter the business market in the eighteenth and nineteenth centuries. The effects of these developments were still making themselves felt in the middle of the twentieth century, when the third transformation, intended to reverse the course of history, was undertaken.

The first legal order: lawyers, attorneys and notaries
(thirteenth century to the present day)
It was the emergence and development of lawyers, attorneys (*procureurs* under the *ancien régime*, and later *avoués*) and notaries, in the second half of the thirteenth century and throughout the fourteenth, that created the first divisions in the corpus of legal knowledge.[1] Although they had been practising in the ecclesiastical courts for a long time, the presence of lawyers in secular courts was first mentioned in the great judicial reforms implemented by St Louis and his successors: proof first by the testimony of witnesses and later by written evidence replaced the judicial duel, while both sides of cases were presented to the court. The possibility now given the litigant of being assisted by a professional whose ability was vouched for by a university diploma, and the officially recognized right to counsel who intervenes by advice and pleading were essential elements of the *justice loyale*, which represented one of the great designs of the monarchy of the time.

The appearance of the attorney testifies to the difficulties caused by the medieval procedure, whose formalism had two main consequences: the parties had to appear personally before the judge, and words, once spoken, could not be retracted. These adverse consequences for the litigant were gradually reduced by the possibility of having himself represented, provided he obtained authorization in a *lettre de grâce*. In the fourteenth century, the practice of granting these letters became widespread, representing as they did a source of revenue for the Crown. In order to take care of the technical side of their case – the procedure – litigants increasingly recruited their representatives from among the 'public writers of the Palais de Justice', who subsequently were to organize in order to obtain a *de facto* monopoly over this sphere of activity. They eventually became the 'scribe-attorneys' and then simply the attorneys, whose intervention became mandatory from the sixteenth century on. The profession of notary, after a long and brilliant evolution in Southern Europe, spread through France from the second half of the thirteenth century. Notaries were responsible for the drafting and the safe-keeping of authentic deeds, but they did not limit their activities to these public services. They also took on the drafting of a broad range of private acts, from deeds of succession and gift to tenancies and contracts of all kinds.

These relatively synchronous historical developments mask the existence of three very different trajectories: the quasi-voluntary creation of the function of lawyer, which was to become one of the mainstays of royal justice; a *sui generis* creation of attorneys; and the successful adoption of a foreign model for notaries. Each of these three professions now addressed itself to a specific activity, which it monopolized (to a greater or lesser extent according to the times): advice and pleading, for lawyers; matters of procedure, for attorneys; drafting of authentic deeds, for notaries. And each of these activities required a specific type of knowledge.

But no technical reason explains the legal order that emerged at the end of the Middle Ages.[2] And this development seems to have represented a serious defeat for lawyers, given their previous assets, as they were effectively cut off not only from the technique of procedure, but also from the legal and socio-economic knowledge upon which the varied business of deeds and contracts was based. How can this development be explained, when lawyers enjoyed far more prestige than attorneys or notaries, since they alone could claim university training, they alone had an intellectual activity as opposed to mere 'activités viles et mécaniques', they alone exercised a function that was permitted to nobles. Whatever the causes, and we shall come to them later, this first split was to continue: the distinction between lawyer and attorney disappeared only in 1971,[3] and that between lawyer and notary continues.

*The first transformation: the split between lawyers and
the world of the state (from the sixteenth century to the
present day)*
Two changes in the organization of the state were dramatically to
reduce the scope of the profession. Until the sixteenth century, the
lawyer had represented both the king and his subjects equally, the
title 'advocate to the King' being an honour and not a special
position. From the sixteenth century on, he was excluded from
defending the interests of the Crown; this function was taken over
by a specialized staff, which was to become known as the 'Parquet'.
Some time later, lawyers fell victim to the separation between
administrative and ordinary courts of justice, the first dealing with
cases to which the state was party, the second being empowered
to deal only with private-party disputes. The creation of the two
jurisdictions, which spotlights the state's refusal to answer to ordinary law, was given its modern form by Napoleon, in 1799. But
this reform simply codified what, in reality, had existed since the
sixteenth century and had accompanied the growing power of the
absolute monarchy: the 'Conseil d'Etat privé' (Privy State Council),
with its justices and its specialized advocates whose office was hereditary, was the direct precursor of the Conseil d'Etat, with its
justices and 'Avocats au Conseil d'Etat et à la Cour de Cassation',
who even today hold hereditary offices and form a professional
body completely distinct from that of the other lawyers.
  Barred from representing the interests of the state and cut off
from the administrative domain, lawyers were excluded from the
skills and thought processes associated with the world of the state;
they were restricted to the activities and knowledge related to
advising and pleading before the ordinary courts.

*The second transformation: refusal to enter the business
market (eighteenth to mid-twentieth centuries)*
In the name of disinterestedness, the profession *voluntarily* refused
to enter the business market. This strategy was first employed
sporadically in the eighteenth century and then systematically from
the nineteenth century on. It took two main forms. On the one
hand, the formulation and application of rules prohibiting trade,
excessive fees, forms of competition characteristic of the capitalist
market, legal redress to recover unpaid fees, and the emphasis
placed on altruism as a counterpoise to material interest constituted
the main ingredients of a specific economic system. On the other
hand, in the middle of the nineteenth century, the bar added to
the already long list of functions incompatible with the profession
of lawyer the holding of high positions in industry and commerce:

in 1865, this development was marked by a decree stipulating that any position of responsibility within a corporation was considered incompatible.[4] These were the two ways the profession used systematically to protect itself from the dynamism of the capitalist market and the desire for unlimited accumulation of wealth.

Just when American lawyers were taking an increasingly active part in economic life, then French lawyers were systematically turning away. Given this choice, they could not help being ignorant of the knowledge and know-how that went hand in hand with the legal and judicial activities of the business world. The profession restricted itself principally to a clientele of families and individuals, to assistance and pleading in civil courts, and to civil and penal law. Such an option could only encourage the emergence and development of legal advisers (*conseils juridiques*) and *agréés*, the two professions which were to cater to the needs of the economic world (consulting, negotiating and drafting private contracts, for the first; the second providing only representation in commercial courts). It was only in the mid-twentieth century that lawyers were to view them as formidable rivals.

The third transformation: can history be reversed?
Lawyers of the 1950s were the product of a historical evolution which, willy-nilly, removed them from the trial procedure and contracts, from the worlds of both state and business. Their monopoly on pleading continued, but the scope of the profession, considering all the functions exercised by attorneys, notaries, *avocats* to the Conseil d'Etat, legal advisers, *agréés* and so on, was substantially reduced. The intense and prolonged state of crisis which, as a result, has been developing since the middle of this century, has given rise to a movement for reform and the conversion of a growing segment of the profession to the world of business. In many guises, with much hesitation and not without serious conflicts with the other legal professions, lawyers are at present engaged in a process of re-defining the contours of their territory and professional knowledge. The results so far are considerable: in 1971 the new definition of lawyer absorbed attorneys and *agréés*; more and more now represent corporations and have gained access to the administrative courts, although they are still excluded from the Conseil d'Etat. However real it may be, though, this recovery remains partial. The fusion of lawyer and legal adviser, the most radical change, was rejected in 1971. Now, some fifteen years later, the problem has arisen again, but in a more acute form. Under pressure from international competition – foreign legal advisers established in France, Anglo-Saxon public accounting firms (the

'Big Eight') – the reorganization of services and knowledge in the judicial, legal, financial and accounting fields has become a crucial issue which concerns not only lawyers and legal advisers, but notaries, auditors, tax advisers and house counsel alike. The door stands open to a variety of manoeuvres and strategies, but the solutions are not immediately apparent.

Political knowledge

Theories already exist to explain the transformations in technical knowledge. And yet such an exercise would be futile for the fundamental reason that, whereas our outline of the evolution of the profession is true enough in what it says, it is invalid by what it leaves out. This is fortunate. For this history, at least down to the mid-twentieth century, would be patently absurd: it lists a series of reallocations of functions and branches of knowledge which, for lawyers, are tantamount to a step-by-step reduction of their territory over a long period of time. In order to explain something of it, we would have to put it down to some strangely suicidal tendency of the entire profession to promote the creation, development and triumph of its rivals.

A more detailed examination of the paradoxical attitudes – the lack of any reaction by lawyers in the fourteenth and fifteenth centuries to the notaries' and attorneys' appropriation of functions and areas of expertise that they could have claimed, and the lawyers' voluntary abandonment of the business market over the course of the 'long' nineteenth century – makes way for another interpretation, which stresses the existence and importance of political knowledge. This new perspective allows us to define the profession in terms of two domains of action, whose relative importance varies over time.

The first paradox: why did lawyers not oppose the rise of notaries and attorneys?
In the fourteenth and fifteenth centuries, the lawyers whose names have come down to us enjoyed esteem because of their knowledge and their talent for pleading, but even more because of their position as Minister of Justice (*Chancellier* or *Garde des Sceaux*), their high-ranking posts in the government or *parlement*, because they served as advisers to princes and kings and so on.[5] This proves that at least one strategy was successful. Lawyers served, simultaneously or successively, as defence counsel in court, as political and legal advisers to princes, as senior civil servants, and as magistrates in the *parlement*. The profession was characterized by its service to

the state as much as to private clients, who were more often than not aristocrats. This tension was a sign of the growing attraction of high public office, which had the advantage of being extremely prestigious and which, moreover, opened the way to ennoblement; it resulted from the dynamics of monarchic power, which expressed itself in terms of territorial stabilization, the concentration and rationalization of the administrative and judicial apparatus, reliance on the law as a means of government and, consequently, the strengthening of the role and position of the jurist at the very heart of the state. With their university education, lawyers belonged to that body of legists who were the builders of the modern state.

Not only did lawyers find access to power within the state incomparably more important than struggling with attorneys and notaries, but they also deemed the two objectives contradictory: their position as part of the power elite could be maintained only by putting the greatest distance possible between their activities and the 'vile and mechanical' activities of attorneys and notaries. Given this priority, we can now understand their lack of interest in the territorial struggle with the other professions, and why the knowledge expected of the professional advocate, at the time, was not limited to the practice of law in court, but included the diverse skills required by senior justices and senior civil servants alike.

The second paradox: why did the profession refuse to enter the business market?

In the sixteenth century, when the selling of public offices replaced their attribution by merit, the link between lawyers and the world of legists came to an end.[6] For the most part without wealth, the profession encountered what had become, with a few rare exceptions, an insurmountable obstacle. The most coveted positions – the offices of parliamentary magistrate, which opened the way to a title – were fast becoming the almost exclusive property of wealthy nobles. The strategy lawyers had been following for two centuries thus ended in disaster and gave way to a crisis of long duration.

The solution lay in a re-definition of the profession, the public expression of which can be seen at the turn of the seventeenth century. Independence became crucial, but its preservation was directly challenged by two opposing forces: the development of commerce, which threatened to make the profession a prisoner of the profit motive, and the increased power of the state, accompanied also by an increasing desire for obedience. In an attempt to overcome these two threats, the profession adopted a strategy of disinterestedness. The term designates the principle which was gradually to unite all aspects of the profession, from the moral to the economic, around a passion for the public good. The relationship was ambiguous, and it was revealing of both the profession's submission to the master it had chosen to serve – the public – and the right it had arrogated to itself to speak for its interests. By opting for disinterestedness and in order to fight the two forces that were threatening it with 'social non-existence', the profession sealed its alliance with the sovereign power, the public.[7]

This strategy explains the multifarious political activity of lawyers in the eighteenth century, the prestige and influence they gained thereby and which could be seen by their prominent representation in the Estates General, which marked the beginning of the French Revolution. It also explains their long-lasting political involvement (from the restoration of the monarchy, in 1814, to the beginning of World War II), which relied on their ability to command recognition as spokesmen for liberal opinion and as a driving force behind opposition to authoritarian regimes. This political commitment, when coupled with a demonstration of devotion to the public (of which the rejection of the business market was the most convincing expression), was an increasingly effective road to political power.[8] Their success knew no limits, and lawyers reached their zenith under the Third Republic, when they occupied all the most powerful positions in government, forming a veritable ruling elite.

Political skills
However, politics was not merely a passing reality; as the longevity of the phenomenon, the priority given it and the collective success it enjoyed attest, it was the second sphere of action of the profession. And to act, to fight, to triumph and to survive, laywers had to invent, to put into practice and transmit specific knowledge. The profession is thus *also* defined by the skills upon which rest the recognition of the profession as spokesman for the public, the skills that win elections and ensure the continued presence of lawyers in high government and parliamentary positions. It is no accident that, under the Third Republic, the bar was considered to be the training ground for power.

French lawyers, at least until the mid-twentieth century, defined themselves by two spheres of activity and two systems of knowledge. According to the period and the divisions within the profession, they tended to favour one area without completely forsaking the other. This duality helps explain how the priority given by lawyers to 'politics' (in the broad sense of the word) for a long time logically kept them 'ignorant' of the emergence and development of attorneys and notaries, and later legal advisers and *agréés*. It also helps explain the introduction of innovations based on 'cross-pollinization' between the two bodies of knowledge: for example, political defence in the nineteenth century and, under the Third Republic, government action clearly marked by the distinctive features of the *esprit juriste*. If, however, lawyers managed to define their position in terms of both these types of knowledge and know-how, this was because the two shared a common reality: law.

By way of conclusion: forces governing the unity and duality of lawyers' professional knowledge

The culture of the profession is a composite one, including both technical and political knowledge.[9] This dualism is not a sporadic phenomenon: it is a fundamental feature of the collectivity. It defines the margin of liberty lawyers have enjoyed, their commitment to one of the two areas of action and their lesser involvement in the other, with the unexpected but logical result of the multiplication of the legal professions. This dualism points up the limits of the conventional definition, which takes for granted what the French profession has for so long rejected: relegation to the sphere of technical knowledge. How can this heterodoxy be accounted for? It will come as no surprise that our interpretation is based on the central place of the state in French society.

To be more precise: the influence of the state does not derive from its organization – centralization – which seems to vouchsafe it an omnipotence which is far from being always confirmed by reality;[10] nor from its forms of action: besides, authoritarian measures which, in spite of everything, have been rare, state intervention in the legal professions has been above all a matter of consecrating spontaneous developments which have satisfied the needs of the state and/or society: rationalization of the relationship between the courts and the public, codification of the private relationship for attorneys and notaries, satisfaction of the legal and judicial needs of the economic sector for legal advisers and *agréés*. To understand the nature of state action, we must once again begin with the unique position of the French lawyer. It is as though, throughout their long history, lawyers had always been the arbiters of the two definitions of social success. On the one hand, the creation of a qualitative distinction with respect to other legal professions, which took a variety of forms; often the result of state-granted privileges, it could, nevertheless, bestow no more than a limited and fragile social superiority. On the other hand, the establishment of a discontinuity, obtained through access to the power elite.

The striking feature is not that the profession has never clearly chosen between the two, but that *it has never been obliged to do so*. What authorizes this constant oscillation between the two domains of action? Or, to put it another way: how can the fact be explained that, often in other countries, lawyers' action is limited to the technical domain?

As the case of American lawyers shows, the two most powerful forces operating to define their sphere of activity are the market and the university: the former imposes on the actors the reality of material survival, the second transforms specific knowledge into a competitive asset.[11] As a result of the late and only partial extension of the market and of a monolithic university system designed to deal with all jurists alike and which, for both these reasons, has not transformed the knowledge transmitted into a differential competitive asset in interprofessional rivalry, French lawyers have been 'protected' from this development and have managed to retain their dual knowledge.

Where market and university are strong enough to impose their logic of functioning, lawyers have no choice but to accept the twofold process of the separation of fields of knowledge and the channelling of their interests, by which the technical sphere, defined by the competition between legal professions, becomes the only reality of the collectivity. Conflicts over where to draw the line, over the various rewards, be they prestige or wealth, serve as a constant reminder of the ultimate threat of disappearance, and as such make it inevitable that all investments be concentrated where the competition takes place. In short, economic struggles give rise to the construction of a symbolic and social discipline that takes the forms of differentiation and specialization; this is accompanied by a new definition of competence and social success. If American lawyers are the most obvious example of the effects of such an historical experience, French lawyers provide the most radical example of resistance, since, because the pressure from the competitive forces was so weak, they were able, until the very middle of the twentieth century, to retain and even strengthen their double sphere of action, and consequently their twofold political and technical knowledge.

This interpretation highlights the differences in historical conditions that are at the root of the various definitions of the profession. It also helps us to explain the two contradictory movements which, over the last decades, have transformed the roles of the French and American lawyer: while the former, as an outcome of the growing influence of market forces, is increasingly relegated to the technical sphere and increasingly committed to the collective experience of uni-dimensionality (whether this is permanent or temporary, no one can say); the latter, conversely, is adding to his technical activities a growing involvement in politics and affairs of the state.[12] This two-pronged evolution, which precludes our indulging in any 'cultural' comparisons, responds, in fact, to a unified interpretation.

The unity or duality of the lawyers' sphere of action and thus of knowledge, derives from the relative influence of the conflicting systems of the state and politics, on the one hand, and of the competitive market and the university, on the other: when the first of these forces dominates the second, duality prevails; in the other case, unity carries the day. Of course there are other contributing causes, but here the hypothesis is that this is the central dynamic. In any case, this thesis makes it possible to combine into a single interpretation the recent developments affecting both French and American lawyers. Having shunned competition for so long, French lawyers now find themselves subjected to an increasingly intense and generalized struggle, which is causing them to fall back on the technical sphere alone. Once the Americans gained complete control of the market, they followed the opposite path: with the disappearance of outside competition, they expanded their activities 'beyond monopoly' and began taking part in the affairs of the state, broadening their range of skills, becoming political actors and turning increasingly to a dual knowledge. There is no reason to think that the same analysis could not be applied to the cognitive configurations of this profession in other countries as well.

Notes

1 The official creation of the advocate to the secular courts was promulgated by the Royal Decrees of 1274 and 1291; that of notaries by the Royal Decrees of 1270 and 1302. Official consecration of attorneys came later, principally in 1378 and 1402. On this phase of history, essential to the creation of the various legal professions, see the short, accurate overview by Lemarignier, 1970:366–373. On lawyers, see Delachenal, 1885. On attorneys: Bataillard, 1866; Bataillard and Nusse, 1882. On notaries: Cipolla, 1973:37–53; Fedou, 1966.

2 For instance, the separation between lawyer and attorney by no means won universal approval, and some royal edicts had even stipulated its abolition in favour of the lawyers. No action was ever taken, however.

3 The law of 31 Dec. 1971, creating the 'new profession of lawyer'.

4 The 1865 decision was taken by the Conseil de l'Ordre des Avocats de Paris, and stipulates that being a lawyer is incompatible with serving on the board of directors of a public or limited liability company, serving on the board of trustees of a limited partnership company or serving as commissioner of a limited liability company.

5 Loisel, 1832.

6 Which probably explains why, at the time, a conflict is recorded between one

group of lawyers and the *procureurs* over control of acts of procedure: see Bataillard and Nusse, 1882:104–105.

7 In this as in the preceding section, I shall limit myself to minimal indications; for further details, I refer the reader to Karpik, 1989:733–752 and Karpik, 1988:707–736.

8 It should be remembered that, in the nineteenth century, the bar systematically developed a policy begun under the *ancien régime*, which was characterized by the incompatibility between the profession of lawyer and the holding of any public or para-public office, *with the exception of political office*. Having two careers was common at the time.

9 This double reference does not mean that the professional status of the lawyer was characterized by the juxtaposition of two areas of knowledge which he would call upon as historical circumstances dictated. Their 'craft' consisted precisely in these categories of perception, classification and judgement, the ensemble of which gave them the possibility of practising duality in a unitary world.

10 As Suleiman, 1987, shows for one of the legal professions.

11 Something Larson, 1977/1979, vigorously pointed out. Even for the USA, however, the primacy of market forces is not universally accepted. See Burrage, 1988:243–277.

12 This is the central thesis of Halliday, 1987.

References

Abbott, Andrew (1981) 'Status and Status Strain in the Professions', *American Journal of Sociology*, 86.

Abbott, Andrew (1988) *The System of Professions: An Essay on the Division of Expert Labor*. Chicago: University of Chicago Press.

Abelshauser, W. (ed.) (1987) *Die Weimarer Republik als Wohlfahrtsstaat*. Stuttgart.

Åmark, Klas (1990) 'Open Cartels and Social Closures: Professional Strategies in Sweden, 1860–1950', in Michael Burrage and Rolf Torstendahl (eds), *Professions in Theory and History: Rethinking the Study of the Professions*. London: Sage.

Andersson, Kerstin (1984) *Omvårdnad. Framväxten av en ny vetenskap*. Stockholm: Esselte.

Anners, Erik (1974/1980) *Den europeiska rättens historia*, 2 vols. Stockholm: Liber.

Aronowitz, Stanley (1973) *False Promises: The Shaping of American Working Class Consciousness*. New York: McGraw-Hill.

Åström, K. (1958) 'Arkitekternas arbetsmetoder', *Arkitekttidningen*, 12.

Bailey, Roy and Brake, Mike (eds) (1976) *Radical Social Work*. New York: Pantheon.

Barbagli, Marzio (1982) *Educating for Unemployment. Politics, Labor Markets and the School System – Italy, 1859–1973*. New York: Columbia University Press.

Barber, Bernard (1952) *Science and the Social Order*. New York: Free Press.

Barnett, R. (1987) 'Teacher Education: A Changing Model of Professional Preparation', *Educational Studies*, 13(1).

Barnett, R., Becher, T., and Cork, M. (1986) 'Models of Professional Preparation', *Studies in Higher Education*, 12(1).

Bataillard, C. (1866) *Les Origines de l'histoire des procureurs et des avoués depuis le Vème siècle jusqu'au XVème (422–1483)*. Paris.

Bataillard, C. and Nusse, E. (1882) *Histoire des procureurs et des avoués 1483–1816*. Paris, vol. 2.

Becher, Tony (1989) 'A Meta-Theoretical Approach to Education Theory', *Cambridge Journal of Education*, 19(1).

Beck, Ulrich (1986) *Risikogesellschaft*. Frankfurt: Suhrkamp.

Becker, Howard S. (1961) *Boys in White: Student Culture in Medical School*. Chicago: University of Chicago Press.

Bell, Daniel (1976) *The Cultural Contradiction of Capital*. New York: Basic Books.

Berlant, Jeffrey (1975) *Profession and Monopoly. A Study of Medicine in the US and Great Britain*. Berkeley, CA: University of California Press.

Bettelheim, Charles (1974) *Les Luttes de classes en URSS*. Paris: Maspero-Seuil.

Blau, J.R. (1984) *Architects and Firms: A Sociological Perspective on Architectural Practice*. Boston: MIT Press.

Bloomfeld, Constance and Levy, Howard (1973) 'Underground Medicine: Ups and Downs of Free Clinics', *Ramparts*, 4.

Bloomfield, Maxwell (1976) *American Lawyers in a Changing Society, 1776–1876*. Cambridge, MA: Harvard University Press.

Blume, S.S. (1977) 'The Role of Credentials for Entry into Certain Professions', in *Selection and Certification in Education and Employment*. OECD.

Bookchin, Murray (1979) 'Marxism as Bourgeois Sociology', *Our Generation*, 13.

Bourdieu, Pierre (1976) 'Le Champ Scientifique', *Actes de la Recherche en Sciences Sociales*, II(2).

Bourdieu, Pierre (1981) 'The Specificity of the Scientific Field', in C. Lemert (ed.), *French Sociology*. New York.

Bourdieu, Pierre and Passeron, Jean-Claude (1970/1977) *Reproduction: in Education, Society, and Culture*. Beverly Hills, CA: Sage.

Bourdieu, Pierre (1979/1984) *Distinction. A Social Critique of the Judgement of Taste*. Cambridge, MA: Harvard University Press.

Boyer, Chammard G. (1976) *Les Avocats*. Paris.

Brante, Thomas (1988a) 'Om konstituering av nya vetenskapliga fält – exemplet forskning om socialt arbete', *Sociologisk Forskning* 4.

Brante, Thomas (1988b) 'Sociological Perspectives on the Professions', *Acta Sociologica*, 31(2).

Braverman, Harry (1974) *Labor and Monopoly Capital*. New York: Monthly Review Press.

Brown, Julie V. (1987) 'The Deprofessionalization of Soviet Physicians: A Reconsideration', *International Journal of Health Services*, 17.

Bucher, Rue and Strauss, Anselm (1961) 'Professions in Process', *American Journal of Sociology*, 66.

Burawoy, Michael (1980) *Manufacturing Consent*. Chicago: University of Chicago Press.

Burchhardt, Lothar (1980) 'Professionalisierung oder Berufskonstruktion? Das Beispiel des Chemikers im Wilhelminischen Deutschland', *Geschichte und Gesellschaft*, 6.

Burrage, Michael (1988) 'Revolution and the Collective Action of the French, American and English Legal Professions', *Law and Social Inquiry, Journal of the American Bar Foundation*, 13(2).

Burrage, Michael (1990) 'Beyond a Sub-set: The Professional Aspirations of Manual Workers in France, the United States and Britain', in Michael Burrage and Rolf Torstendahl (eds), *Professions in Theory and History: Rethinking the Study of the Professions*. London: Sage.

Calhoun, Daniel (1965) *Professional Lives in America: Structure and Aspirations, 1750–1850*. Cambridge, MA: Harvard University Press.

Carr-Saunders, A.M. and Wilson, P.A. (1933) *The Professions*. Oxford: Clarendon Press.

Cipolla, C.M. (1973) 'The Professions: the Long View', *Journal of European Economic History*, 2.

CNAA (1983) *Initial BEd courses for the Early and Middle Years: A Discussion Document*. CNAA.

CNAA (1984) *Perspectives on Postgraduate Initial Training: The CNAA-validated PGCE*. CNAA.

Cohen, Marcia B. and Wagner, David (1982) 'Social Work Professionalism: Reality and Illusion', in Charles Derber (ed.), *Professionals as Workers*. Boston: G.K. Hall & Co.

Collins, Randall (1979) *The Credential Society: An Historical Sociology of Education and Stratification*. New York: Academic Press.

Collins, Randall (1981) 'Crises and Declines in Credential Systems', in *Sociology Since Midcentury: Essays in Theory Cumulation*. New York: Academic Press.

Cooley, M. (1976) 'Contradictions of Science and Technology in the Production Process', in Hilary Rose and Steve Rose (eds), *The Political Economy of Science*. London: Macmillan.

Corrigan, Philip and Sayer, Derek (1985) *The Great Arch: English State Formation as Cultural Revolution*. Oxford: Basil Blackwell.

Crane, Diana (1980) 'Science Policy Studies', in P.J. Durbin (ed.), *A Guide to the Culture of Science, Technology and Medicine*. New York: Free Press.

Cullen, John (1978) *Structure of Professionalism*. New York.

Delachenal, R. (1885) *Histoire des avocats au Parlement de Paris 1300–1600*. Paris.

Derber, Charles (1982) *Professionals as Workers: Mental Labor in Advanced Capitalism*. Boston: G.K. Hall & Co.

Disco, Cornelis (1982) 'The Educated Minotaur', *Theory and Society*, XI (6 Nov.).

Disco, Cornelis (1987) 'Intellectuals in Advanced Capitalism: Capital, Closure and the New Class Thesis', in R. Eyerman, L. Svensson, and T. Söderquist (eds), *Intellectuals, Universities, and the State in Western Modern Societies*. Berkeley, CA: University of California Press.

Edwards, Richard (1979) *Contested Terrain*. New York: Basic Books.

Ehrenreich, Barbara and Ehrenreich, John (1977a) 'The Professional-Managerial Class', *Radical America*, 2(2).

Ehrenreich, Barbara and Ehrenreich, John (1977b) 'The New Left and the Professional-Managerial Class', *Radical America*, 2(3).

Elster, J. (1974) *Stat, organisasjon, klasse*. Oslo.

English National Board for Nursing, Midwifery and Health Visiting (1985) *Professional Education and Training Courses: A Discussion Document*. ENB.

Eraut, M. (1985) 'Knowledge Creation and Knowledge Use in Professional Contexts', *Studies in Higher Education*, 10(2).

Evans, Peter, Rueschemeyer, Dietrich, and Skocpol, Theda (eds) (1985) *Bringing the State Back In*. Cambridge: Cambridge University Press.

Eyerman, R., Svensson, L. and Söderquist, T. (eds) (1987) *Intellectuals, Universities, and the State in Western Modern Societies*. Berkeley, CA: University of California Press.

Fedou, R. (1966) *Les Hommes de loi lyonnais à la fin du Moyen Age*. Annales de Lyon.

Field, M.G. (1957) *Doctor and Patient in Soviet Russia*. Cambridge, MA: Harvard University Press.

Forester, J. (1983) 'Critical Theory and Planning Practice', in J.R. Blau, M. Gory, and J.S. Pipkin (eds), *Professionals and Urban Form*. New York: State University of New York Press.

Foucault, Michel (1971) *L'Ordre du Discours*. Paris: Gallimard.

Foucault, Michel (1972) *The Discourse on Language*. Translated by Rupert Swyer, Appendix to *The Archaeology of Knowledge*, translated by A.M. Sheridan Smith. New York: Pantheon.

Foucault, Michel (1978) *Discipline and Punishment*. New York: Vintage.

Foucault, Michel (1981) Translation of 'Questions de Méthode', *Ideology and Consciousness*.

Franzen, G. (ed.) (1977) *Byggnormer* (Standards of Construction). Lund.

Freidson, Eliot (1970a) *Profession of Medicine. A Study of the Sociology of Applied Knowledge*. New York: Dodd & Mead.

Freidson, Eliot (1970b) *Professional Dominance*. New York: Atherton Press.

Freidson, Eliot (1973a) 'Prepaid Group Practice and the new Demanding Patient', *Milbank Memorial Fund Quarterly* (Health and Society).

Freidson, Eliot (1973b) 'Professionals and the Occupational Principle', in Eliot Freidson (ed.), *The Professions and their Prospects*. Beverly Hills, CA: Sage.

Freidson, Eliot (1975) *Doctoring Together: A Study of Professional Social Control*. New York: Elsevier.

Freidson, Eliot (1984) 'Are Professions Necessary?', in Thomas L. Haskell (ed.), *The Authority of Experts*. Bloomington, IN: University of Indiana Press.

Freidson, Eliot (1986) *Professional Powers: A Study of the Institutionalization of Formal Knowledge*. Chicago: University of Chicago Press.

Fromm, Erich (1941) *Escape from Freedom*. New York: Farrar & Rinehart.

Galbraith, John Kenneth (1967) *The New Industrial State*. Boston: Houghton Mifflin.

Galper, Jeffry (1978) 'What are Radical Social Services?' *Social Policy* (Jan.–Feb.).

Gaudry, J.A.J. (1864) *Histoire du barreau de Paris. Depuis son origine jusqu'à 1830*. Paris: (reprint: Geneva, 1977).

Geertz, Clifford (1983) *Local Knowledge*. New York: Basic Books.

Geison, Gerald (ed.) (1984) *Professions and the French State, 1700–1900*. Philadelphia: University of Pennsylvania Press.

Gibbons, Michael and Wittrock, Björn (eds) (1985) *Science as a Commodity*. Harlow, Essex: Longman.

Ginger, Ann (1973) *The Relevant Lawyers*. New York: Simon & Schuster.

Glaser, N. (1979) 'The Schools of the Minor Professions', *Minerva*, 12(3).

Goldstein, Jan (1984) 'Moral Contagion: A Professional Ideology of Medicine and Psychiatry in 18th and 19th Century France', in Gerald Geison (ed.), *Professions and the French State, 1700–1900*, Philadelphia: University of Pennsylvania Press.

Gorz, André (1964) *Strategy for Labor*. Boston: Beacon Press.

Gouldner, A.W. (1957) 'Cosmopolitan and Locals', *Administrative Science Quarterly*, 2.

Gouldner, Alvin (1978) 'The New Class Project', *Theory and Society*, 6(2).

Gouldner, Alvin (1979) *The Future of Intellectuals and the Rise of the New Class*. New York: Seabury Press.

Gross, Ronald and Osterman, Paul (eds) (1972) *The New Professionals*. New York: Simon & Schuster.

H 1971:3, 'Formerna för auktorisation av revisorer mm.' *Betänkande avgivet av Auktorisationsutredningen* (1971).

Habermas, Jürgen (1973) *Legitimationskrise im Spätkapitalismus*. Frankfurt: Suhrkamp.

Habermas, Jürgen (1981) *Theorie des kommunikativen Handelns*, vol. 2. Frankfurt: Suhrkamp.

Halliday, T.C. (1987) *Beyond Monopoly: Lawyers, State Crises and Professional Empowerment*. Chicago: University of Chicago Press.

Haug, Marie (1973) 'Deprofessionalization: An Alternative Hypothesis for the Future', in P. Halmos (ed.), *Professionalization and Social Change*. Keele: University of Keele.

Haug, Marie (1975) 'The Deprofessionalization of Everyone?' *Sociological Focus*, 8.

Haug, Marie (1977) 'Computer Technology and Obsolescence of the Concept of

Profession', in M. Haug and J. Dofny (eds), *Work and Technology*. Beverly Hills, CA: Sage.

Hayward, J. (1982) 'Universities and Nursing Education', *Journal of Advanced Nursing*, 7.

Hazard, John N. (1964) *The Soviet System of Government*. 3rd edn. Chicago: University of Chicago Press.

Hellberg, Inga (1978) 'Studier i professionell organisation. En professionsteori med tillämpning på veterinäryrket'. Dissertation, Göteborg.

Hirst, P.H. (ed.) (1983) *Educational Theory and its Foundation Disciplines*. London: Routledge.

HMI (1983) *Teaching in Schools: The Content of Initial Training. An HMI Discussion Document*. DES.

Hoff, J. (1985) 'The Concept of Class and Public Employees', *Acta Sociologica*, 3.

Hortleder, Gerd (1970) *Das Gesellschaftsbild des Ingenieurs*. Frankfurt.

House, V.G. (1977) 'Survival of the Fittest: A Summary of an Attempt to Evaluate Experimental Schemes of Nurse Training', *Journal of Advanced Nursing*, 2.

Hubert, Henri and Maus, Marcel (1902–1903/1975) *A General Theory of Magic*. New York: Norton.

Hunt, J. (1981) 'Indicators for Nursing Practice: The Use of Research Findings', *Journal of Advanced Nursing*, 6.

Illich, Ivan, Zola, I.K., McKnight, J., Caplan, J. and Shaiken, H. (1977) *Disabling Professions*. London: Marion Boyars Publishers.

Jarausch, Konrad (1982) *Students, Society and Politics in Imperial Germany: The Rise of Academic Illiberalism*. Princeton, NJ

Jarausch, Konrad H. (1986a) 'The Perils of Professionalism. Lawyers, Teachers and Engineers in Nazi Germany', *German Studies Review*, 9.

Jarausch, Konrad (1986b) 'Professionalization German Style', The Swedish Collegium for Advanced Study in the Social Sciences (SCASSS), Uppsala.

Jarausch, Konrad, Siegrist, Hannes, and Burrage, Michael (1990) 'An Actor-based Framework for the Study of the Professions', in M. Burrage and R. Torstendahl (eds), *Professions in Theory and History: Rethinking the Study of the Professions*. London: Sage.

Johansson, O. (1971) 'SYLF 50 en tillbakablick med glimtar från de gångna årens verksamhet', in *Läkartidningen*, 51.

Johnson, Jeffrey (1987) 'Academic, Proletarian, . . . Professional? Shaping Professionalization for German Industrial Chemists, 1887–1920', MS, Villanova, PA.

Johnson, Jon (1987) *Retten til juridisk bistand*. Oslo.

Johnson, T. (1982) 'The State and the Professions: Peculiarities of the British', in A. Giddens and G. Mackenzie (eds), *Social Class and the Division of Labour*. Cambridge: Cambridge University Press.

Karpik, Lucien (1988) 'Lawyers and Politics in France, 1814–1950: The State, the Market, and the Public', *Law and Social Inquiry*, 13.

Karpik, Lucien (1989) 'Le Désintéressement', *Annales*, 3.

Kater, Michael (1985) 'Professionalization and Socialization of Physicians in Wilhelmine and Weimar Germany', *Journal of Contemporary History*, 20.

Kirschner, Don S. (1986) *The Paradox of Professionalism*. New York: Greenwood Press.

Klegon, Douglas (1978) 'The Sociology of Professions. An Emerging Perspective', *Sociology of Work and Professions*, 5.

Konrad, György and Szelenyi, Ivan (1979) *The Intellectuals on the Road to Class Power*. New York: Harcourt, Brace, Jovanovich.

Kornhauser, William (1962–1963) *Scientists in Industry: Conflict and Accommodation*. Berkeley, CA: University of California Press.

Korpi, Walter (1988) 'Makt, politik och statsautonomi i det sociala medborgarskapets framväxt. En jämförande studie av 18 OECD-länder', *Sociologisk Forskning*, 4.

Kotschnig, W.M. (1937) *Unemployment in the Learned Professions*. London: Oxford University Press.

Ladinsky, Jack (1963) 'Careers of Lawyers, Law Practice, and Legal Institutions', *American Sociological Review*, 28.

Larson, Magali Sarfatti (1977/1979) *The Rise of Professionalism: A Sociological Analysis*. Berkeley, CA: University of California Press.

Larson, Magali Sarfatti (1979) 'Professionalism: Rise and Fall', *International Journal of Health Services*, 9.

Larson, Magali Sarfatti (1980) 'Proletarianization and Educated Labor', *Theory and Society*, IX(1) (Jan.).

Larson, Magali Sarfatti (1984) 'The Production of Expertise and the Constitution of Expert Power', in Thomas L. Haskell (ed.), *The Authority of Experts*. Bloomington, IN: University of Indiana Press.

Larson, Magali Sarfatti (1986) 'The Rise and Fall of Professionalization', The Swedish Collegium for Advanced Study in the Social Sciences. MS.

Lasch, Christopher (1978) *Haven in a Heartless World*. New York: Basic Books.

Ledford, Kenneth (1987) 'Lawyers, Liberalism, and Freie Advokatur: The German Legal Profession, 1879–1936', Ph.D. dissertation, in progress, Baltimore, MD: Johns Hopkins University.

Lemarignier, J.F. (1970) *La France médiévale. Institution et société*. Paris: A. Colin.

Lipstadt, Hélène (1979) *Polémique, Débat, Conflit: Architecte et Ingénieur dans la Presse*. Paris: Corda.

Loisel, A. (1832) 'Pasquier ou dialogue des advocats du Parlement de Paris (1604)', in Ainé Dupin, *Profession d'Avocat. Recueil de Pièces*. Paris.

Lundequist, E.J. (1984) 'Ideologi och praxis'. Department of Architecture, College of Technology, Stockholm.

McClelland, Charles (forthcoming) *The German Experience of Professionalization. The Development of Modern Learned Professions and their Organizations, 1840–1940*. New York and Cambridge.

McCloskey, Joanne Comi (1981) 'The Professionalization of Nursing: United States and England', *International Nursing Review*, 28(2) (March/April).

MacDonagh, O. (1977) *Early Victorian Government*. London: Weidenfeld and Nicolson.

McGlynn, J. (1984) 'The Quest for Nursing Knowledge', *Nurse Education Today*, 4(2).

McKinlay, John B. (1982) 'Toward the Proletarianization of Physicians', in Charles Derber (ed.), *Professionals as Workers*. Boston: G.K. Hall & Co.

McKinlay, John B. and Arches, Joan (1985) 'Towards the Proletarianization of Physicians', *International Journal of Health Services*, 15.

Mallet, S. (1975) *Essays on the New Working Class*. St Louis: Telos Press.

Manasse, M.R. and Groves, M.J. (1985) 'A Descriptive Review of Pharmacy Education in England and Wales', *American Journal of Pharmaceutical Education*, 49.

Mannheim, Karl (1935/1940) *Man and Society in an Age of Reconstruction*. New York: Harcourt, Brace.

Marsh, N. (1978) 'Development of the Undergraduate Nursing Course in the University of Manchester', *Journal of Advanced Nursing*, 3.

Marshall, Thomas H. (1950) *Citizenship and Social Class and Other Essays*. Cambridge: Cambridge University Press.

Marson, S.N. (1982) 'Ward Sister – Teacher or Facilitator? An Investigation into the Behavioral Characteristics of Effective Ward Teachers', *Journal of Advanced Nursing*, 7.

Mattick, Paul, Jr. (1983) 'Foreword' to Paul Mattick, *Marxism – Last Refuge of the Bourgeoisie?* Edited by Paul Mattick, Jr., Armonk, NY: M.E. Sharpe, Inc.

Mattick, Paul (1983) *Marxism – Last Refuge of the Bourgeoisie?* Edited by Paul Mattick, Jr., Armonk, NY: M.E. Sharpe, Inc.

Merton, Robert K. (1949) *Social Theory and Social Structure*. Glencoe, IL: Free Press.

Merton, Robert K. (1967) *On Theoretical Sociology*. New York: Free Press.

Modéer, K.A. (1987) *Festskrift till Sveriges Advokatsamfund 1887–1987*.

Motpol, 4–5 (1986).

Mottram, D.R. (1985) 'Trends in Continuing Education', *Pharmaceutical Journal* (12 Oct.).

Murphy, Raymond (1983) 'The Struggle for Scholarly Recognition: The Development of the Closure Problematic', *Theory and Society*, 12.

Murphy, Raymond (1984) 'The Structure of Closure: A Critique and Development of Weber, Collins, and Parkin', *British Journal of Sociology*, 35.

Murphy, Raymond (1985) 'Exploitation or Exclusion?', *Sociology*, 19.

Murphy, Raymond (1988) *Social Closure. The Theory of Monopolization and Exclusion*. Oxford: Clarendon Press.

Nelkin, Dorothy (1987) 'Universities in the Year 2000', Lecture held at the University of Arizona, Phoenix.

Norberg, Astrid (1984) 'Nursing Science – a New Field of Research', in Looking and Learning (UHÄ – National Board of Universities and Colleges), Stockholm.

Nordiska Hälsovårdshögskolan (1987) 'Nya tjänster vid Nordiska Hälsovårdsskolan', Göteborg.

Ödman, E. (1986) *Bakom fasaderna: Om arkitekelevers kunskaper och värderingar*. Stockholm: Liber.

Oppenheimer, Martin (1970) 'White Collar Revisited: The Making of a New Working Class', *Social Policy* (July-Aug.).

Oppenheimer, Martin (1973) 'The Proletarianization of the Professional', *Sociological Review of Monographs*, 20.

Oppenheimer, Martin (1975) 'The Unionization of the Professional', *Social Policy*, 5.

Östnäs, A. (1984) 'Arkitekterna och deras yrkesutveckling i Sverige', College of Technology, Gothenburg.

Östnäs, A. and Svensson, L. (1986) *Arkitektarbete*, Department of Architecture, College of Technology, no. 5, Gothenburg.

Owen, G.M. (1984) *The Development of Degree Courses in Nursing Education – in Historical and Professional Context*, Polytechnic of the South Bank, Occasional Paper no. 4.

Parkin, Frank (1979) *Marxism and Class Theory: A Bourgeois Critique*. London: Routledge.

Parsons, Talcott (1939) 'The Professions and Social Structure', *Social Forces*, 17.
Parsons, Talcott (1949) *Essays in Sociological Theory, Pure and Applied*. New York: The Free Press of Glencoe.
Parsons, Talcott (1951) *The Social System*. Glencoe, IL: Free Press.
Parsons, Talcott (1977) *The Evolution of Societies*. Jack Toby (ed.), Englewood Cliffs, NJ: Prentice-Hall.
Patry, Bill (1978) 'Taylorism Comes to the Social Services', *Monthly Review*, 30(5).
Perrucci, Robert and Gerstl, Joel (1969) *Profession without Community: Engineers in American Society*. New York: Random House.
Pharmaceutical Society (1980) 'Council Approval of Degrees in Pharmacy', Mimeo, 19 Dec.
Pharmaceutical Society (1984) 'First Report of the Working Party on Pharmaceutical Education and Training', *Pharmaceutical Journal* (28 April).
Pharmaceutical Society (1985) 'The Schools of Pharmacy', *Pharmaceutical Journal* (12 Oct.).
Pharmaceutical Society (n.d.) 'Entrance Requirements to Schools of Pharmacy', Pharmaceutical Society.
Pitkin, Hanna F. (1967) *The Concept of Representation*. Berkeley, CA: University of California Press.
Poulantzas, Nicos (1978a) *Classes in Contemporary Capitalism*. London: Verso Press.
Poulantzas, Nicos (1978b) *State, Power and Socialism*. London: Verso Press.
Preuss, Ulrich (1986) 'The Concept of Rights and the Welfare State', in Günther Teubner (ed.), *Dilemmas of Law in the Welfare State*. Berlin/New York: Walter de Gruyter.
Quinn, F.M. (1980) *The Principles and Practice of Nurse Education*. London: Croom Helm.
Quinn, Robert and Staines, G.L. (1979) *The 1979 Quality of Employment Survey*. Ann Arbor, MI: University of Michigan.
Ramsey, Matthew (1984) 'The Politics of Professional Monopoly in Nineteenth-Century Medicine: The French Model and Its Rivals', in Gerald L. Geison (ed.), *Professions and the French State 1700–1900*. Philadelphia: University of Pennsylvania Press.
Ringer, Fritz K. (1979) *Education and Society in Modern Europe*. Bloomington, IN.
Riska, Elianne and Wegar, Katarina (1988) 'Feminisering av läkarprofessionen. Kommer hälsovården att förändras?', *Naistutkimus – Kvinnoforskning*, 2 (8 Dec.).
Roberts, David (1960) *Victorian Origins of the British Welfare State*. New Haven, CT: Yale University Press.
Roberts, K.I. (1985) 'Theory of Nursing as Curriculum Content', *Journal of Advanced Nursing*, 10.
Roemer, John (1982a) 'New Directions in the Marxian Theory of Exploitation and Class', *Politics and Society*, 11.
Roemer, John (1982b) *A General Theory of Exploitation and Class*, Cambridge, MA: Harvard University Press.
Rogers, Martha (1961) *Education Revolution in Nursing*. New York.
Rogoff Ramsöy, Natalie and Kölsröd, Lise (1985) *Velferdsstatens yrker*. Oslo.
Rorty, Richard (1979) *The Mirror of Nature*. Princeton, NJ: Princeton University Press.
Rose, Hilary and Rose, Steve (1976) *The Political Economy of Science*. Cambridge, MA: Schenkman.

206 The formation of professions

Ross, Alf (1953) *Ret of Retfaerdighed*. Copenhagen: Gyldendals.

Sarason, Seymour B. (1979) *Work, Aging, and Social Change*. New York: Free Press.

SCB, 1977, 'Tendenser och prognoser från Statistiska Centralbyrån', Stockholm.

Schön, D.A. (1983) *The Reflective Practitioner: How Professionals Think in Action*. Part I, London.

Schudson, Michael (1980) 'Review Article: a Discussion of Magali Sarfatti Larson's "The Rise of Professionalism" ', *Theory and Society*, 9.

Selander, Staffan (ed.) (1989) *Yrke eller profession*. Lund: Studentlitteratur.

Sheahan, J. (1980) 'Some Aspects of the Teaching and Learning of Nursing', *Journal of Advanced Nursing*, 5.

Siegrist, Hannes (1985) 'Gebremste Professionalisierung – Das Beispiel der schweizer Rechtsanwaltschaft im Vergleich zu Frankreich und Deutschland im 19. und 20. Jahrhundert', in Werner Conze and Jürgen Kocka (eds), *Bildungsbürgertum im 19. Jahrhundert*. Stuttgart.

Slagstad, Rune (1987) *Rett og Politik. Et liberalt tema med variasjoner*. Oslo: Universitetsforlaget.

Smigel, Ervin O. (1964) *The Wall Street Lawyer*. New York: Free Press.

Smith, L. (1983) 'Nursing: An Embryonic Discipline of Knowledge?', *Nurse Education Today*, 3(3).

SOU, 1981:57, 'Djurens hälso- och sjukvård'.

Spangler, Eve and Lehman, Peter M. (1982) 'Lawyering as Work', in Charles Derber (ed.), *Professionals as Workers*. Boston: G.K. Hall & Co.

Spiegel-Rosing, Ina (1977) 'The Study of Science, Technology and Society', in Ina Spiegel-Rosing and Derek de Solla Price (eds), *Science, Technology and Society*. Beverly Hills, CA: Sage.

Starr, Paul (1982) *The Social Transformation of American Medicine*. New York: Basic Books.

Statistics Canada, Education in Canada: A Statistical Review for 1982–83. Cat 81–229. Ottawa, 1984 (Ministry of Supply and Services).

Steinfels, Peter (1979) *The Neo-Conservatives*. New York: Simon & Schuster.

Suleiman, E.N. (1987) *Private Power and Centralization in France. The Notaires and the State*. Princeton, NJ: Princeton University Press.

Sutherland, G. (ed.) (1972) *Studies in the Growth of Nineteenth Century Government*. London: Routledge & Kegan Paul.

Svensk Veterinärtidning.

'Svenska Läkaresällskapet 175 år: dess sektioners tillkomst och utveckling' (1983). *Swedish Statistical Yearbook, 1988*.

Szelenyi, Ivan (1986–1987) 'The Prospects and Limits of the East European New Class Project', *Politics and Society*, XV(2).

Taylor, W. (1981) 'Teacher Education – into the 1990s', *Education Review*, 33(2).

Therborn, Göran (1986) 'Karl Marx Returning: The Welfare State and Neo-Marxist, Corporatist, and State Theories', *International Political Science Review*, 7.

Tigar, Michael (1961) 'A Lawyer for Social Change', *Center Magazine*, 4(6).

Tocqueville, Alexis de (1945) *Democracy in America*, Phillips Bradley (ed.), New York: Vintage.

UHÄ (1978) *UHÄ Report 1978:14*. Stockholm: National Board of Universities and Colleges.

Vårdfacket, 18(1986). *Vårdfacket* is the journal of the Swedish nurses' union which carries many features and news items on the development of nursing science in Sweden.

Vårdfacket, 22(1988).

Walzer, Michael (1983) *Spheres of Justice*. New York.

Weber, Max (1922/1968) *Economy and Society*. Guenter Roth and Klaus Wittich (eds), New York: Bedminster Press.

Weber, Max (1977) *Vetenskap och politik*. Göteborg: Korpen.

Weber, Max (1978) *Economy and Society*, vol. 2. Berkeley, CA: University of California Press.

Weiss, John (1984) 'Bridges and Barriers: Narrowing Access and Changing Structure in the French Engineering Profession', in Gerald Geison (ed.), *Professions and the French State, 1700–1900*. Philadelphia: University of Pennsylvania Press.

Wilensky, Harold L. (1964) 'The Professionalization of Everyone?' *American Journal of Sociology*, 70.

Wilson, Rand (1979) *Professionals as Workers*. Cambridge: Policy Training Centre.

Withorn, Ann (1979) 'Radical Social Work', in Rand Wilson, (ed.), *Professionals as Workers*. Cambridge: Policy Training Centre.

Wood, V. (1985) 'Nursing Education: A Descriptive Examination of the Effects of Moving from Hospitals to Colleges', *Nurse Education Today*, 5(3).

Wright, E.O. (1985) *Classes*. London: Verso.

Yankelovich, Daniel (1974) 'Corporate Ownership and Control: The Large Corporation and the Capitalist Class', *American Journal of Sociology*, 79.

Yura, H. and Walsh, M.B. (1978) *The Nursing Process: Assessing, Planning, Implementing, Evaluating*. New York: Appleton-Century-Crofts.

Index